99 paper 19.95

9.95

Win, Lose, or Draw

Win, Lose, or Draw

Domestic Politics and the
Crucible of War

Allan C. Stam III

Ann Arbor

THE UNIVERSITY OF MICHIGAN PRESS

First paperback edition 1999
Copyright © by the University of Michigan 1996
All rights reserved
Published in the United States of America by
The University of Michigan Press
Manufactured in the United States of America
⊗ Printed on acid-free paper

2002   2001   2000   1999   5   4   3   2

A CIP catalog record for this book is available from the British Library

Library of Congress Cataloging-in-Publication Data

Stam, Allan C.
    Win, lose, or draw : domestic politics and the crucible of war /
Allan C. Stam III.
        p.   cm.
    Includes bibliographical references (p.   ) and index.
    ISBN 0-472-10682-1 (cloth : acid-free paper)
    1. War.   2. Strategy.   3. International relations.   I. Title.
U21.2.S68   1996
355.02 — dc20   96-10152
                                                                CIP

ISBN 0-472-08577-8 (pbk. : alk. paper)

To Fritz Tibbs and Kolbe Kahn

Contents

Tables

Figures

Preface

In 1990 the prevalent view among political scientists was that the topic of war outcomes was "boring," "passé in the post-cold-war world," and "not political science." The Gulf War in 1991 changed this widely held belief. War—its origins, its prosecution, and its endings—has never been boring. If anything, it is an area of study where we still have more questions than answers, an area for research that is both fascinating and crucially important. The end of the cold war has not led to an era of peace and harmony throughout the world; if anything, just the opposite. Finally, while war is fought by militaries using apolitical machines, every decision along the way to and during war is laced with politics.

Using quantitative data and historical illustrations from the early 1800s to the late 1980s, this book investigates the relative effect on war outcomes of both the choices leaders must make during war and the resources they have at their disposal. States' strategy choices are among the most important decisions we can study. Strategy choices, along with decisions about troop levels and defense spending are not made in a vacuum; rather, they are made in the crucible of domestic politics. As military organizations begin to draw down their forces and troop levels from the high levels maintained during the cold war, we have realized that the so-called peace dividend may disappear in the morass of pork-barrel politics and logrolling. The need to satisfy domestic constituencies during peacetime has far-reaching consequences during times of war. As I show in this book, there are optimal ways for states to fight during war. These optimal strategies and resource allocations are, however, very expensive. The costs lie both in the financial resources required to purchase and maintain the necessary equipment and in the human requirements—the number of soldiers and high levels of training required to successfully execute the strategies when needed. While there are best ways to fight, because of domestic political constraints, states must frequently make suboptimal choices, a trade-off of security in the international arena for political gains at home.

Many of the results presented in the chapters that follow confirm the conventional wisdom regarding war. As most readers would assume, military and industrial capabilities are quite important. But I show that it is not the resources alone that enable states to exercise effective power in the international system. Rather, the process by which states use these resources, or the strategy that they employ, is the most important determinant of who will win or lose. I also show that some wars in some locations simply will not have decisive outcomes—regardless of the desires of the political leaders and mass publics in the warring states. Terrain, distance, and time all conspire to drag some wars into violent draws, in many cases due to factors outside the control of the leaders at hand. While this is not a cheery finding, it is a critical one if we are to be able to understand why some wars such as the recent conflict in the Balkans are unlikely candidates for decisive and successful military intervention and why some, such as the Gulf War, are.

Acknowledgments

While writing this book I received an unusually broad range of help and advice from both academics and military practitioners. Along the way, Steven Rosenstone, Douglas Dion, and Chris Achen made sure that I was as rigorous as possible, both in terms of maintaining a theoretical framework throughout and also in ensuring that the tests of the various propositions were as unbiased as possible. Former army teammates Randy Kinnunen and Jim Lowder, from my short days in the Special Forces, provided both inspiration and more than a little prodding to ensure that I did not forget about what actually takes place on the ground in a war. Serving in various jobs in the U.S. Army Armor Corps as a reservist also convinced me that John J. Mearsheimer was correct in his analysis of the brutal effectiveness of the blitzkrieg strategy. There I also learned firsthand (in training) about the high risks associated with mobile strategies and the tremendous demands they place on the training of those who must execute the strategy.

Scott Gartner and Dan Reiter read multiple complete drafts of the book along the way to publication. Their insights and criticisms have led to a much better book than I could have written on my own. David Lalman, Scott Bennett, Shoon Murray, David Leblang, Scott Tarry, and two anonymous referees for the University of Michigan Press also provided suggestions that have vastly improved the theoretical arguments and the presentation of the empirical results.

Special thanks are reserved for Ken Organski. Without his unfailing support through all aspects of this project it is quite likely that I would not have finished. He is everything anyone could ever ask for in a teacher, a mentor, and a friend. Bruce Bueno de Mesquita is also deserving of special thanks. He never complained about reading several drafts of various chapters and always provided penetrating observations, which have made this a far better book than it would have been otherwise. Bill Zimmerman facilitated financial support at a critical juncture at the outset of the process that has led to this book. Without his assistance and willingness to entertain ideas that went against what was popular at the time, again, this project would have never been completed.

There are also several people outside of the academic and military worlds who made contributions to this book. Without the support of my parents, Julia Petrakis and Allan Stam Jr., I would never have made it out of the trailer park in Spring Lake, North Carolina, or many of the other pitfalls I found myself in as I made my way through both school and life. Skip Peterson has been a role model and confidant through both good times and bad. Finally, I want to thank my wife Cyndi whose friendship, love, and unflagging support have made the last five years spent writing this book an adventure rather than a time to be endured.

CHAPTER 1

War Outcomes and the Study of International Relations

Introduction

This is a book about war. It is about what determines the winners and losers of the most salient events that take place within the international system. While the statement that wars are important events might seem so patently obvious as to be trivial, political scientists, for the most part, have focused their efforts on the causes or correlates of the outbreak of war rather than investigating the process by which winners and losers are determined. In Gibbs and Singer's (1993) comprehensive review of the empirical literature on world politics, of the over eighty journal articles on war and peace that they review, only one is directly concerned with estimating the outcomes of interstate wars.

This orientation is certainly justifiable. Wars have been among the most destructive forces introduced by man in the history of civilization. Just as medical researchers seek to eliminate diseases such as smallpox or AIDS by trying to understand the vectors by which the diseases are transmitted, political scientists have sought a way to contain or eliminate the scourge of war by better understanding its origins. But, in addition to studying the transmission of disease, medical researchers devote equal or greater effort to understanding the processes by which diseases progress and the likelihood that individuals will recover or suffer lasting effects from a particular illness. Social scientists have expended a great amount of energy investigating the correlates of war initiation and expansion, while comparatively little work has been done on the process by which states prosecute them with an eye toward being able to anticipate their likely outcomes.

For some readers, political scientists' relative lack of attention to what occurs after the initiation of wars may be quite puzzling. Few of us, for example, would argue that war and conflicts have little effect on international relations. Whether we are focusing our attention on the world system or on smaller regional systems, the politics of the relations between states depend a great deal on how conflicts between and within those states begin and end. In an anarchic international system, competition between states and nongovernmental actors determines the distribution of goods available in the system. Because actors in the international system are competing for shares of a finite pool of resources, conflict is inevitable. Many political scientists take this conclusion to an extreme and argue that the study of politics is *solely* about conflict (Jackman 1993; Krasner 1983). Robert Jervis argues that studying the outcomes of wars is critical to being able to understand how the international system functions. This is because wars, to a large degree, "determine the course of later events. Who wins and who loses, who is destroyed and who comes out with resources intact, who decides that the gains are worth fighting for again and who feels that the burdens are too great—all have a great impact on the future of international politics" (Jervis 1985, 11).

In the following chapters, I show how both the distributions of power between states and the nature of the internal political systems of the particular states involved in a conflict affect the outcome of wars. In doing so, I hope to convince the reader that we must concern ourselves not only with international system-level variables as Kenneth Waltz and realist scholars suggest but also with how the political cultures, types of societies, and issues being disputed affect the ultimate outcome and resolution of wars. In turn, this leads to conclusions about which theoretical approaches to international relations may be considered the most useful in trying to understand conflict between nation-states.

War and the International System

Regardless of perspective, all must agree that occasionally the conflicts that arise between states over the distribution of resources escalate to the point of war.[1] To the winners, whether determined through the use of force or solely through negotiation, go the spoils. As regime theorists have pointed out, these spoils may be territorial goods or the right to set the rules and norms that govern the behavior of other actors in the system (Young 1980; Puchala 1984; Ruggie 1984; Krasner 1985; Strange 1985). Changes in the status quo and in the distribution of resources also frequently stem from the ways conflicts between actors are resolved. From most any theoretical perspective in world politics, understanding the outcomes of wars is critical to being able to understand the underlying mechanisms in the international system.

If war outcomes depend only on the military-industrial capabilities of the two sides, as most authors assume for the sake of their studies on dispute initiation, the analysis of the conflict process would not be terribly interesting. But if the process were simple and the outcomes obvious and easily understood, there would probably be far fewer wars. Geoffrey Blainey (1973), writing from a historical perspective, maintains that wars are likely when the two sides disagree as to the likely outcome. He argues that if both sides in a war or dispute knew what the outcome would be ahead of time, there would probably be fewer conflicts.

While the majority of wars are won by the states that initiate them, the international system's status quo has changed almost constantly over time, usually through challenge and conflict (Bueno de Mesquita 1981). To understand the nature of change within the international system, we must be able to answer two important questions: one, how conflicts begin, and, just as importantly (if one believes that we cannot eliminate conflict), two, how conflicts end.

For example, we can imagine a far different world if the outcome of World War II differed from what actually happened. At the regional level, the conditions in the Middle East during the postwar period would be very different if Israel had not prevailed in its conflicts with the radical Arab states. Within a country, conflicts and their outcomes affect both the daily lives of the state's citizens as well as the international politics of the states involved (Bueno de Mesquita and Siverson 1994).

Unfortunately, we really do not have a good and systematic understanding of what contributes to states winning or losing wars and what does not. Both the institutional characteristics and the political processes taking place within the combatant states contribute to wars' outcomes. In addition to the characteristics of the states themselves, the process by which states prosecute wars or, more simply, how the states fight has a powerful influence on determining winners and losers. To be sure, historians have generated an astoundingly rich literature that recounts and describes interstate wars through the millennia. But the conclusions one draws from idiosyncratic or anecdotal case studies and rich description may or may not apply to broader sets of cases.

What Matters: Domestic- versus System-Level Variables

Before diving headlong into a study of winners and losers, it is important to review how scholars of international relations approach world politics. Because decision makers typically think about wars' outcomes when they debate their initiation, the research on the initiation of war holds important clues to the way we should expect states to behave during wartime. The themes that emerge in more generic studies of world politics are likely to be found or ignored in the study of war as well. One of the first puzzles in this regard is whither domestic politics? Many theoreticians in world politics look at the domestic affairs of states as matters of little importance. Hans Morgenthau and Kenneth Waltz, the two standard-bearers of the realist and neorealist paradigms, go to great lengths to convince us that reductionist theories of world politics that look to the roles of the individual and societies have little utility (Morgenthau 1978; Waltz 1979). For them, and many others, the nature of the distribution of power within the international system is of the utmost importance (Kaplan 1962; Mearsheimer 1990). But what mechanism establishes and then clarifies the nature of the system to the actors participating in the system? What determines the distribution of power that is accepted by the states in question? I believe it to be the outcomes (or anticipated outcomes) and the resolution of conflicts and wars that establish and alter the nature of the world system and smaller regional systems. Wars are fought for many reasons, all of which have to do with gaining the opportunity to create or maintain sets of rules, whether they are at the individual state level or at the international system level.

Unlike the realists, I am convinced that domestic political factors are of critical importance in determining the winners and losers in war. Of course, the outcomes do not result solely from the interaction of state-level factors, but in this book I will argue that they are among the most important ones for security specialists to focus their research efforts on. This is not to say that the core propositions of the realist paradigm have no use. Rather, the point here is to show how either approach, whether it is realism, which advocates a myopic focus on the power relations among states, or liberalism, which urges a focus on the role that institutions and domestic politics play in world affairs, on its own cannot provide a complete view of how states actually behave during war. To make this point, I develop and test a model of war outcomes using quantitative regression techniques. This allows me to present and analyze the relative effect of the factors that more system-oriented scholars point to, such as relative military-industrial capacity, as well as those factors emphasized by scholars that focus on the state level of analysis, such as democratization and political repression.

Approaches to International Relations

Realism

> It is sufficient to state that the struggle for power is universal in time and space and is an undeniable fact of experience. (Morgenthau 1978, 36)

Realism has been and remains the dominant viewpoint of modern international relations. In 1939, E. H. Carr identified Machiavelli as the first true realist, but it was Carr's *The Twenty Years' Crisis* that clarified the debate between idealists, or utopians as Carr referred to them, and people who argued for "realistic" views of international relations. More than fifty years later, the debate between realists and their opponents is still going strong. Frank Wayman and Paul Diehl, in *Reconstructing Realpolitik*, laid out the basic theoretical propositions of realism in order to see how well they stood up to the historical record. Many of the core assertions or propositions of the realist framework have to do with the initiation of war and as such will only be covered here briefly. In order for power-based theories to be considered valid, they must be able to explain those particular events in the international system that are most clearly about the application of state power, that is, international wars. Realists, or scholars working in the realpolitik tradition, are not just concerned with how states behave with regard to the choice of whether or not to initiate conflict or war. Realism provides a basic set of principles from which an almost endless list of questions about the basic behavior of states flows. In a sense, realism is a well from which we may draw basic propositions about how states can be expected to behave.

In *Politics among Nations*, Morgenthau lays out the six basic principles of his realist paradigm:

1. Politics is governed by objective laws.
2. The main signpost of international politics is the concept of interest defined by power. Political realism contains not only a theoretical but also a normative element.
3. Realism assumes that its key concept of interest, defined as power, is an objective category that is universally valid.
4. Political realism is aware of the moral significance of political action.
5. Political realism refuses to identify the moral aspirations of a particular nation with the moral laws that govern the universe.
6. Intellectually, the political realist maintains the autonomy of the political sphere. He thinks in terms of interest defined as power. The political realist asks: "How does this policy affect the power of the nation?"

While useful as starting points, these basic principles leave many questions about the behavior of states unanswered. Morgenthau, as the prototypical realist, proved to be a very savvy writer. By ordaining his approach to politics "realism," he managed to give the impression that all other approaches were somewhat less than worthwhile, or "unreal." The policy prescriptions that flow from Morgenthau's work are then seen as "realistic," and the prescriptions of those that argue differently, somehow "unrealistic." Anticipating just this sort of reaction, he noted that "[t]hus it is inevitable that a theory which tries to understand international politics as it actually is and as it ought to be in view of its intrinsic nature rather than as people would like to see it, must overcome a psychological resistance that most other branches of learning need not face" (Morgenthau 1978, 15).

Morgenthau frames his theory of political realism in terms of both how the world works and how he believes it ought to work. He buttresses his approach by condemning those who would criticize the theory by asserting that the reason why one might challenge realism is not because realism describes the behavior of the world incorrectly, or in a bad way from a normative perspective, but because people will simply have a psychological resistance to the ideas contained therein, because in some way the uninformed will find his ideas distasteful, but once they "understand," they will see the realist light. In a way, realism is not so much a consistent paradigm but something of a catechism. We will see though, that the arguments of realists prove less efficacious than does a more inclusive approach, whether we view realism as a normative framework for policy makers or as a positivist theory for policy analysts.

The debate between realists and their critics frequently comes down to how one believes that domestic politics should be treated. Morgenthau addresses the junction of international and domestic politics and urges that we should keep them separate:

> An economic, financial, territorial, or military policy undertaken for its sake is subject to evaluation in its own terms. . . . What are the consequences of a change in military policy for education, population, and the domestic political system? The decisions with respect to these policies are made exclusively in terms of such intrinsic considerations. (Morgenthau 1978, 16)

Morgenthau implies that domestic political decisions are made without regard to how they might affect a state's power. Therefore, Morgenthau is asserting that analysts should ignore domestic politics in their analysis of international politics. Morgenthau goes on to allege that states should and will make domestic policy choices that might not be the most fortuitous domestically but can be justified in that they will pay dividends in the international arena:

An economic policy [for example] that cannot be justified in purely economic terms might nevertheless be undertaken in view of the political policy pursued. When the objectives of these policies serve to increase the power of the nation pursuing them in relation to other nations, these policies and their objectives must be judged primarily from the point of view of their contribution to national power. (Morgenthau 1978, 6)

Morgenthau envisions situations where domestic political concerns might impinge upon the international pursuit of power, but he argues that in these cases the policy chosen will be the one that maximizes that country's national power and international influence, regardless of the cost to its citizens. It is the implicit assumption that states choose policies that provide a net benefit to their power capabilities that leads Morgenthau to the conclusion that as students of international politics, we can and should ignore domestic politics and morality as constraints on a state's power: "what decides (not 'what should decide') the issue is the probable effect of these policies upon the power of the nation" (Morgenthau 1978, 35). The following comment of Khrushchev's about the Russo-Finnish war is an example of this type of politics: "There's some question whether we had any legal or moral right for our actions against Finland. Of course we did not have any legal right" (Trotter 1991, 17).

Unfortunately, Morgenthau plays fast and loose with the distinctions between normative and positivist theory, using either one depending on which best fits his purpose. To some, this might appear to be an advantage for the theorist. It certainly makes testing the theory a bit easier. It is problematic, however, if we want to set up testable propositions about how states *will* behave versus how they *ought* to behave. Though the ground is muddied, from either perspective he is fairly clear that policy makers should ignore domestic concerns in determining their foreign policy and resulting pursuit of power and that analysts should ignore domestic politics and focus on how states maximize their power and how international power imbalances lead to potential conflict between nations. Beyond this rather simple credo, several questions about the ways in which states relate to one another come to mind. Wayman and Diehl develop a fairly comprehensive list of the questions that realism raises. Among these and other questions are the following, which are the basic questions relating to wartime behavior:

> While realists agree that states are the key actors in world politics, can states be treated as unitary actors, or must some account be

taken of conflicting groups within them and of the need of state
leaders to mobilize support from these groups?

While such power maximization, survival, or maneuvering requires
calculation of the relative power (and supporting capabilities) of
other states, can such a calculation be precise and accurate, or is
it likely to be unreliable and invalid?

To what degree do states augment their own power by relying on
that of allies? When one relies on allies and war breaks out, how
reliably do they come to one's aid?

How deterministic is the link between superior capabilities and victory in war?

While realists agree that states pursue their self-interest, is their
goal best expressed as maximizing their own power, maximizing
their chance for survival, or maneuvering to weaken dangerous
opponents? (Wayman and Diehl 1994, 7–8)

Each of these questions will be directly addressed in the chapters
that follow. However, it should be noted that some might argue that
Morgenthau is too dated to be taken seriously. More recently, a new
group of realist scholars emerged to modify and extend Carr's and
Morgenthau's work.

Neorealism

By 1979, political science had progressed in both its methodological and
its theoretical sophistication. In an attempt to revive and upgrade the
basic tenets of realism, Kenneth Waltz emerged as the leader of the
neorealist wave with his *Theory of International Politics*. But rather than
broadening the depth and scope of Morgenthau's theory, Waltz narrows
it significantly. In doing so, Waltz also mistakenly alleges that if we
include the domestic level of politics in our studies of international
politics, we immediately reduce our work to the level of mere description. He states that "it is not possible to understand world politics simply
by looking inside of states. If the aims, policies, and actions of states
become matters of exclusive attention or even of central concern, then
we are forced back to the descriptive level; and from simple descriptions
no valid generalizations can logically be drawn" (Waltz 1979, 65). He
reaches this conclusion in part as a result of deductions from a somewhat
misguided assumption: namely, to explain every new event we would
have to include another unit-level variable as its cause. It seems a bit
puzzling that this assumption of the intellectual or analytic slippery slope
would not apply to system-level variables as well. But perhaps this is

why Waltz insists upon an essentially monocausal explanation (international system structure) for the events of world politics.

It is likely that Waltz and other system-level theorists persist in their arguments against the inclusion of domestic politics because they see the analytic process in a different way than those working from a deliberate choice perspective. Realists like Waltz see wars and other international events as caused by, or resulting from, a change in some outside constraint or force that inevitably leads to some potentially faraway reaction. Waltz probably is correct in asserting, assuming that the events we are interested in are caused, and are not simply occurring as the result of some stochastic process, that by focusing on the unit level we would be hard-pressed to account for the staggering degree of continuity in the international system given the equally staggering degree of flux and change at the unit level (Waltz 1979, 64). If we view these events from a perspective of rational choice, we can understand how we can see a fluid domestic environment and a relatively static international system and not be forced to conclude that the system alone should account for the events taking place within the system itself:

> So long as one leaves the structure unaffected, it is not possible for changes in the intentions and the actions of particular actors to produce desirable outcomes or to avoid undesirable ones. The only remedies for strong structural effects are structural changes. . . . Structural constraints cannot be wished away, although many fail to understand this. The international interest must be served; and if that means anything at all, it means that national interests are subordinate to it. (Waltz 1979, 108–9)

This is a clarion call to ignore the effects of domestic- or unit-level politics in our attempts to forecast and understand the behavior of states within the context of the international system. The most vivid example of interstate behavior is war. The logical conclusion one should draw here is that Waltz is trying to show that to understand international politics we should subjugate our interest in the unit level to a focus on the environmental structure that states operate in.

Waltz reaches the final deduction about theoretical perspectives of world politics by concluding that "[o]nly through some sort of systems theory can international politics be understood. To be a success, such a theory has to show how international politics can be conceived of as a domain distinct from the economic, social, and other domains one may conceive of" (Waltz 1979, 79). Figure 1 sketches out Waltz's (and the realists') approach:

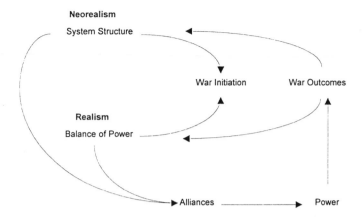

Fig. 1. Relationships between realism, neorealism, and war

The causal loop in figure 1 operates as follows: if we start with the system structure, the allies a state chooses will be strongly influenced by the nature or distribution of power in the international system. Alliances, according to realists and neorealists, are critical components of state power, which in turn determines war outcomes. It is the outcomes of wars that then clarify the nature of the international system, which in turn serves, according to Waltz, as the critical key in our attempts to understand the initiation of war. Of all of the relationships illustrated in figure 1, the relationship between power and outcomes is perhaps the least studied by political scientists.

In this model, Waltz envisions a world where a state's power is a function of its military and industrial capabilities and its alliance portfolio. The most powerful states, those likely to win major wars, are termed "poles," the number of which determines the system's structure. It is this system structure that Waltz argues determines the likelihood of war. This assertion about the omnipotence of systems theory is what Waltz uses to bolster his unwillingness to quantify power. If Waltz were to quantify power, he would necessarily contradict his statement that "only by ignoring unit level characteristics can we understand international politics." Waltz *must* finesse the definition and measurement of poles and power because he also argues that power is a function of many domestic state characteristics.

By arguing that we have no need to include domestic politics, Waltz significantly weakens his ability to construct a positivist theory. He ends up with one that requires the clarity of historical hindsight, relying on historians who have reached a consensus about the number of great powers in a particular period. This problem is similar to that illustrated by arguments about revealed preferences in economics. Until the revelation occurs, we cannot accomplish anything without either assumptions about the nature of preferences or a theory of where preferences come from.

Policy makers must make decisions based on what they see to be the likely outcomes of potential conflicts between states. This leads to a need for a theory of conflict or war outcomes, a way to aggregate the various factors contributing to a state's power, be it a process or a goal— a need that Waltz argues is peripheral to the study of world politics but which I believe to be central.

Domestic-Level Variables and War

Of the various factors that may contribute to deciding war outcomes, why should we be concerned particularly with domestically determined ones? One reason lies in the fact that the social structure of a nation-state permeates its government, regardless of whether that government is a democratic or an authoritarian one. It is the nation-state's government that is responsible for making the decisions that affect the progress that wars take. Given this, it is reasonable to assume that the state's social structure will influence the process by which governments choose to initiate and prosecute wars, which in turn will affect the outcomes of wars. Ethnic biases, class conflict, and inequitable distribution of resources (such as education) within a society may severely affect the state's chances of successfully achieving its military goals. Besides the possible adverse effects of some societal factors, many domestically determined factors such as military strategy are manipulable in the short run, whereas the structure of the international system is not.

Standard notions of outcomes in the political science literature depend on variables that affect both war outcomes and war initiation (national- and systemic-level variables like gross national product [GNP], population, and the international distribution of power), which states cannot manipulate in the short run. As far as international systemic variables go, some, such as alliance portfolios, are manipulable in the short run, but others, such as the polarity of the system, may not be manipulable even in the long run.

In contrast to many of the systemic factors, many domestic-level factors are far more malleable. A state may alter its military strategy relatively easily and significantly change the way it prepares to fight wars or to prevent them. A state may change its strategy quickly compared to raising its GNP, for example. Because of this, states may be inclined to use strategy changes as a way to improve their capabilities more cheaply or more quickly than if they sought improvement in military performance through more structural or fundamental changes.

Aside from simply being manipulable, factors such as military strategy affect the efficiency of a state's armed forces. In other words, different strategies designed to reach the same goals (winning wars) may require more resources to execute than others. In the absence of assumptions about the role of a state's military-industrial complex (another domestic-level variable), states should be inclined to pick the strategy that meets their security needs at the lowest cost. By understanding the implications of these potential strategy changes we may be better able to understand the longer-term costs and benefits beyond the superficial short-term monetary savings associated with strategy and mobilization choices.

Understanding how domestic-level variables such as strategy affect outcomes may also allow us to better understand the sometimes puzzling relationships of these same variables to war initiation. Domestic factors such as organizational inertia may also be an important factor in a state's decision to go to war. As Stephen Van Evera (1984) points out, when many states share offensive strategies and believe that conflict with an adversary is likely some time in the future, the incentive to fight a preventive war may be overwhelming.[2] As a result, states may become involved in wars that they really do not desire to be in. Jack Snyder and Robert Jervis (1991) expand on this theme by investigating the domestic sources of empire overexpansion and conclude that political logrolling within legislative bodies lies at the root of imperial overexpansion and collapse. In this way (and in others detailed later) domestic-level variables become powerful factors determining both the outcome and origins of war. By understanding their relationship to outcomes, we will be better able to understand why states sometimes make choices that appear to reduce their security by increasing the risk of war, a risk balanced in leaders' minds by a greater chance of success should war actually come.

Of course, concerns about the links between domestic-level variables and international politics are not novel. A. F. K. Organski and Jacek Kugler's (1980) power transition theory and Robert Gilpin's (1981) hegemonic stability theory seek to explain the initiation of war by great powers as resulting from changes in the international distribution of power. But where realists frequently decline to address where these shifts in power come from, Organski and Kugler argue that shifts in power distributions come from changes in states' domestic characteristics, particularly their political development and economic decline. These authors are concerned primarily with understanding the onset of war rather than closely investigating the links between the political culture and domestic politics of various states, on the one hand, and the nature of the international system, on the other. Even strict rational choice writers such as Bruce Bueno de Mesquita (1981) focus on integrating domestic factors into models of decision making to better understand how wars begin. These initial steps taken to link domestic factors and international processes miss the critical area that this book addresses. It is not the initiation of wars and conflicts that alters the international system so much as it is the resolution and outcomes of these wars and conflicts.

Studies on the relation between domestic politics and states' ability to wage war have been largely historical and anecdotal, the work of Klaus Knorr (1962) being a notable exception. While Bueno de Mesquita and Siverson (1995) discuss the relationship between war outcomes and domestic political institutions, they do not investigate the differences in the process by which democracies fight; rather, they investigate the different types of wars that democracies choose to fight in. It is this selection effect that they argue accounts for much of the variation in outcomes. While this is an important argument that we should be aware of, there are examples where the domestic political unrest or lack of support for a war affect *how* the state fought in the war and not just whether the state became involved in the war or not. The United States' behavior during its war with Vietnam is an often cited example.

**Examples of Domestic Politics and
War-Fighting Efficiency**

The depth of the domestic unpopularity of the United States' war in Vietnam profoundly affected U.S. military behavior in Asia and at home. Realizing the limited stakes in Vietnam, U.S. presidents from Eisenhower to Nixon strictly limited the number of soldiers that the military could call up from either the reserves or through the draft. Due to shortages of trained soldiers even during the early years of the Vietnam War, the U.S. Army cut military training courses by several weeks in length to assign soldiers more quickly to rapidly alerted units. According to Shelby Stanton, "(t)raining standards slipped due to rapid turnover" (1985, 25). He points out that during the war, compressed and accelerated training programs became the norm. This situation was aggravated by the decline in the quality of recruits compared to those recruited during peacetime. These changes, Stanley Karnow (1983) argues, were instrumental in the failure of U.S. policy in Southeast Asia. Due to personnel considerations and to the fact that the war was far from home where domestic support eroded steadily over the years, the army insisted upon one-year, fixed-duration tours for the soldiers fighting in Vietnam. This was in contrast to the standard of "duration plus six months" in place during previous wars. This personnel policy, reflecting domestic political concerns, had a deleterious effect on the army's efficiency. Stanton argues that just as soldiers became proficient at fighting in the foreign terrain of Vietnam, they were yanked from the theater. Replacements needed to become acclimatized to the area and had to immediately learn all the skills needed to survive in the jungle that the departing soldiers had mastered over the course of their yearlong tour. "A popular military adage summed it up: the United States never fought in Vietnam ten years, it fought in Vietnam one year ten times" (Stanton 1985, 27).

States that face domestic instability during wartime may find their ability to project force into the interstate war they are involved in significantly reduced. The source of this instability is not terribly important. What is important is how it may detract from the overall war effort. As a result, states may resort to draconian policies at home during wartime to reduce their domestic security commitments while the foreign security commitments are being tested in war. Domestic instability resulting from the racial divisions within the United States tapped into the United States' military strength and affected its ability to project its power abroad. During the riots in Detroit in 1967 alone, the U.S. government stationed fifteen thousand federal troops in Detroit. The army's elite Eighty-Second Airborne Division fought primarily during the Vietnam War, not on the front line as overseas shock troops as they had during World War II, but in burnt-out laundromats or returning sniper fire from abandoned buildings in Washington D.C., Detroit, and Newark (Stanton 1985, 203).

If we ignore domestic politics and its connections to a state's power (during war, state power might be thought of as the ability to win), we will frequently miss critical events in the internal affairs of states that may have significant international repercussions. In an example from the Soviet Union, David Holloway points to Stalin's purges of the Red Army during the late 1930s, which, while they served Stalin's domestic political agenda, certainly affected the operating efficiency of his army as well. During the 1930s, Stalin was forced to strike a balance between the external demands of ensuring the security of his state and the need to maintain control over his domestic rivals, whether real or imagined. In 1937, the Red Army became Stalin's target for investigation and purge. The majority of brigade-level and higher commanders were shot or arrested. Field-grade and junior-level officers also suffered enormous losses, many being shot or sent to camps in Siberia. "The Red Army lost more officers in these peacetime years than any army ever did in war." Stalin's purges destroyed the reform movement that had been underway for years after the disastrous war against the Japanese. Most of the military innovators, including General Tukhachevsky, who was responsible for a novel way of integrating infantry and armor in a mobile defense in depth, were arrested and then replaced by men far less capable (Holloway 1985, 10). The military innovations associated with the men arrested or shot were then viewed with suspicion and dropped from the Soviet doctrinal plans. "The resulting loss of direction was reflected in the general disarray of the Red Army in 1938–41 and contributed to its poor showing in the war with Finland in the winter of 1939–40." As a result of the purges, driven by domestic political needs, the Red Army was not ready for the German attack in 1941, and the German army was quickly able to occupy large parts of the Soviet Union. By late 1941, the outcome of the war between Germany and the Soviet Union was very much in doubt, arguably due in large part to domestic unrest during the interwar period (Holloway 1985, 10–11).

The relationship between domestic politics and the outcomes of war also fits into a broader literature that investigates the so-called democratic peace. Much of the more recent work attacking the realist paradigm focuses on the role that democratization plays in the probability of observing conflict behavior.

Integrating Realist and Domestic Approaches: Rational Choice

The rational choice paradigm is an attractive alternative to realism and strict institutionalist or domestic political models. There is no compelling reason to assume that some vaguely operationalized mechanism causes international events. Using the rational choice approach, we can understand the role of the various and often complex factors that affect the decision makers' preferences for various outcomes (likely determined by unit-level factors). We can also better understand the payoffs associated with various outcomes that are determined by a combination of system structure and domestic political effects. While decision makers' choices affect the nature and timing of the outcomes in question, these outcomes are things that state leaders cannot choose directly. For instance, we typically would not think that leaders can choose to win wars, otherwise there would never be losers. The choices made will affect the timing of the outcome and whether the war began in the first place. The structure of the environment, both at the unit level and the system level, plays a powerful role in determining the likely outcomes.

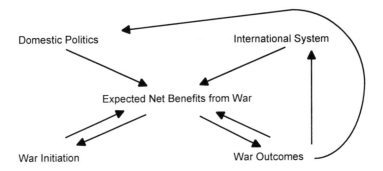

Fig. 2. Relationships between domestic politics, expected net benefits of war, and war initiation and outcomes

In this way, we can accommodate both the structuralists and the scholars who argue that domestic-level incentives and constraints cannot be ignored either. The structure will affect the probabilities associated with the various outcomes that a particular policy choice might lead to (victory, loss, ties). Domestic-level incentives will affect the preferences of the actors for the particular outcomes and their willingness to bear the costs associated with the payoffs and probabilities of the various outcomes in question. Figure 2 shows several of the approaches to studying war that rational choice scholars have adopted. It is important to realize that there is not one single rational choice theory but rather a large group of work that ranges from formal theory to case study work. The common theme of this approach is that these scholars all believe that deliberate choices made by self-interested egoists drive much of the behavior we observe in the international system (Green and Shapiro 1994). While Green and Shapiro see this flexibility as part of the "pathology of rational choice," I believe it to be the most profitable way that we can develop and test increasingly complex models without degenerating into a one-case, one-theory mentality. At the same time, a rational perspective allows us to maintain a unified theoretical structure to guide us toward solutions when history does not match our expectations.

In figure 2, each arrow represents a causal relationship and a significant area of study within the international relations literature. The relationship between the utility or expected net benefits from war and war initiation (rather than outcomes) has been the primary focus of rational choice scholars, with a few notable exceptions (Wittman 1979; Morrow 1987). This book focuses on these net costs and benefits and their collective relationship to war outcomes.

From the rational actor perspective, Bueno de Mesquita and Siverson (1995) build on a rapidly expanding literature in their attempt to show how states' domestic politics affect the international system by investigating the relationships between domestic politics, war initiation, and war outcomes (see also Bueno de Mesquita and Lalman 1992; Organski and Kugler 1980; Kilgour 1991). Following this line of argument, others have shown that, at least in the case of the United States, domestic political factors have more influence on a president's willingness to use force than do international ones (Gaubatz 1991; Morrow 1991). Randolph Siverson and Juliann Emmons (1991) argue that democracies have significantly different alliance patterns (which will be shown to influence outcomes) than nondemocracies.

Also from a rational choice perspective, Christopher Mitchell argues that the timing of the ending of the war, an event that will certainly affect the war's outcome, is the result of states' preferences, which are the aggregation of preference orderings or utility functions across a wide set of groups. The problem is that the different groups' utility functions may vary significantly from the "national interest" or the interests that the realists identify. "If this situation arises frequently—and recent research indicates that it does—then classical utility models require modification if they are to help in analyzing the empirical process of war termination" (Mitchell 1991, 51).

Bueno de Mesquita et al. (1992) find strong support for the argument that war will have significant effects on the domestic politics of states. They make the empirical ex post observation that domestic groups typically punish regimes for poor wartime performance. They conclude that anticipation of the effect will affect the likelihood of war initiation, which in turn will affect the type of wars that democracies become involved in, which in turn affects the types of outcomes we should expect to be associated with democracies and nondemocracies (Bueno de Mesquita et al. 1992, 644). These findings buttress the increasing criticism of the realist paradigm. Using a rational choice approach, Bueno de Mesquita and Lalman have shown in *War and Reason* (1992) that domestic politics directly affects states' utility for war initiation and that outcomes of war have significant effects on domestic politics as well.

Realists dismiss studies that demonstrate links between domestic politics and war initiation on normative grounds. They argue that if states would only ignore domestic pressures, they would then be able to pursue more "realistic" and by implication, better, foreign policies. Realists also argue that those studies that demonstrate the connection between war and domestic political change are irrelevant to the question they find most interesting: what causes the initiation of major wars

(Wayman and Diehl 1994; Waltz 1979, 65). From the realist perspective though, links between domestic politics and war outcomes, if they exist, cannot be ignored. By shifting back and forth from a positivist to a normative perspective, realists have been able to dodge difficult questions about persistent gaps between theory and reality. But in the pursuit of security and the application of power, war is the ultimate test in international relations. I argue that war emerges as *the* critical case with which we can investigate the relative merit of the realist paradigm. By showing that domestic politics and political structures both critically affect war outcomes, this book, along with other recent works, suggests a significant, but redressable, flaw in the realist paradigm.

The Interaction of Choices and Structural Constraints

One advantage of the rational actor perspective is that it allows us to explicitly combine both the choices that leaders make and the constraining characteristics of the political structure that they operate within. In the following chapters I will demonstrate that the complex interaction of the choices that leaders and participants make (both before the beginning of the war and during the war) and the structure in which the decisions are made determine the outcomes of wars.

To illustrate this notion of the interaction between choice and structure, consider the following example: few would argue that an army's choice of military strategy would have little effect on the outcome of a battle or war, but the choice alone will not determine the outcome. Various structural factors affect the relative efficiency of a state's choices or its ability to make the choice at all. States fight on some sort of terrain, whether that terrain is on the ground, in the air, or under the sea. The terrain on which the states fight will have an impact on which types of strategies will be most likely to succeed. In this notion, terrain, a factor that the states at war cannot alter (although they may choose to take the fight to a different venue), serves as a structure within which the strategies of the two sides interact. One way to think of structure is to think of the factors that states' leaders cannot change in the short run. An example of this type of factor is the role that a state's population plays in determining outcomes. In the short run, states cannot change the population that they have available to mobilize. The state can choose to mobilize fewer or more combatants, but its ability to mobilize is constrained or limited by the size of the state's population, which serves as a structural constraint on military mobilization. In large part, this book is an investigation of the relationship between the choices that leaders of states and armies must make and the constraining physical and political structures in which the choices are made.

War Outcomes

Military and defense organizations invest heavily in war gaming or operations research in attempts to forecast the outcomes of battles. However, these models typically ignore or assume away the political variables that I argue will have significant effects on the eventual outcomes. Standard models of attrition and outcomes find that wars continue until one side or the other, typically referred to as the vanquished, cries "Enough!" But finding or predicting the point at which a state makes the necessary plaintive cry is exceedingly difficult. In almost all wars, further resistance is possible until the last person is dead. It is not necessary, typically, with perhaps the exception of the nineteenth-century war in Paraguay, to kill all the men in a country to defeat it in a war. "All that is usually necessary is to destroy the enemy's force as a force. . . . To scatter and dissipate an organized force is the equivalent of destroying it," if the organization's effectiveness relies critically upon its ability to control and regulate the ebb and flow of supplies and communications (Calahan 1944, 229). The other problem with finding the critical point at which a state will quit is that the point varies over time and by regime. During World War I, France lost six hundred thousand men at Verdun and stayed in the war. During World War II, France lost fifty thousand men over a five-week period and quit, giving up the entire country (Calahan 1944, 231).

Jacek Kugler and William Domke argue that the fundamental test for any measure of a state's power is "the accurate anticipation of the outcome of conflicts in which contestants are fully committed to victory" (Kugler and Domke 1986, 43). While this makes sense at first review, the problem with this sort of logic is that it may degenerate into a tautology. Wars with unanticipated outcomes will have occurred because one actor or the other did not "fully commit" themselves. It is an obvious proposition that a country with greater resources will win against an opponent with fewer resources if both sides use all the resources available to them efficiently. The problem is that, even during the world wars, the vast majority of actors were never fully committed down to the last dispensable person and efficiency levels vary tremendously from state to state.

The more challenging and interesting test is to be able to construct a model of war outcomes that will account for the majority of instances where either one or both of the combatants are not fully mobilized but nonetheless involved in a major war. In this regard, Zeev Maoz (1983) compares the relative efficacy of a power model versus a model incorporating resolve. The power politics model is a simple representation of the argument that in interstate disputes it is the balance of military capabilities that is the critical determinant of the outcomes. In contrast, the resolve model that Maoz develops and tests argues that the outcomes are the result of the balance of motivation rather than the balance of capabilities (Maoz 1983, 199).

One of the more notable attempts to construct a deductive model of war outcomes comes from Organski and Kugler's *War Ledger* (1980). Their two major findings are as follows:

1. Existing measures of national capabilities evaluate inaccurately the strength of the contestants in three of the four conflicts they studied. Given the outcomes of the wars, estimates that South Vietnam was stronger than North Vietnam, that South Korea was stronger than North Korea, and that the Arabs were stronger than the Israelis were obviously erroneous.

2. By combining socioeconomic indices with direct measures of political performance they correct many of the deficiencies of existing measures. The correction that this political index introduces into overall models of national capabilities is substantial (Organski and Kugler 1980, 101).

Unfortunately, Organski and Kugler's model is dependent on a somewhat arbitrary transformation of the two sides' GNP. Each side's power is estimated by adding their internal national capabilities to the capabilities contributed by other actors. These capabilities are weighted by population and the state's relative tax effort, raised to the 1.75 power. The exponent of 1.75 results from a desire to give greater weight to the domestic component than the external components of power (Organski and Kugler 1980, 85).

From logic about the willingness of nations to suffer, Steven Rosen (1972) suggests a simple model that incorporates both capabilities and willingness to suffer:

Power Ratio: = Power of Party A / Power of Party B
= (Cost-Tolerance of A/Strength B)/(Cost Tolerance of B/Strength A)

This identity captures the trade-off that allows an opponent to compensate for shortcomings in the ability to inflict punishment by a greater

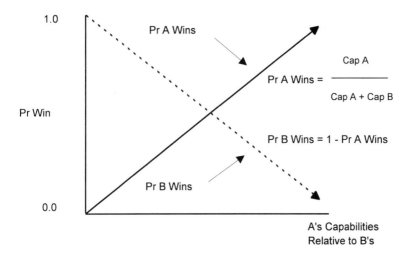

Fig. 3. Forecasting zero-sum outcomes: A simple ratio of the two actors' capabilities

willingness to suffer during the conflict. Figure 3 presents a graphic interpretation of Rosen's and Organski and Kugler's theories of outcomes. First, notice that the notion of outcome is zero-sum in that as one side's chances of victory increase, the other side's chances decrease at exactly the same rate. Another potential shortcoming visible in the graph is the problem of how to anticipate draws. According to this type of approach, draws can only occur at the point of intersection between the two sides' capabilities lines or when the two sides' capabilities are exactly equal. Because this point is infinitesimally small, draws, for all practical purposes, should not occur. I will address this problem in the model developed later in the text.

Rosen's test of the model relies on GNP as an indicator of strength. He bases this less upon a theoretical argument than on a reading of the literature and by identifying the consensus of "GNP as the most useful simple measure of physical strength in war" (Rosen 1972, 259). He does admit that "none [of the studies] has validated the GNP measure of war power by showing that it correlates with the winning of wars" (Rosen 1972, 259). After deciding upon GNP as a measure of strength, Rosen then tackles the problem of measuring the willingness to suffer and settles on an ex-post indicator: battle deaths.

Maoz measured the notion of a side's willingness to escalate a dispute at a faster rate than the opponent. The advantage of the Maoz technique is that it allows for policy prescriptions for future situations. Rosen's approach is a bit more inductive. He argues that "we do not . . . have a good way of gauging the cost-tolerance attitudes of parties in wars of the past." Instead of using a measure that might have greater ex ante predictive power, Rosen used the ratio of battle deaths of the two sides, something that can only be observed ex post.

> If there is a very strong correlation between losing fewer lives and winning, then we may infer that cost-tolerance is not major factor since the party that inflicted greater harm usually won. If on the other hand there is not a strong tendency for the party losing fewer lives to win, then the hypotheses are at least not disconfirmed. (Rosen 1972, 261)

Rosen found that there were no "very strong" correlations regarding battle deaths. In 30 cases, the winner lost more lives, and in 18 cases the loser did. Interestingly, in 28 out of 40 cases, Rosen found that the side with the larger population won. While Rosen's work is interesting, it is not surprising that his results were inconclusive insofar as his many measures were simply tested using bivariate correlations, not controlling for the effects of multiple factors simultaneously.

Continuing our review of the potential indicators of outcomes, Blainey, in *Causes of War* (1973), identifies a series of factors that he believes influence states' abilities to wage war. He suggests that nations, in assessing their relative strength, are influenced by seven main factors:

1. Military strength and the ability to apply that strength efficiently in the chosen zone of war.
2. Predictions of how outside nations would behave in the event of war.
3. Perceptions of internal unity and of the unity or discord of the enemy.
4. Memory or forgetfulness of the realities and sufferings of war.
5. Perceptions of prosperity and of ability to sustain, economically, the kind of war envisaged.
6. Nationalism and ideology.
7. The personality and mental qualities of the leaders who weighed the evidence and decided for peace or war (Blainey 1973, 123).

While each of these factors would appear to be logically linked to war outcomes, Blainey offers no real theory of outcomes, just a set of logical arguments and a series of illustrative historical case studies.

While most political scientists have expended little effort to estimate models of war and battle outcomes, military organizations and researchers under their contract have developed sophisticated models of battle dynamics. Working principally in what is known as the operations research area, Joshua Epstein notes:

> The Lanchester equations have for decades dominated the dynamic assessment of conventional land balances. The United States Army, the Joint Chiefs of Staff, and analytic directorates within the Office of the Secretary of Defense employ Lanchester-based models to assess theater balances and to aid in the selection of weapons systems. Theater-level combat modeling conducted under contract to the Pentagon is also dominated by Lanchester theory and its extensions. Lanchester models are employed by prominent independent defense analysts, they are central to force planning curricula at major universities and post-graduate service schools, and they form the core of the scholarly literature on conventional war gaming and simulation. (Epstein 1987, 9–10)

Epstein offers a complex alternative model of battle engagements, but not one that forecasts the wars' outcomes. To do so, he would have to incorporate political constraints on decision making, something that is noticeably absent from the operations research part of the field.

While the various research approaches noted earlier offer useful insights into the conduct of war, none integrates the military aspects of the operations research field with the more political components found in models of domestic conflict developed in the political science field. A theory that did this would present a strong challenge to the realists' arguments about the role of states' domestic politics as determinants of international relations.

To demonstrate the validity of my earlier assertions, we must develop a general theory of how wars end and a systematic way to test the hypotheses that flow from the theory against a broad set of cases. This approach is not intended to be the final word on this subject but rather to complement the work on dispute initiation that shows us when the states will be likely to challenge the international status quo. This study will help us understand, given a challenge, when the status quo will be altered. Others have shown how different types of status quos can have different implications for how states will interact and for the role the states' governments will have in shaping the nature of their states' relationships (McKeown 1983; Krasner 1985; Milner 1988).

For the security field, interstate wars provide a rich research environment in which to develop and test hypotheses about competition, conflict, and outcomes. By adopting a part of the theoretical approach of political economists who investigate the role of process in determining outcomes with the methodological approaches frequently found in quantitative security studies (Bueno de Mesquita 1981; Huth 1988; Bueno de Mesquita and Lalman 1986, 1992), I hope to broaden our understanding of the important factors at work in determining the outcomes of cases relevant to security studies in particular and to international relations in general.

Systematically Building a Model of Outcomes

The rest of this book proceeds in methodical fashion, starting with a very simple approach followed by a series of arguments that allow us to build in more of the apparent complexity observed in the real world. In the next chapter, I will present a simple model of the choices that leaders make at the end of a war that determines its outcome. The point of this chapter is not to develop a complete theory of war but rather to develop a set of hypotheses about how the outcome variable should be coded (win, lose, draw), what type of statistical model should be used to test the hypotheses, and what general types of variables are needed to adequately model outcomes. In chapters 3 and 4, I identify and develop sets of indicators or predictors for the costs and benefits that states incur while waging war. I also develop and test a simple model of war duration. Following the arguments in chapter 2, the various factors discussed are split into two principal groups:

1. Factors that affect the costs associated with fighting, which are determined by the actors' choices both prior to and during the war.
2. Factors that are structural constraints or factors that the actors do not get to choose, such as population, democracy, and so on.

Additionally, I identify each variable as not only a choice or structural variable but also as a realpolitik variable or domestic political variable. Each of the two sets of variables are operationally defined, and the hypothesis associated with each will be laid out as they should affect the outcomes of wars. The information is arranged into the same two categories as earlier, choices and structural constraints, with similar distinctions between realpolitik and domestic variables.

In chapter 5, I present the empirical results of a statistical model of outcomes. Following the discussion of the overall statistical model fit to the data, in chapter 6, I discuss the results for the choice variables (strategy, repression, initiation, surprise, and doctrine), highlighting the difference between realpolitik variables and domestic political variables. Chapter 7 presents the results for various structural constraint variables (capabilities, democracy, population, terrain, time, allies, and distance) and discusses the difference between the relative effects of the variables identified on outcomes. Here it becomes clear that neither the domestic politics approach nor the realpolitik approach alone allow us to best understand war outcomes.

In the concluding chapter, I explain how the various choices leaders must make (strategy, mobilization, repression, etc.) fit together with the various types of structural constraints they face during a war. This discussion illustrates the relationship between choices (things that decision makers can control) and constraints (things that they cannot control).

CHAPTER 2

Hypotheses on the Outcomes of War

Introduction

In 1961, America's president, John F. Kennedy, told the nation in his inaugural address that Americans should "(l)et every nation know, whether it wishes us well or ill, that we shall pay any price, bear any burden, meet any hardship, support any friend, oppose any foe to assure the survival and success of liberty." If this statement had proved true, the outcome of the Vietnam War would likely have been far different than it was. In the end, the United States was unwilling to bear the hardship and the costs of an unpopular war thousands of miles away against a seemingly overmatched foe. Many in the policy-making and military communities seemed perplexed by the inability of the United States to defeat a clearly weaker foe. The following conversation between Colonel Harry G. Summers and one of his North Vietnamese counterparts sums up the thoughts of many on both sides of the war:

> "You know," he [Summers] boasted to a North Vietnamese colonel after the war, "you never defeated us on the battlefield." To which the Communist officer replied, "That may be so, but it is also irrelevant." (Karnow 1983, 19)

Ultimately, the decision makers in a state at war must ask themselves if the potential gains from victory are worth the costs of continuing to fight. This is precisely the problem that the United States faced in Vietnam, where the insurgents in the south and their allies in the north were prepared to accept substantial punishment rather than abandon their goal of destroying the U.S.-backed regime in Saigon. "In fact, the level of violence the Americans inflicted against the Vietnamese in their attempt to compel them to stop fighting in the south increased so enormously that it eventually unnerved not the recipients, but the deliverers" (Rothgeb 1993, 104). This willingness or ability to inflict punishment is not an absolute. Rather, the willingness to participate in the use and reception of force varies according to the issue at stake. In the war against the Japanese in 1945, the United States did not hesitate long to use the most massive display of force in the history of mankind when it dropped nuclear bombs on Nagasaki and Hiroshima.

This chapter will make three very basic and important points that serve as the theoretical basis for the rest of the book. First, war is a mutual attempt at coercion, meaning it is about imposing costs and seeking benefits. This means that war continues when, for both sides, the prospect of accruing benefits exceeds the prospect of accepting more costs. Second, wars end when one or both sides see costs as exceeding benefits. The implications of this is that we must be able to measure how costs are imposed and what the prospective benefits would be. This also means that time is crucial, as more time means more costs (one could also argue that more time leads to the discounting of benefits, as one doesn't receive the benefits until a longer and longer time in the future). Third, outcomes include victory, loss, and draw, which leads to the deduction that an increasing probability of victory for one actor does *not* necessarily mean decreasing probability of defeat for the other.

In order to make these points and to generate empirical support for them, I make three basic assumptions about the nature of decision makers and the information available to them. First, I assume that decision makers are rational. By this I do not mean that they have access to perfect information. During a war, one of the greatest problems leaders face is a shortage of useful information. Typically, leaders are awash in data that they cannot process quickly enough to make completely informed decisions. When I say that decision makers are rational, I mean that the choices they make are deliberate and that they prefer fewer costs to greater, and greater benefits to fewer. Second, states also have incomplete information, which means they do not know the costs they must inflict upon their opponent to drive it out of the war. Third, there is genuine uncertainty about the outcomes due to the stochastic nature of highly complex systems.

Theoretical Outline

The model of outcomes I develop here and in the following chapters is essentially structural, based not on a strategic decision-making or game theoretic model but rather on the structure of capabilities and resolve present at the outset of a war. While it might be tempting to try and model war outcomes using a game theoretic approach, a simple analogy illustrates the likely futility of that approach.

The game of chess has long been viewed as a particularly apt analogy for war. When writers describe chess strategy, they frequently refer to what occurs on the chessboard as "war." Similarly, military historians frequently bring to mind chess analogies when they discuss strategic choices made during wartime, talking about gambits and endgames. But chess is, of course, a game. Compared to what occurs during war, chess is actually quite simple. There are only two sides, and no others may join during the game. There are a known and equal number of pieces on each side. The sixteen pieces that are at the disposal of each player move according to known and agreed upon rules. Also, rules clearly establish what it means to win, lose, or agree to a draw in a game of chess. Both players have the complete history of the game they are playing along with the records of all the moves made in thousands of prior games available to them. Serious players may spend years studying the strategies and outcomes of previous games, all played using the same rules under the same conditions. From this view, we might expect chess to be a rather trivial game, similar to tic-tac-toe perhaps. While we might expect such a simple and rigidly structured game to yield a simple solution, chess has proved far more complex and intractable than one might imagine.[1]

In theory, the solution to chess should exist. But because of the possible number of combinations of moves, no one has been able to specify what the best strategy is. Some of the greatest minds in history have tried, and failed, to find the solution or the best way to play chess. Computer programs designed to exploit the speed and data processing capabilities of the latest supercomputers have also failed to yield the solution to chess. Because the initial positions are known and the number of pieces and rules fixed, there should be a "best" or winning strategy, or we should be able to predict that the "best" strategy results in a draw. Unfortunately, because the possible permutations are so large, no one has been able to discover the optimal strategy.[2] "When chess players talk of strategy, they mean something like 'open with the king's Indian Defense and play aggressively.' In game theory, a strategy is a much more specific plan. It is a complete description of a particular way to play a game, no matter what the other player(s) does and no matter how long the game lasts" (Poundstone 1992, 48).

War is far more complex than chess. In chess, the rules are known. In war, while there are rules or general standards of behavior (the Geneva Convention for example), there is no enforcement mechanism even for the basic guidelines that do exist. In chess, if the pieces return to the same position three times, the game is declared a draw. In war, states make up the ending rules as they go along, with neither side knowing, for certain, if the one side is using the same rules as the other, or if the decision rules have changed during the course of the game. In chess, because the number of pieces is fixed along with the number of sides and the location where the pieces can be placed, we can specify or know the opening strategies. In war, states deliberately try to introduce new strategies, tactics, and technologies during the contest. In war, the sides in effect hide some of their pieces, introducing them into parts of the game where the opponent does not suspect they will appear. In short, if a game as simple as chess has resisted a game theoretic solution, it is unlikely that game theory would be the most profitable approach for studying war outcomes.

Now, we should note that while chess has remained "unsolved" despite the best efforts of millions of players, we do know a great deal about what types of general approaches work better than others. The outcomes of chess matches are not random. Just because Bobby Fischer does not know how to deductively solve a chess game, it does not follow that Bobby Fischer cannot be expected to win most matches against most opponents. Just because we cannot solve the game theoretically does not mean that we do not know a tremendous amount about how to best play the game. From empirical analysis, that is, by reviewing thousands of games that have been played in the past, we know that opening with the center pawns tends to be more successful than opening with a knight's pawn or a rook's pawn. Chess experts can tell us with strong assurance that if we move our queen around during the opening our chances of winning will be greatly reduced. How do they know this? By analyzing previously played games. In a sense, this is the approach that I take in this book. I will systematically investigate the wars that have occurred in the past to learn which strategies work best and which do not, much as chess masters have tried to provide insight into the game of chess.

Coercion, Compellance, and War

During any type of conflict at least two sides try to change the policies or behaviors of the other.[3] Whether the two sides are groups within a state, a group trying to change a recalcitrant government's policies, or two states fighting in a war, the various actors attempt to manipulate the other side's policies to bring them more in line with their own preferences. Prior to the initiation of conflict, states and other actors may try negotiation, incentives, or diplomacy. After a conflict begins, however, actors use different, more forceful, methods to coerce the opponent to change the policy at the root of the dispute.

Actors try to coerce others by inflicting punishment on them (Schelling 1966). This punishment can take many forms. Military force may come to mind when we think of interstate disputes (Art and Waltz 1983). Political repression, using both violent and nonviolent behavioral

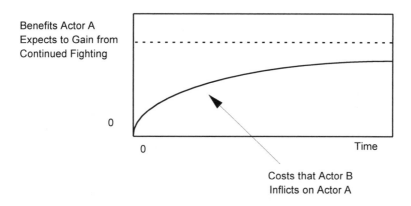

Fig. 4. Scenario one: Actor A does not quit. The costs inflicted by B do not exceed the benefits A expects to receive

control measures, is also an example of the tools of intrastate coercion (Miles 1984). According to Thomas Schelling, a state will be successfully coerced when it can no longer afford to absorb the punishment being inflicted upon it by its adversary. But this view only presents half the story. Traditionally, studies of coercion look at one actor trying to coerce another (Pape 1990). But this misspecifies the problem; war is an example of mutual coercion.

States go to war to compel or coerce an adversary to do something. The actor in the war that has been attacked is also trying to execute a policy of coercion once the war has begun, at a minimum trying to get its adversary to stop waging the war against it. This is not a universally accepted way of defining war, however. Glenn Snyder argues that there is a conceptual difference between compellance or coercion and defense. He argues that defense is largely the process of damage limitation: "Defense means reducing our own prospective costs and risks . . . defense reduces the enemy's capability to damage or deprive us; the defense value of military forces is their effect in mitigating the adverse consequences for us of possible enemy moves" (Snyder 1968, 33). The problem with this notion of defense is that it precludes the idea that some defenses may look suspiciously like good offenses. Because of this, and because Schelling's argument makes equal sense for both the titular defender and aggressors, inasmuch as both are trying to change the policies of their respective opponents, I argue that war is best thought of as an instance of simultaneous or mutual coercion.

We might represent this mutual coercion in the following way. In figures 4 and 5, Actor B is trying to coerce Actor A into choosing some

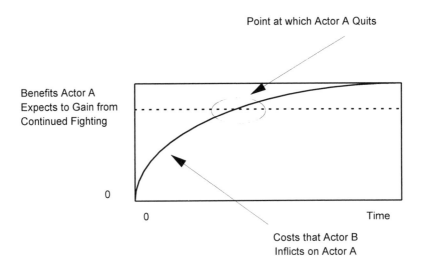

Fig. 5. Scenario two: Actor A quits. Costs inflicted by B have exceeded the benefits A expected to receive

policy by waging war against, or inflicting costs on Actor A. The two scenarios are graphic representations of what happens during war as one actor tries to compel the other actor to quit fighting. In scenario 1 there is some threshold or set of benefits that state A expects to gain from winning. That threshold is represented by the dotted line in figure 1. Over time, the costs that Actor B inflicts upon Actor A rise monotonically. The slope of the cost curve represents the rate at which costs accrue to Actor A. The height of the cost curve represents the total costs at a particular time that Actor B has inflicted on Actor A. As long as the costs that Actor B has inflicted upon Actor A remain below Actor A's benefits threshold, Actor A will continue to fight. Scenario 2 (fig. 5) demonstrates how wars come to a conclusion. Actor A quits fighting when the costs imposed upon it by Actor B cross A's benefits threshold.

In scenario 2, Actor A quits at the circled point in time, where B's punishments have exceeded the benefits A expected to receive. The notion of the two sides in a war having some capacity to absorb punishment or costs and their respective opponents trying to cross that threshold derives principally from Schelling's arguments about the coercive use of force. Schelling argues that

War appears to be, or threatens to be, not so much a contest of strength as one of endurance, nerve, obstinacy, and pain. It appears to be, and threatens to be, not so much a contest of military strength as a bargaining process—dirty, extortionate, and often quite reluctant bargaining on one side or both—nevertheless a bargaining process. (Schelling 1966, 7)

As an exemple of this punishment by one side against another, Schelling points to the terror tactics of the Jews in Palestine during the 1940s. He argues that the Jews could not expel the British, but they could inflict so much punishment on them that by crossing the threshold of Britain's willingness or ability to absorb punishment the Jews were able to influence the British decision-making process and compel them to leave the Jews alone (Schelling 1966, 6).

While Schelling and others preached the subtle virtues of coercion, in practice the sophisticated logic that underpinned his arguments frequently fell apart. To a large extent this is likely because Schelling's theory of coercion and compellance was so one-sided. The United States' strategy in the Vietnam War is an illustrative case. The U.S. policy of combining negotiations with threats, which were sometimes carried out and other times not, would appear to be just the kind of coercive diplomacy Schelling was talking about. The policies failed, however, because U.S. decision makers were unable to understand the beliefs and resolve of their North Vietnamese counterparts, who in turn had a more sophisticated understanding of the United States' cost threshold. We are left then with a need to develop a more sophisticated approach to mutual coercion outcomes. As Jervis points out, "although current theories of coercion can, then, explain why the policy was adopted, they cannot tell us why it failed or why the decision makers were so slow to see the problems" (Jervis 1985, 8).

According to my approach, one actor's ability to coerce another to change its policy depends on two factors, similar for each actor. In order to be able to coerce or compel another, an actor must be able to inflict some form of punishment on the opponent, thereby raising the opponent's costs and reducing its expected net gains for fighting. At the same time, in order to be successful, this actor must also be able to absorb any potential punishment or cost its opponent might deal out. Each actor then must have some capacity to inflict costs upon the other. My theory of coercion is necessarily two-sided. The step from one side trying to coerce the other to both sides trying to coerce each other simultaneously may seem trivial, but it allows us to see the world more accurately. It also helps us develop a parsimonious theory from which we can deduce hypotheses about which side should prevail in a conflict (Bueno de Mesquita and Lalman 1992). In the next section, I lay out my general argument for two-sided coercion. Based on this, I present a graphical representation from which I deduce hypotheses about (1) what types of outcomes we can expect to observe and (2) what kinds of indicators will allow us to predict which side should prevail in an interstate war.

War as Mutual Coercion

States and other actors usually try negotiations, incentives, or diplomacy before resorting to force. After an armed conflict begins, however, states focus on different methods to coerce an opponent to change the policy at the root of the dispute. As noted above, most of the work on coercion examines the decision calculus of one side or the other in a particular conflict. Robert Pape, for example, looks at the factors that affected the United States' ability to coerce North Vietnamese during the later part of the Vietnam War. But Pape only looks at the punishments the United States inflicted upon the Vietnamese and ignores any simultaneous attempts by the Vietnamese to coerce U.S. leaders. By ignoring half of the conflict at any point we might draw erroneous conclusions about the changes in the likely outcome of a potential conflict between two actors. It is this type of logic that leads us to accept the standard notion of the security dilemma, where increases in one state's security necessarily come at the expense of the other actor in a dyadic relationship. Using a more realistic notion of conflicts and their outcomes, we will see how two adversaries may be able to increase their respective security simultaneously.

This theoretical finding is a dramatic and critical one. Most political scientists, including those who specialize in conflict studies, take the presence of the security dilemma for granted. The desire to find a way out of or around the security dilemma drives much of the recent work in security and peace studies. By developing and testing the model presented later in this text I will demonstrate empirically that the security dilemma does not necessarily need to be the overriding concern of either states or political scientists.

Making the transition from the one-sided notion of coercion demonstrated in figures 4 and 5 to mutual coercion is quite straightforward. It also allows us to deduce how many different types of outcomes we can expect to see at the ends of wars. Because each actor in a war is making the type of calculation pictured in figures 4 and 5, we simply need to combine the two pictures for each actor, Actor B inflicting costs on Actor A and vice versa, into a single diagram. Figure 6 illustrates the simultaneous choices that are going on during a war that lead to four possible outcomes at any given time.

In figure 6, the choice that the two actors, A and B, have to make is

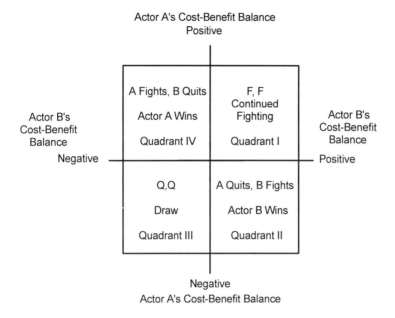

Actor A's Cost-Benefit Balance
Positive

	A Fights, B Quits	F, F
		Continued
Actor B's	Actor A Wins	Fighting
Cost-Benefit		
Balance	Quadrant IV	Quadrant I

Actor B's Cost-Benefit Balance

Negative — Positive

Q,Q	A Quits, B Fights
Draw	Actor B Wins
Quadrant III	Quadrant II

Negative
Actor A's Cost-Benefit Balance

Fig. 6. Actors' cost-benefit balance that they associate with fighting

the same as the choice shown in figures 4 and 5. Both actors, at any time, must decide whether to fight or quit. They will continue to fight as long as their respective benefit threshold is not exceeded by the costs that their opponent inflicts upon them during the war.

From this assumption, we can deduce that once a conflict between two actors starts, it will continue until one of the two actors wins or a draw is reached, three possible discrete outcomes. A side wins if its opponent is forced to accept a change in the prewar status quo that favors the side that did not choose to stop fighting. A draw occurs when both sides are willing to accept a status quo outcome through some form of negotiated settlement. Unless the expected costs of fighting exceed the expected benefits of victory, given the choice between fighting (F) and quitting (Q), states will prefer to continue to fight because in doing so they do not have to change their policies to conform to their opponent's wishes. In this sense, fighting is a dominant strategy for both sides. For the moment, I am not making any distinctions between the various ways in which states can pursue a fighting strategy. Later, I address the different ways in which states try to punish their opponents. If we assume for a moment that we can hold the costs and benefits of fighting constant for both sides, we can set up a simple game that will lead to a hypothesis about the relative likelihood of seeing one type of outcome versus the others. If two sides are faced with the two choices, at any time there will be four possible outcomes, in order of preference for the first player (again, F = fight, Q = quit):

1. F, Q: Actor A wins and does not change its policies; Actor B must change its policy.
2. F, F: Fighting continues; neither actor must change its policy.
3. Q, Q: Both players choose to quit, which results in a draw.
4. Q, F: Actor A loses and is forced to change its policies by Actor B, who wins.

Putting these four possible outcomes into a two-by-two table, along with the associated ordinal payoffs, allows us to see which types of outcomes we might expect to see. Table 1 represents the simple game in the normal form, with 1 being the best payoff and 4 being the worst.

Given the preferences stated above, both players will stay in the conflict as long as the cost of the opponent's punishments do not outweigh the anticipated benefits, the Nash equilibrium being, F, F.[4] In this instance, neither player can make itself better off by changing its behavior of fighting. Truces or draws are unstable as long as either side is capable of resisting. Both sides have unilateral incentives to reopen the conflict if they can. We see this type of behavior often, particularly in conflicts where both sides can absorb the opponent's punishments fairly easily, as in limited wars or civil insurrection. The payoff structure above is also known as deadlock (Snyder and Diesing 1977, 45). Cooperation under deadlock is impossible to sustain even without the inherent distrust present when two adversaries are involved in an active war. Some might argue that we should switch the preferences of the second and third outcomes, continued fighting and draw. If this were the case, the

TABLE 1.   The Combination of Choices for the Two Actors in a War along with the Actors' Ordered Preferences for Each Combination

	Actor B	
Actor A	Fight	Quit
Fight	2,2	1,4
Quit	4,1	3,3

Payoffs to: (Actor A, Actor B)

equilibrium would be the same (F, F), but we would expect to see more instances of cooperation resulting because, as presented here, wars are iterated games with the outcomes resulting from a series of choices over time. Robert Axelrod (1984) and others have shown that in iterated prisoners' dilemmas cooperation can evolve and be stable under certain conditions. But, returning to my original assumptions about the actors' preferences, it seems unreasonable to assume that an actor that could continue to resist in war (where costs remain below expected benefits) would be unwilling to do so.

An actor's ability to continue on in a war depends on its ability to absorb the punishment that its opponent is meting out. As long as an actor can absorb its opponent's punishment, it will continue to try to change its opponent's policies, if only the opponent's policy is to continue to fight. Both sides will be absorbing the punishments of the other. While both sides in the war are trying to absorb their opponent's punishments, they will both also be trying to impose costs on their opponent. This punishment can range from rhetoric to the use of nuclear weapons. For each of the two sides in the conflict, there exists some net, or balance, between the amount of punishment they can absorb and the amount their opponent can inflict. As long as a state or actor maintains a positive balance, they can stay involved in the conflict. If both sides have a positive balance, they will both stay involved and the conflict will continue.

If the two actors are virtually certain about their own ability to absorb costs as well as their opponents, then we would expect the outcomes to be certain, not probabilistic.[5] In other words, the boundaries separating the four quadrants would be critical values, corresponding to the thresholds in the diagrams above. For example, on one side of the boundary separating Quadrant II from Quadrant IV we would see Actor A winning and on the other side of the quadrant dividing line, Actor B.

It seems unlikely that the actors possess the perfect information that would lead us to deduce hypotheses of deterministic outcomes versus probabilistic ones. More likely, an actor can only guess the strategy its opponent will choose and how much it values the outcomes, which will determine how much punishment it can or will be willing to absorb. Each actor will not know precisely where its opponent will be located on the quadrant diagram. Along either axis, when the net balance between what an actor can absorb and what its opponent can inflict is near zero, the actor may be uncertain as to whether or not it will be able to continue to absorb its opponent's punishments. Similarly, if the two actors are on the border between Quadrants II and III, a situation in which Actor B would either win or suffer a draw, Actor A may be uncertain as to whether Actor B will continue to fight or quit.

Because of the actors' uncertainty (the uncertainty the two actors have about each others' capabilities and willingness to bear costs) and because of our uncertainty about the actors' beliefs, I can only make probabilistic estimates of the players' behaviors. The farther away from the origin the players are, the less uncertainty (both ours and theirs) there should be about the players' actions and hence about the outcomes. Because I can also only estimate the two players' capabilities using crude measures, it makes sense to also make probabilistic predictions as to their actions. These probabilities are based on the assumption that an actor is more likely to stay in a conflict the greater its advantage over its opponent is, holding benefits equal. When the actor's opponent has the advantage, the greater this advantage is, the greater the probability it will quit is, which is positively related to the size of the disadvantage. Referring to the quadrant diagram, this assumption means that the farther away from the borders between the quadrants an actor is, the higher the probability that it will either continue to fight or quit due to its greater certainty about its own capabilities and those of its opponent.

If we could visualize a third axis in figure 6 extending straight out of the page, it would represent the objective probability of a particular outcome for a particular actor. For instance, in the lower right-hand corner of Quadrant II, the expected probability of Actor B winning is at its maximum. This is because Actor B expects the gains from fighting to far outweigh the costs and as a result is very unlikely to quit. For Actor A, just the opposite holds true, and as such, it will be very likely to quit. The combination of the two choices leads to likely victory for Actor B.

One way to represent this change in objective probability would be to create a three-dimensional chart. Figure 7 is just such a diagram. The bottom floor of the figure is identical to figure 6, with the same cost-benefit balances and outcome quadrants. The vertical third axis represents the relative probability of the outcome in question, in this case Actor A's chances of victory. The plotted surface represents the expected probability of Actor A winning. The highest expected probability is in the far corner of Quadrant IV where Actor A's expected net gains are highest and Actor B's lowest.

The farther the actors find themselves from a border between the quadrants (the greater the costs they can inflict relative to the benefits their opponent may expect to receive, for example) the less uncertainty about the outcomes there should be. Because we also can only estimate the two actors' capabilities and how they see the expected benefits, it makes sense to also make probability predictions as to their actions. When the actor's opponent has the advantage, and the greater this advantage is, the greater the probability will be that the actor will quit. If

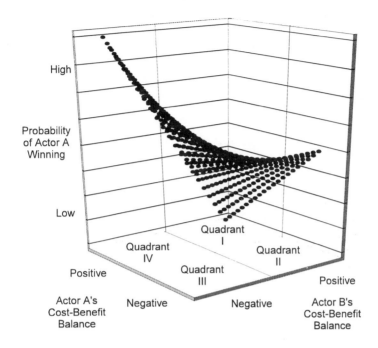

Fig. 7. A three-dimensional representation of Actor A's relative probability of winning as the two actors move through the four quadrants of the cost-benefit diagram

we think of the threshold diagrams (figs. 4 and 5), the greater its opponent's ability to inflict costs, the more likely an actor can be expected to quit. Referring to the quadrant diagram (fig. 7), this assumption means that the farther away from one of the borders between two quadrants an actor is, the higher the probability that it will either continue to fight or quit due to its greater certainty about its own capabilities and those of its opponent.

Using these assumptions about costs and the likelihood of an actor quitting, we can predict the conditions (in terms of costs and benefits) when both sides' chances for prevailing are the greatest and the least. Let X be equal to the net balance of the amount of punishment Actor B can absorb (B's expected benefits) minus the costs Actor A can inflict, and let Y equal the balance of the amount of punishment that Actor A can absorb (A's expected benefits) minus the costs that Actor B can inflict. If we assume that the probability that an actor will continue to fight is proportional to the net of the benefits an actor expects to receive minus the costs its opponent can inflict, we can specify the conditions under which the four outcomes are the most likely. When the balance is positive, the actor will be more likely to continue fighting. When the balance becomes negative, the more likely it is that the actor will quit.

X = Actor B's capacity to absorb costs − Actor A's capacity to inflict costs.
Y = Actor A's capacity to absorb costs − Actor B's capacity to inflict costs.

The probabilities associated with each of the four outcomes can then be derived from the combination of the two actors' cost-benefit balances, or their position on the quadrant diagram.

If the probability that Actor B continues to fight $= X$, and the probability that Actor A continues to fight $= Y$, and $(1 - X)$ is the probability that Actor B quits, and $(1 - Y)$ is the probability that Actor A quits, then:

Eq. 1 Probability of Continued fighting $= X \times Y$
Eq. 2 Probability of Draw $= (1 - X) \times (1 - Y)$
Eq. 3 Probability of Actor A Winning $= Y \times (1 - X)$
Eq. 4 Probability of Actor B Winning $= X \times (1 - Y)$

These four equations tell us who will win or lose depending on the decisions that are made; but under what conditions will the two actors decide to continue to fight or quit? An actor's decision to stay in a conflict is dependent upon the factors identified in the threshold diagrams: the height of the benefits line, the slope of the cost curve, and the length of time the war has been going on, or more generally, the costs and benefits an actor associates with the outcomes, given its opponent's capabilities to inflict punishment on it. So far I have identified two of the three basic points of this chapter:

1. That the basic factors that determine war outcomes are the expected benefits of victory, the rate that the two actors are able to impose costs upon each other, and the duration of the war.
2. At any moment during a war, there are four possible outcomes: one of the two sides winning, a draw, or the war continuing on. At the conclusion of the war, there are then three possible outcomes—win, lose, or draw.

The final point to be made is that war outcomes are not necessarily zero-sum, meaning that changes in capabilities or duration may increase

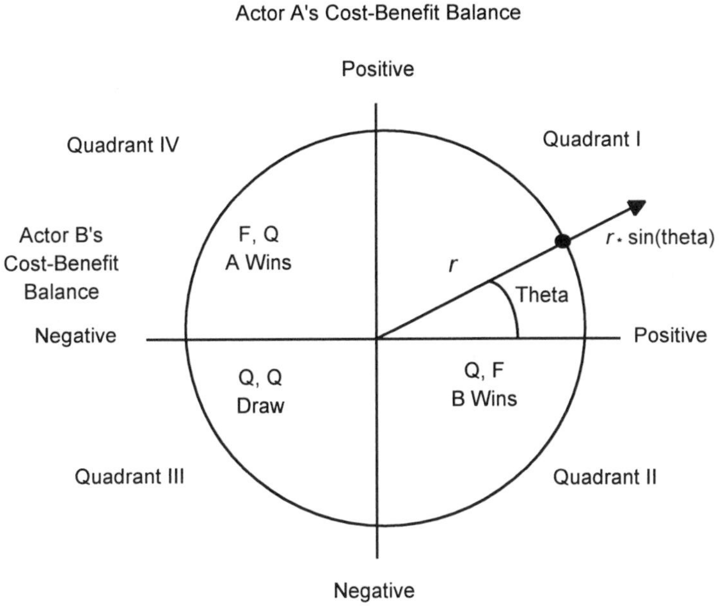

Fig. 8. An actor's outcome quadrant using a polar-coordinate system rather than a cartesian mapping system

(or decrease) both side's chances of victory simultaneously. In order to illustrate this, we need to be able to see how the probabilities of the various outcomes can covary.

Probabilistic Outcomes

In order to display how the probabilities of the four outcomes vary together, I would need to construct a three-dimensional plot showing all four separate planes, each representing the expected probability of a particular outcome. Needless to say, a chart of this nature would be exceedingly cluttered and difficult to interpret. Another way of seeing one of the many ways in which the probabilities of the four outcomes can vary together is to look at how they vary as we move around the outcome diagram in a circle, rather than trying to look at the probabilities across the entire surface. Using a circle, I can represent the relative probabilities with a two-dimensional graph rather than a three-dimensional one. Figure 8 is the same as figure 6, except that I have inscribed a circle onto the diagram, and the position on the outcome Cartesian is now measured by θ

and r rather than by X and Y. This different mapping system, polar-coordinates versus a Cartesian system, simplifies the presentation of the arguments but does not change the substance.

As I mentioned previously, for each point on the chart, there are four probabilities, one for each of the final outcomes and one for the likelihood the war will continue. This is why a change in the likelihood of victory for one actor may not change the likelihood of victory for the other actor. Thus, as we move around the circle, the expected probabilities change systematically, as a function of the location of the particular point relative to the two axes. It is important to note that there is nothing special about the circle. I could have inscribed a square on the diagram and shown how the probabilities might vary around its parameter. The point is not that the differences in the probabilities associated with each of the outcomes must change this way, but simply that they can. By examining possible combinations of outcome probabilities and how they may covary we can gain insight into some of the theoretical questions in the war initiation and outcome literature. For example, much of the literature on war initiation depends on the idea that the two sides in a potential war can, over time, see their power increasing. Typical zero-sum approaches to war outcomes, based on simple capabilities indices such as that shown in figure 3, cannot capture this notion of power. I discuss the importance of this illustration in greater detail later. The following figures illustrate the changes in the relative probability that result from using a model with three ultimate outcomes rather than the more conventional two.

Using the assumption that the probability of fighting is proportional to a player's position on the diagram, the X and Y discussed earlier, I can calculate and predict where both sides' chances for prevailing are the greatest and the least (within the constraint of the circle).

Eq. 5 $Y = P_A = f(r \times \sin \theta)$
Eq. 6 $X = P_B = f(r \times \cos \theta)$

By substituting P_A and P_B from equations 5 and 6 into equations 2 through 4, we can derive equations for the final outcomes as a function of the actors' positions in the quadrant diagram. Note that these are the polar coordinate equivalents of equations 1–4.

Eq. 7 $P_{draw} = f(1 - r \cos \theta)(1 - r \sin \theta)^6$
Eq. 8 $P_{Actor\ A\ wins} = f(r \sin \theta)(1 - r \cos \theta)$
Eq. 9 $P_{Actor\ B\ wins} = f(r \cos \theta)(1 - r \sin \theta)$

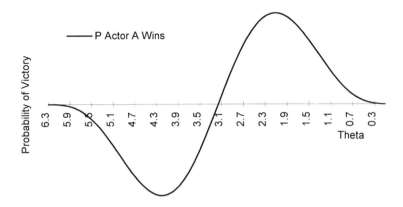

Fig. 9. The relative probability of victory for Actor A as a function of theta measured in radians

These functions allow us to calculate under what conditions an actor has the maximum and minimum chances of prevailing in a conflict. I can plot the changes in the outcome probabilities as we move around the circle. For the sake of clarity in the following figure, I have fixed $r = 1$. This does not change the relationship of the curves to each other or the location of the various maxima or minima, but only the absolute amplitude of the curves. Because no absolute probability scale is assumed, using a fixed r does not affect the arguments that follow. Figure 9 is a plot of the relative probability of Actor A winning as its position changes, moving around a unit circle inscribed on the quadrant diagram. Because r is fixed, θ becomes the variable that describes the position on the quadrant chart. In turn, θ then represents the net balance of costs and benefits for the two sides at war with one another. As θ changes (moving around the unit circle), we are simply allowing the net balance between the two sides to vary systematically from the situation where one actor anticipates much greater benefits than the other to the situation where both actors expect to have negative benefits and so forth.

Figure 10 shows that the two sides' probabilities of victory are not simple mirror images of each other, as many authors maintain. This point, which may appear trivial to some, is quite important in distinguishing this model of outcomes from the more typical zero-sum models. By including the outcome draw in the model, we have made a fundamental change in the nature of the relationship of the two sides' outcomes. Many authors assume that the probability of one actor winning is simply one minus the probability of the other's chances (Blainey

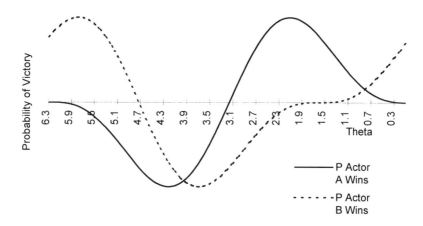

Fig. 10. The relative probability of victory for Actor A and Actor B as a function of theta in radians

1973; Bueno de Mesquita 1981). We can see that in my approach this is not the case.

Figure 10 shows a graphic representation of how the two actors' chances of winning vary simultaneously as the two players' positions move simultaneously around a unit circle transcribed on the quadrant diagram. The horizontal scale is θ in radians, which represents the two actors' location on the unit circle found in figure 6. The vertical axis is a scaleless indicator of the two sides' relative chances of victory.

It is interesting to note that in figure 10 as θ moves from 4 to 6 Pi radians, *both* Actors A and B have increasing chances of victory, a finding that fits closely with the power cycle literature on war initiation (Doran and Parsons 1980; Levy 1982).[7] This is an important finding. The theory developed here allows us to understand how both actors could have increasing chances for victory simultaneously, a notion that is inconsistent with most conceptions of the relationship between victory and loss in war and standard notions of the security dilemma. It is also interesting to note with θ near 6 Pi radians, both actors hit a plateau in their relative power; Actor B is near the apex of its ability to absorb Actor A's punishment or potential punishments, and Actor A is at an inflection point that could easily be confused with a peak in power or ability to absorb punishment. It is at just this point in the relationship of power between two actors that many writers predict conflict to be most likely. Organski and Kugler's power transition theory depends on the idea that different growth rates among competing states can lead to situations in which one actor's power can overtake another's, even while

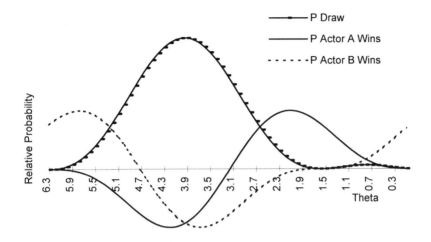

Fig. 11. The relative probability of Actor A winning, Actor B winning, and a draw occurring as a function of theta in radians

both actors' power is increasing. While Organski and Kugler's theory is strong, their test is weak, depending as it does on a zero-sum notion of war outcomes that cannot capture the idea of both sides having increasing power. This problem, where the empirical tests fail to correspond to the theoretical construct at hand, is a common one in the security studies literature. The conceptual model developed here attempts to address this concern.

In figure 11, I have added the likelihood of a draw occurring along with the likelihood of the two actors winning. We can see how, as the probability of a draw rises, the probability of either side winning falls dramatically. Situations of this type may correspond to the arms races that end in peace versus those that end in war, a situation more likely captured in the section of rising probability of victory for both actors shown in figure 11. Another important point to note is that the shape of the "Draw" curve is different than the shape of the "Win" curves. I will return to this point in chapter 4 when I outline the functional form of the empirical tests. For now, this simply means that changes in the costs that one side can inflict on the other do not have identical effects on the relative likelihood of a draw occurring as opposed to one side or the other winning. In order to account for this in the empirical tests we will need separate equations for draws as compared to wins.

One potential objection to this model of outcomes is that the assumption of outcomes as being truly probabilistic is unrealistic. While everyone would agree that during wars we make probabilistic judgments because of informational sources of uncertainty, I believe that the outcomes of wars have a stochastic component that would render them probabilistic even if we possessed perfect information. Some, like Blainey, might argue that wars are not probabilistic, but rather our understanding of the decisions that lead to wars are. I believe that we can reasonably think of outcomes as probabilistic as a result of both the leaders' uncertainty (an information problem) and of wartime friction. Carl von Clausewitz (1976), considered by many to be the principle authority on the conduct of war in the modern era, first mentions friction in his book *On War*. Friction is the risk entailed not so much from actions taken by the enemy but rather the unintended problems and delays caused by unanticipated failures of individuals and equipment to behave as expected.

Large military organizations are highly interdependent organizations. The ability of one part of the organization to execute its mission at a particular time and place depends critically on the behavior of many other parts of the organization doing their jobs as expected at the time expected. Each individual acts, in a way, as a fail-safe mechanism. If an individual fails to do his or her job, other individuals who rely on that person's behavior or work output to do their own work are hindered from completing their jobs. In turn, others are barred from completing their tasks, and so on, until the entire organization grinds to a halt. Because it is unrealistic to expect that all members of the organization will be in the precisely correct place at the correct time, unintended reactions will occur. For instance, we cannot anticipate which trucks will fail to start, which tank sights will fall out of alignment, or which lieutenants will get lost. What we do know is that these events will occur, and the other dependent parts of the organization will be unable to complete their own tasks unless they have been able to anticipate the failures in advance and develop contingency plans for possible breakdowns in planning. But, as I discussed in the chess analogy, one of the problems of modeling war outcomes is that decision makers try to deliberately inject uncertainty into the decision-making calculus of their opponent by changing tactics and introducing various kinds of innovations onto the battlefield. The successful prosecution of war is a massive attempt to control this notion of friction. We cannot control it with certainty, but we can make estimates as to when states will have greater or smaller probabilities of successfully overcoming the timing and equipment problems inherent in large organizations.

This general probabilistic approach or model is suitable for any war between two sides. In this study, I focus only on interstate wars. In this chapter, I have demonstrated that if we assume each side can either fight or quit, three outcomes will eventually be observed. The decision to fight or quit is based on the costs that an actor's opponent inflicts, the rate at which those costs are imposed (the slope of the cost curve in the threshold diagram), and how long the war has been going on. The relationship between the three possible outcomes and changes in the costs that each side imposes are not identical however. The outcome plots show that we may expect there to be different relationships among the three outcomes and the costs, benefits, and durations associated with fighting wars. To test the model's fit with reality, in chapters 3 and 4 I construct a statistical model that will incorporate the following factors for both actors:

An actor's ability to punish another, and hence the ability to raise the costs for its opponents and the rates at which those costs can be imposed.

The expected benefits of the various outcomes for each of the actors.

The ability of each actor to communicate the expectations of benefits from winning to its mass public and to be believed.

The different effects of costs and benefits on victories as compared to draws.

The next chapter deals with developing indicators for the actors' ability to inflict costs on their opponents. I discuss the role of various factors such as strategy and the quality and quantity of resources available to an actor in determining the costs and benefits of fighting for each actor, which forms the backbone of this study.

CHAPTER 3

Indicators of Costs and Benefits

In the previous chapter, I developed a theoretical model of war outcomes. Based on the two opponents' balance of the costs and benefits that they associate with fighting, the theoretical model is necessarily somewhat abstract. Empirically however, we cannot directly observe or measure a state's estimate of the costs it is willing to absorb or inflict. It is simply a hypothetical construct. We must identify other observable variables to serve as indicators for this and other latent factors. There are two approaches to estimating the components of an actor's cost-benefit function. One method would be to *assume* what the relative contributions of the anticipated costs and benefits are and then generate a capabilities index as others have done in the past. Using the index we would then compare the anticipated outcomes with the actual outcomes to confirm or reject the theoretical approach. Alternatively, we can infer the relative impact of a variety of indicators using econometric techniques. In addition to being able to gauge the relative usefulness of the entire model, by using econometric techniques we can also infer the relative effect of each of the factors I will identify as having a direct effect on outcomes. I will use the latter technique to estimate the effects of the indicators of costs and benefits.

In order to be able to test the conceptual model of war outcomes developed in the previous chapter, we need to be able to identify the various factors that will affect each actor's willingness to fight. As shown earlier, the probability of the various war outcomes occurring is some function of the combination of the two actors' cost-benefit balance or their position on the quadrant diagram:

War Outcomes = f (probability Actor A quits and probability
Actor B quits)

More specifically, when X = Actor B's capacity to absorb costs minus Actor A's capacity to inflict costs—or, letting A stand for Absorb and I for Inflict, $X = A_B - I_A$; and Y = Actor A's capacity to absorb costs minus Actor B's capacity to inflict costs—or, letting A stand for

Absorb, and I stand for Inflict, $Y = A_A - I_B$; then from the equations in chapter 2:

Eq. 8   Probability of Draw = $[1 - (A_B - I_A)] \times [1 - (A_A - I_B)]$
Eq. 9   Probability of Actor A Winning = $(A_A - I_B) \times [1 - (A_B - I_A)]$
Eq.10   Probability of Actor B Winning = $(A_B - I_A) \times [1 - (A_A - I_B)]$

Looking more closely at equation 9, the probability of Actor A winning, we can see that factors that increase Actor A's ability to absorb costs from Actor B (A_A) and increase Actor A's ability to inflict costs on Actor B (I_A) both will increase Actor A's chances of victory. From equation 8 we see that when each side's ability to inflict costs is close to its opponent's ability to absorb costs, the likelihood of draws increases. The greater the imbalance between the costs and benefits for the two sides, the greater the likelihood of a decisive outcome. The more closely the net costs and benefits for the two sides are matched, the more likely a draw is to occur. Therefore, to test the arguments about war outcomes, we need indicators of each actor's ability to inflict costs upon its opponent as well as each actor's ability or willingness to absorb the costs of fighting.

A factor may have a direct impact on the rate that costs are imposed or may have an indirect impact by affecting the duration of the war, which in turn affects the cumulative costs associated with fighting. The factors or indicators of a side's ability to absorb or inflict costs are grouped in two ways. First, a factor can be something that the decision maker gets to choose (to form an alliance, for example) versus something that is a constraint on the capacity of the states, that is, something that cannot be manipulated in the short run (e.g., population). Second, within each of these two groupings, indicators are further differentiated by whether they fall into a realist approach or a domestic politics approach as discussed in the first chapter. The next sections of this chapter present in detail the justification for the inclusion or exclusion of the many factors identified in the relevant literature as having a significant impact (or likely impact, as is more common) on the outcomes of interstate war.

Figure 12 provides a general schematic of the variables that affect a state's ability to inflict costs on its opponent. The variables identified in figures 12 and 13 are those that have been identified in the earlier literature review from both the realist perspective and the domestic politics perspective. They represent the most commonly referred to factors that military historians and political scientists alike have identified as being the likely candidates to affect war outcomes. Figure 13

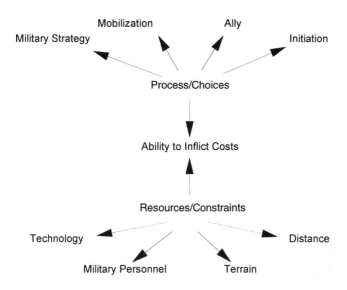

Fig. 12. Indicators of a state's ability to inflict costs

diagrams the factors that affect a state's ability or willingness to absorb costs. I discuss each variable's relationship to the costs and benefits that the two sides associate with fighting in the next section. I first address the various factors that states' leaders get to choose or directly manipulate in the short run. Following these indicators, I address those factors that are identified in the literature as affecting states' costs and benefits but which are constraints or things that decision makers cannot manipulate easily, at least in the short run.

Choices that Affect the Costs and Benefits of Fighting

Realpolitik Factors

Strategy and Doctrine: Affects Rate and Location of Costs
Military strategy has frequently been ignored in political scientists' quantitative studies of international conflict. Previous analyses suggest that strategy plays a key role in determining war outcomes (Dupuy 1979; Epstein 1987). Strategy matters because it determines, in part, how fast and how heavily costs are imposed. Strategy is also a main variable by which leaders can affect the duration of a war, which is a key concern of decision makers.

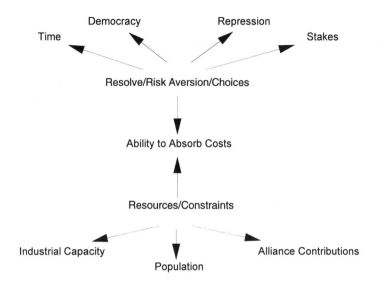

Fig. 13. Indicators of a state's ability to bear costs

I define military strategy as the general way in which a state uses its military forces in a war. I classify the three basic types of strategy as maneuver, attrition, and punishment. Strategy differs in my terminology from doctrine, or a state's foreign policy goals and plans for attaining them. Doctrine can be fundamentally offensive or defensive depending upon whether state objectives are to maintain or to alter the status quo. Regardless of doctrine, states can use any of the three types of strategy.

The interaction of the two sides' military strategies has an important impact on the length of a war and on the costs that each side expects to bear as a result of fighting. Maneuver strategies offer the potential for, and anticipation of, the quickest outcomes and the fewest casualties for the side executing the strategy. Maneuver strategies concentrate on a narrow point of attack. Once a narrow salient has been opened, mobile forces speed as quickly as possible toward rear areas where they have the potential to cause enormous disruption to the opponent. Mobile strategies entail significant risk, however, because the advancing columns and their following logistical trains are themselves quite vulnerable (Luttwak 1987, 100–101). A maneuver strategy will tend to end relatively quickly, as its rapid success or failure becomes apparent. Attrition strategies rely upon wearing the opponent down and are not predicated on speed in the same way that the maneuver strategies are. There is less need to move quickly as long as damage is being inflicted on the opponent. Attrition strategies do not depend on the success or failure of any individual battle to as great an extent as a sequential movement strategy does, and as a result they are less risky than maneuver strategies. States using punishment strategies count on their opponents having difficulty adapting to the long-term imposition of costs during a war. The aim is for the target state to ultimately suffer political defeat through the erosion of political resolve among elites and/or mass publics. As the strategy counts on erosion of support rather than destruction or defeat of forces, wars in which one side or both use punishment strategies will last longest of all.

Maneuver Strategy. Maneuver strategies are those in which states focus on the use of speed and mobility to disarm the opponent by disrupting the opponent's ability to effectively organize its forces. Maneuver strategies are often referred to as "blitzkrieg" strategies. When used under an offensive doctrine, the attacking state seeks to occupy as much of the defending state's territory as possible through a series of sequential actions in which physically occupying enemy territory may be more important than destroying enemy forces. Germany defeated France in World War II with this strategy. When used under a defensive doctrine, the defending state will use mobile forces to seek out, destroy, or disarm attacking forces wherever they are rather than set up a relatively static defensive line.

Attrition Strategy. Attrition strategies seek to destroy or capture opposing forces, making them incapable of continuing to fight, without necessarily using mobility to achieve this. Typically, an attrition strategy seeks large confrontations with the enemy (Mearsheimer 1983, 34). Hitler adopted an attrition strategy in the Soviet Union, ordering his forces to take as many prisoners as possible and to destroy as many forces as they could rather than bypass large battles as they had in France. Under a defensive doctrine, the defender using an attrition strategy will attempt to deny the attacker the ability to cross the defender's border with a forward defense. The French Maginot Line in World War II exemplifies this type of strategy.

Punishment Strategy. Punishment strategies attempt to inflict such high costs on an opponent that they either cease an attack or surrender even though their military forces may not actually be defeated in battle. Unlike maneuver and attrition strategies, a punishment strategy is not necessarily a counterforce strategy. The punisher is simply counting on being able to break the resolve of the enemy. In the West, punishment strategies developed from the theoretical work of Douhet and Mitchell (Mitchell 1921) and are exemplified by the logic behind mutual assured destruction (MAD). Another type of offensive punishment strategy is the guerrilla warfare strategy. Mao Tse-tung maintained that guerrilla forces should seek to avoid large military confrontations with the enemy and instead inflict damage on the enemy where and when they could to avoid suffering significant costs themselves.

How Strategy Affects Outcomes: Via the Ability to
Raise Opponent's Costs
While it may be self-evident from the military history literature that military strategy is an important factor in determining war outcomes, few authors investigate why it matters. I argue that strategy matters because it directly affects the costs that the two sides at war must bear, the rate at which those costs accrue, the length of time the costs are imposed, and the physical location where the costs are incurred. The German strategy in World War II illustrates some of the logic quite nicely. One of the stunning strategic innovations of the twentieth century was the German blitzkrieg of World War II. The essence of the blitzkrieg and many other related strategies is mobility.

> The blitzkrieg is predicated upon the assumption that the opposition's army is a large and complex machine that is geared to fighting along a well-established line. In the machine's rear lies a vulnerable network, which comprises numerous lines of communication along which the various lines intersect. Destruction of this central nervous system is tantamount to destruction of the army (Mearsheimer 1983, 36)

The logic behind the advantage of the mobile offense (or defense for that matter) involves being able to exploit the initiative that mobility can provide. The proposition that some strategies convey inherent advantages is controversial. While those on the defensive may enjoy the advantage of fighting into their supplies, the offense fights away from its logistical base. Many authors argue that, in fact, offensive doctrines or mobile strategies convey no net advantage. The idea that there are optimal strategies for the conduct of war is a disputed one within the political science literature. Jack Snyder, one of the chief "Cult of the Offensive" protagonists, argues that in its execution "offense is virtually never easier than defense" (Snyder 1985, 158). For evidence of this assertion, Snyder simply cites in a footnote invaluable "discussion of the question with John Mearsheimer" (Snyder 1985, 256). But Snyder later admits that

It is an empirical question whether the material advantages of the defense outweigh the countervailing advantages conferred by seizing the advantage. No doubt there are combinations of circumstances where the offense has an overall advantage because its characteristic advantages operate strongly, whereas the defender's operate weakly. (Snyder 1985, 159)

This is one of the important questions that I will answer in the following chapters. The lack of empirical rigor in investigating a critical assertion such as the one Snyder poses in the quotation just cited, illustrates a problem with much of the work on strategy and war outcomes in political science. Because of the paucity of empirical and quantitative work on war outcomes, much of what we think we know about the effects of strategy and the traditional indices of power is known through assertion, not through carefully controlled empirical testing.

While Snyder admits that attackers often win in war, he maintains that the use of offensive military strategies has little to do with the final outcome. In fact, given his argument, states win on the offense, in spite of the fact that they use offensive strategies. "Of course, attackers often win, but this is because they are stronger, not because offense makes their task easier. People who believe that the offense confers a net advantage are simply failing to control for the effects of quantity and especially the quality of the opposing forces" (Snyder 1985, 158). Unlike the members of the "Cult of the Offensive" school, I believe (and will show) that it is the combination of the two or more states' strategies that is crucial. If one state's strategy is able to exploit a potential weakness in another's (all strategies have some weakness and some strengths), then the former will be likely to prevail over the latter, all other factors held constant.

$H_{Maneuver}$:   Actor who uses a maneuver strategy will have greater chances of victory.

$H_{Punishment}$:   Wars in which one or both sides use a punishment strategy will be the longest and the most likely to end in a draw.

Ally Contribution: Disperses Costs and Reduces Benefits

As the number of participants in a war increases and the benefits of potential victory become distributed among more actors, the potential gains or benefits from victory for any individual state shrink. When many states are involved in fighting, some of them may receive no tangible benefits from victory at all. Because of smaller and possibly more abstract benefits, the leader of an individual state in a coalition will thus be less able to convince domestic audiences to continue fighting than when the state is fighting alone. I expect that when more states are fighting in a war, the more quickly a coalition will fall apart, leading to a shorter war with lower costs for all sides. This is offset by the actor's increased ability to inflict costs on the opponent because the actor now has access to greater resources than it would have had otherwise.

The contribution of alliance partners to the outcomes of wars and disputes is one that has largely been assumed, an unsupported assumption made necessary by the basic tenets of the realist paradigm. The vast majority of work on the effects of alliance patterns has been to investigate the role of alliances in the onset of war. Maoz notes, however, that frequently allies get an actor into trouble and then desert the actor, leaving it hanging when a war breaks out or continues (Maoz 1983, 201). Mancur Olson and Richard Zeckhauser (1970) have investigated the degree of alliance effectiveness and have found that it varies tremendously. Maoz points out that history contains many examples of alliance partners effectively leaving each other in the lurch (Maoz 1983, 213).

$H_{Alliance}$: Due to collective action problems, allies' contributions to victory will be less than each state's own but will still be positively correlated with winning.

Surprise: Increases Ability to Inflict Costs

Many scholars "argue that surprise is a universal phenomenon sought by any state planning to initiate an act of aggression against one or more adversaries. Surprise is sought because it reduces the costs of facing a fully alerted adversary and the chances of being preempted" (Hybel 1986, 25). Military strategists often discuss the importance of surprise (Clausewitz 1976; Dupuy 1979; Axelrod 1979; Sun Tzu 1991). Strategic surprise occurs when a state is forced to change significantly how it has planned to fight the overall war based on a sudden military move by its opponent. For example, the enemy could suddenly increase its military commitment or change its strategy. Several scholars, among them Alex Hybel (1986) and Barry Posen (1984), argue that unanticipated initiation is of paramount importance. Hybel goes on to argue that because the result of surprise is to increase the advantage to the attacker, an advantage that would not be secured otherwise, we should expect the incentives for surprise attack to be greatest among the weakest states, they being the ones in which a marginal change in capabilities would have the greatest net benefit. If this is true, then we should be able to see the systematic influence of surprise on the outcomes of war.

This hypothesis stems from the logic that the initiator gets to pick the time and place of the first battle. Because the initiator also gets to pick how the first battle will be fought, it is usually assumed that leaders will pick a strategy that, in combination with the opponent's strategy, will give the greatest benefit. Again, the initiator should accrue a significant advantage, but this advantage fades with time. Over time, the opponent can either force a change in how the war is being fought or adapt to the current tactics being used in the war (Maoz 1990, 143).

Note that both sides can achieve strategic surprise at different times in a single war. In the Korean War, the North Koreans surprised the United States and South Korea with their initial attack, the United States achieved surprise with the Inchon landing, and the Chinese surprised the United States with their sudden entry into the war.

$H_{Surprise}$:   If a state achieves strategic surprise, it will be more likely to win.

Mobilization: Increases Ability to Inflict Costs
States' ability to mobilize their resources for war is perceived to be a key factor in their ability to prevail in a conflict (Trachtenberg 1991). Differences in states' mobilization rates have also been blamed as a cause of war, particularly in World War I (Snyder 1984; Van Evera 1984). The argument that mobilization significantly influences war outcomes or duration has not to my knowledge been broadly tested. While I am *not* able to test propositions about preemptive motives resulting from anticipated short-term advantages at the outset of a war or preventive motives prior to a power transition, I am able to test the effect of long-term mobilization during a war.

The number of troops that a state has available to fight should be a critical component of the state's ability to successfully prosecute a war. States with smaller armies will be at a disadvantage, particularly when the two sides are fighting using attrition strategies, by far the most common strategy observed. In attrition strategies the principle goal is to wear down the opponent's base of soldiers. Having a larger pool of soldiers to draw from means that a state can more easily absorb the costs associated with fighting. Alternatively, a state that has not adequately mobilized its population, and as a result has no surplus of soldiers to draw from, may find itself in a critical situation if the initial battles do not go as planned. Having soldiers in reserve should convey a powerful advantage to the side with a large standing army.

> H$_{Mobilization}$:   States that mobilize larger numbers of soldiers will be more likely to win.

Military Quality: Better Technology and Training
Increases Rate that Costs Accrue to Opponent
When one state's military has better-trained troops and higher technology equipment than that of the other, it can inflict relatively higher costs on the adversary in a given amount of time than the adversary can inflict on it. A better-equipped military can also absorb more costs than a lower-quality military before collapsing. As a result, when the disparity between the quality of two adversaries' militaries is high, the side with the better training and technology will be more likely to win.

Technological development and realistic training are the principal ways in which states try to overcome the insidious effects of wartime friction, which limits a state's ability to inflict costs on its opponent and to be able to defend itself against the costs its opponent is trying to inflict upon it. Clausewitz explains the notion of friction in *On War*:

> Everything in war is very simple, but the simplest thing is difficult. The difficulties accumulate and end by producing a kind of friction that is inconceivable unless one has experienced war. . . . Countless minor incidents—the kind you can never really foresee—combine to lower the general level of performance, so that one always falls far short of the intended goal. . . . Friction is the only concept that more or less corresponds to the factors that distinguish real war from war on paper. The military machine—the army and everything related to it—is basically very simple and therefore seems easy to manage. But we should bear in mind that none of its component parts is of one piece: each part is composed of individuals, every one of whom retains his potential of friction. (Clausewitz 1976, 119)

> H$_{Quality}$:   The greater the difference in the two sides' military quality, the more likely it is that the side with the more advanced technology will win.

Domestic Politics: Choices that Affect Costs and Benefits

Having reviewed the realpolitik choices that confront leaders, we will now move to the principal domestic political choice that leaders must make during a war, namely, whether or not to repress dissent within the state's borders. Unlike the previous factors, repression clearly falls outside the realist approach to world politics, but it is a factor that in the next section I show to be potentially one of the more potent tools available to decision makers in states at war.

Political Repression: Allows Leaders to Hide Costs and Maintain Legitimacy

One of war's byproducts within states is the domestic dissent it generates, which increases over time. States in which the leaders can effectively hide this dissent, which is the result of rising costs, through political repression will be more likely to win because they are able, in effect, to reduce the costs that the state's mass publics must pay in the war. The costs are there, but because of the repression most members of the mass public are unaware or less aware of them than they would have been otherwise.

It is the state's mass public that ultimately decide whether the benefits justify the costs. If the mass publics conclude that the costs of fighting exceed the possible gains from victory and the state cannot alter this calculus through either coercion or inducements, then the mass publics will withdraw their support for the war. This consequence of mass public action is the state's loss of one of its principal means of waging war. A good example of this kind of collapse of mass support might be the outbreak of the Russian Civil War in 1917, which was a reaction to the draconian domestic politics that the Russian czar and his backers believed necessary to sustain the war effort against the Germans. As a result, the state's ability to manipulate the mass publics' perceptions will be of paramount importance to its ability to wage effective and successful war.

The logic behind the argument that war inevitably leads to domestic conflict is a bit complex. According to Michael Stohl (1976), wartime economic mobilization brings new groups into the productive process and enhances the economic positions of some groups relative to others, thus intensifying domestic economic conflict and violence. Wartime social mobility increases the status position of one-time underdog social groups relative to the dominant segments, which increases the hostilities between them. As a result, the economic and social changes driven by war generate upward demands within segments of the once ignored mass publics for the reallocation of political power and rewards. This demand may intensify conflict and violence between the political top and bottom segments of society. Somewhat paradoxically—at the same time—success in war provides a greater number of goods that can be distributed by dominant segments of society, while simultaneously increasing these segments' power and prestige. This typically leads to an intensification of their efforts to maintain control of the political system while increasing their ability to do so. The result is an increase of violence directed downward by dominant segments during successful war efforts (Stohl 1976, 64).

> Lack of success in war decreases the power and prestige of dominant segments and provides no additional goods to distribute. This intensifies their efforts to maintain control of the political system without increasing their ability to do so. The result is an increase in violence directed upward by lower segments attempting to maintain the relative gains accrued to them during the war. (Stohl 1976, 64–65)

Either way, according to Stohl, in successful or unsuccessful wars there will be an increase in dissent and threats to the legitimacy of the state. It becomes critical for the state to be able to convey the belief that the expected benefits of the war will outweigh the costs to the mass publics. By repressing the dissenting voices, at least in the short run, leaders will be able to effectively hide the costs of war and allow the state to continue fighting. Without this ability to maintain the legitimacy of the state, the decision maker's choice to continue fighting would become irrelevant.

$H_{Repression}$:   Highly repressive states will be able to hide the costs of fighting and hence be more likely to win.

Resource Constraints that Increase or Limit the Costs of War

Having discussed the choices that leaders must make in the process of waging war, I will now investigate the resource constraints or structures within which choices are made. As I mentioned previously, there are a variety of important factors in war that leaders simply cannot control, at least in the short run. While these may not be selected, they still play a critical role in determining outcomes. The first set of resources or structural constraints will be the realpolitik factors; following these, I will address the domestic political structure in which the choices mentioned in the previous section are made.

Realpolitik Factors

Balance of Capabilities: Greater Capacity to Absorb
Industrial Losses
When one side is stronger than its adversary, it will be able to inflict more damage on the adversary in a given period of time than the adversary is able to inflict on it and may be able to quickly overwhelm its opponent. This will lead to the weaker side surrendering relatively sooner than it otherwise would as it recognizes that the probability of winning the ongoing conflict is small. When two states are relatively equal in size, however, neither side is likely to collapse quickly, which will lead to a longer and more costly war.

$H_{\text{Balance of Capabilities}}$:   The greater the imbalance of capabilities, the greater the chances of victory.

Relative Military Capabilities: Greater Capacity
to Absorb Military Costs
The relative size of military forces also affects war outcomes. As realists commonly assert, states are rightly interested in relative power, not necessarily absolute power. When countries have larger militaries, they can absorb more damage before they are forced to give up or otherwise seek to end the war. Additionally, it simply takes more time for any military to fight through a large opposing army than through a small opposing army.

$H_{\text{Total Capabilities}}$:   The greater a side's relative military forces, the greater the chances of victory.

Population: Greater Capacity to Absorb the Costs
of Manpower Losses
When countries are involved in a war, they draw upon both material and human resources to fight the war. Larger countries have more human resources that they can draw on than do smaller countries. They can thus absorb more costs in terms of casualties and mobilize more people than smaller countries. According to John Mearsheimer, a successful attrition offense is similar to a steamroller, or perhaps a more apt analogy would be to a belt sander, where the two opponents simply try to wear down their opponents. The side with the greatest supply of "sandpaper" and "wood" will be the likely winner (Mearsheimer 1983, 34).

Katherine Organski and A. F. K. Organski outline the theoretical arguments for the inclusion of population as a critical indicator in the equations modeling war outcomes. They argue that the transition of states from small professional armies to the mass mobilization of states' population for war by political and military organizations led to the need to consider population as an indicator, both from the perspective of a state's ability to inflict and to absorb punishment and a state's ability absorb the costs of fighting. The replacement of mercenaries and completely professional armies by systems of mass recruitment led to two changes in warfare. First, the need to fill out the ranks of a mass army required a large population. Second, large mass armies typically lead to large losses on the part of the belligerents during wars. The side that has sufficient population to be able to absorb and replace large numbers of losses from its military ranks will enjoy an advantage in war (Organski and Organski 1961, 13).

Additionally, the social dislocations of mass mobilization mean that states that have high levels of legitimacy and that are efficient at extracting resources from the mass publics will have an advantage as well.

> Because the social reorganization required to fill the jobs men leave behind is one that only a nation of the greatest efficiency can manage, underdeveloped nations can tap only a fraction of their human resources for military service. Nonetheless, it is the size of the total population that sets the limit. Though few nations arm to the hilt, the size of the sword is significant (Organski and Organski 1961, 15).

The ability to constantly sharpen the sword when dulled in battle is also a valuable asset. This ability is conferred through a limitless population committed to the cause at hand; this commitment flows from the state's legitimacy and the mass publics' belief that it will share in the benefits of victory. This leads to the second hypothesis about population. While the relative size of the two sides' population may be correlated with victory for one side or the other, the absolute size of a state's population will be positively correlated with draws or defeat. If we hold the benefits of victory constant, as one side's population grows the benefits per capita shrink, hence the fewer costs the mass publics will be willing to bear on an individual basis, leading to an earlier than might otherwise be expected withdrawal from the war.

$H_{Population}$:   The greater a state's population, the less the likelihood of victory.

Distance: Harder to Inflict Costs on the Opponent
Distance is often declared to be an important factor in determining war outcomes. The argument is that the farther away a state must send its forces the more difficult it will be for that state to inflict costs upon its opponent. Several reasons for the effect of distance have been advanced. Most of them will be accounted for directly. One of them will not be. Bueno de Mesquita argues in *The War Trap* that a state's power declines over distance as a result of four factors:

1. Long distance introduces organizational and command problems.
2. Distance threatens military morale.
3. Long-distance wars invite domestic dissension.
4. Fighting afar debilitates soldiers and their equipment. (Bueno de Mesquita 1981, 41)

These potential problems appear to be important factors that may affect a state's ability to raise the costs of war for an opponent or to be able to minimize its own costs. Some of the factors will be controlled for directly; others I will not control for. For example, much of the difference in a state's ability to fight close to home as well as its ability to fight far from home would more likely seem to be a function of the issue over which the war is being fought. The farther away from home a soldier fights, the less likely the issue at stake will be one next to the "pole of power" where the state's survival is in question. Wars fought in distant lands tend to be over issues of empire or abstract government policies. As I argue later and show in the following empirical chapters, the issue at stake has a significant effect on the war outcome. Likewise, the effect of the distance from home on domestic dissension is likely to be related to the issue being fought over rather than the intrinsic effect of distance itself. Finally, the argument that somehow distance from home debilitates soldiers seems somewhat specious. Aside from the problems of acclimatizing to a foreign environment, the debilitating effects of which last for no more than a matter of weeks, this line of argument appears weak. The organizational problems that result from distance I am unable to control for directly so I do expect to observe an effect. For the effects of distance that we can expect to observe, small states should be at a greater disadvantage than larger, wealthier states. Wealthy states will be better able to afford the technological advances in communication and transportation that ameliorate the effects of distance. Distance also affects the likely duration of a war and hence the costs that the states can impose upon each other. The farther away from each other the two sides are, the more difficult it is to inflict costs, which will lead to a higher likelihood of a draw.

$H_{Distance}$:   The farther away from its borders a state fights the lower the chances of victory.

$H_{Distance\ and\ Size}$:   The effects of distance will have a larger effect on small states' ability to project power than large states.

Terrain: Reduces Rate at which Costs Can Be Imposed

Terrain affects the prosecution of war in two ways. The first effect is on mobility and the second on the ability to locate and engage the enemy. Both of these factors affect a state's ability to inflict costs upon its opponent. Strategies that are predicated on the mobility of the attacker (or defender), whether the aim is to deeply penetrate the opponent's rear and to wreak havoc upon the communication and logistical networks therein or to avoid initial contact and encircle the enemy's main forces, depend upon the ability to move across terrain quickly. "A blitzkrieg can only operate in terrain that is conducive to mobile armored warfare. In other words, the attacker requires terrain that will facilitate his penetration of the defender's front and will then allow his columns to race forward with a minimum of interference" (Mearsheimer 1983, 43). In this way, terrain may have a direct effect on the war's outcome.

Terrain may have an indirect effect as well, in that it may make it exceedingly difficult for the two opponents to find each other. This thereby limits the costs that the two sides can impose upon each other and therefore extends the time required to wage the war, in turn leading to a greater chance of a draw occurring. Dense jungles and steep mountains, in addition to limiting strategic options in that they prohibit or limit quick movement and maneuver, also allow defenders to hide and attackers to execute ambushes with impudence. Frequently though, states try to overcome the constraints that terrain and other factors place on them by compensating with technological solutions.

$H_{Terrain}$:   Wars fought on flat, open terrain will be decisive. Wars fought on inhospitable terrain will be associated with a higher probability of draws.

Strategy and Terrain Interaction

Terrain and strategy choice also interact as mentioned earlier. Decision makers and military leaders typically anticipate that terrain and strategy will affect their ability to inflict costs on the opponent and will pick a strategy to match the terrain in which they are fighting. For example, states that are located in areas with rough terrain such as jungles or mountains will be more likely to fight with punishment strategies than maneuver strategies in that the rugged terrain hinders rapid movement but will allow forces to inflict costs upon their opponent with relative impunity.

It is possible, though, for leaders to choose an "inappropriate" strategy for a given terrain. If a state tries to fight using a punishment strategy in open terrain, for instance, it will typically find it difficult to sustain the secrecy necessary to fight with a Maoist-style guerrilla strategy. Without the cover and concealment of rough terrain, more time will have to elapse between operations as the military units struggle to maintain the necessary level of secrecy in the open. Given the mismatch of strategy and terrain, the war will be paradoxically longer than when punishment can be applied almost continuously. Similarly, states that try to fight using a maneuver strategy in terrain that cannot support the quick transportation of soldiers and supplies will end up having difficulty implementing their strategy, which will lead to a longer duration for the war. In all cases, wars fought with punishment strategies should last longer than wars fought using movement strategies, but within the context of a single strategy choice, a mismatch of strategy with terrain will slow the war.

$H_{Interaction}$:   Wars fought on the appropriate terrain will be associated with victory.

Domestic Political Factors

Democracy: Increases Legitimacy and Willingness to Incur Costs, Selects Low Cost Wars

Two plausible arguments can be made to support the hypothesis that democratic states will be more likely to win than nondemocratic states. The first argument assumes the democracy is a proxy for state legitimacy and that mass publics in highly legitimate states will be more willing to bear costs than in illegitimate states. In legitimate states, the mass publics are less likely to believe that they will be excluded from the gains from victory and more likely to believe that the costs they must bear will be fairly distributed throughout society.

The second argument suggests that wars involving democracies will be more likely to end in defeat for the nondemocratic state because of choices that are made prior to the outbreak of war. Because they face more certain sanctions following a flawed choice, leaders in highly democratic states are likely to avoid, whenever possible, wars in which they anticipate a long duration and the associated high political costs. Democratic leaders will choose not to initiate wars that they believe will be either highly costly or of long duration. This prewar selection effect of aversion to risky wars may account for the observed difference in outcomes.

In *Power and Discontent*, William Gamson lays out the theoretical underpinnings of the notion of trust or legitimacy as a characteristic of state power. Gamson points out that we would need little convincing to argue that a lack of trust or political discontent is important in the study of domestic politics. But by breaking the notion of trust into two components, that of social control and influence, he sheds some light on the problem of how a legitimate state can reasonably be considered more powerful than one that is illegitimate or lacks the trust of its population. As Gamson explains:

> For authorities to be effective, they must have a good deal of freedom to commit resources without the prior consent of those who will ultimately supply those resources. Such freedom to invest or spend the resources they have "borrowed" from members allows leaders to generate additional resources and thus, in theory, provide the leaders with a generous return in the form of public goods or increased resources. (Gamson 1968, 43)

Gamson goes on to argue that the ability of the government's political leadership to secure the necessary cooperation of the mass publics "without having to specify in advance what such cooperation will entail" is of critical importance to the state's ability to wage war. The logic continues with the importance of political trust being revealed in what is lost along with the potential loss of the trust itself: "The loss of trust is the loss of system power, the loss of a generalized capacity for authorities to commit resources to attain collective goals" (Gamson 1968, 43).

In a discussion of the origins of state legitimacy, "Rousseau argued that it was basically the consent of the governed which could make it legitimate that people are 'in chains,' that is, subject to government" (Friedrich 1972, 89). This idea, however, is a challenge to more traditional or historically rooted notions of legitimacy. During the eighteenth century and before, legitimacy typically stemmed from some divine right or from the will of the gods or, possibly later, as a result of an election. Not so much theory as experience shows that to the winner go the political spoils or that nothing breeds support like success, which has often served as the source of legitimacy. Success, that is, lies in establishing a government or in making it work satisfactorily (Friedrich 1972, 88–89).

How should we go about thinking of legitimacy in more concrete terms? Traditionally, within the fields of comparative and American politics democracy emerged as the proxy for government legitimacy. H. B. Mayo takes a small step toward linking democracy and legitimacy:

> One might plausibly assume then that nearly everybody would accept this value—that ceteris paribus, it is better to coerce fewer people than more, to get voluntary observance rather than coerced obedience, to substitute what Wordsworth called the "discipline of virtue" for the "discipline of slavery": "order else cannot subsist, nor confidence nor peace." (Mayo 1960, 224)

In this sense, democracies are all the stronger because their soldiers and supporters are willing participants, fighting to keep something they value, relative to others in repressive systems who are possibly defending values they see as worth less than those values of the state they are fighting off. An example of this might be the Germans in World War II, fighting to be able to surrender to the Americans rather than being forced to give in to the Soviets.

In an interesting counter to Alexis de Tocqueville's concerns that democracies would be ineffective in the area of foreign policy, Barry Holden explains why democracies should perform better than authoritarian regimes, where leaders are appointed rather than selected. "Although each individual may be deficient in the qualities necessary for political decision making, the people collectively are not deficient in this way. They are, indeed, better endowed than any 'experts,' since the combined qualities of all the individuals add up to a far from deficient totality" (Holden 1988, 181). Mayo then links the logic of effective collective decision making with the willingness of mass publics to follow and support the decisions or choices either made by the masses directly or through their proxies, the republican state:

> The normal democratic policy is in a sense a decision which gives no claimant everything he asks for; is not a mere mechanical compromise but a new policy, shaped from the continuing dialogue and struggle of the political process. Some go so far as to call the method "creative discussion." From this it is only a short step to saying that there is more value in decisions which we make, or help to make, than in having "wiser" decisions made for us, and which we must be compelled to obey. (Mayo 1960, 223)

Dahl argues that democratization is critical to the understanding of government effectiveness, but that it will be difficult to show. "One might . . . demonstrate that in a given time and place . . . no ethical rules other than those embodied in popular sovereignty and political equality would convey legitimacy of governmental decisions" (Dahl 1956, 46). With this in mind, and assuming that government legitimacy could be shown to be linked with the successful achievement of governmental goals, Dahl argues that democracy would be the only government system truly capable of succeeding. "Given governmental indoctrination though, it would be difficult to show, however, that a full shift to populist democracy would therefore increase the legitimacy of governmental decisions" (Dahl 1956, 46).

$H_{Democracy}$:   The more democratic the state is the more likely it will be to win.

Repression and Democracy
Somewhat paradoxically, I believe that both highly repressive and highly democratic regimes will be associated with increased chances of victory. This may seem counterintuitive to most readers. Typically, we assume that repression is a behavior of illegitimate regimes, the types of states that should fair poorly in war. Democracies are assumed to be legitimate states that would have no ability to repress because of domestic institutional restraints. There are two basic ways in which these two factors are both associated with stronger chances of victory. First, democracy and repression affect the process by which the wars are fought and as such affect the two sides' ability to absorb costs. These two variables also will have a selection effect, meaning that highly repressive and democratic states will initiate different types of wars than other kinds of states. I will address the notion that democracy may act as a constraint on a state's ability to repress its mass publics in chapter 6.

Issue Salience: Determines Height of Benefits Line
Wars are fought over issues that reflect different potential benefits. It is the benefits, or the height of the cost threshold, that determines the costs one state must inflict upon another to drive it out of the war. The greater the benefits at stake in a conflict, the more costs rational leaders will be willing to accept in that conflict (Zimmerman 1973). The greater the benefits, the longer state leaders will be able to convince domestic audiences to continue fighting.

In different wars, states pursue different goals. As a result, the potential benefits of victory vary as well. In the Vietnam War, the United

States was fighting the spread of communism and hoped for the fall of the Minh regime and actually went to great lengths to destabilize it through thousands of assassinations carried out under the Central Intelligence Agency's (CIA) Phoenix Project. In the Gulf War with Iraq, President Bush went to great lengths to point out that while the United States would not be upset if Hussein fell from power that was not a primary goal of the war. Removing the government from power was not the principal U.S. goal in Iraq as it had been in the war against North Vietnam. The United States' issue area for the two opponents differed.

When Clausewitz discussed the nature of limited war, he came away unimpressed with its potential (Clausewitz 1976; Dupuy 1983). Many states in the twentieth century, in contrast, became convinced of the utility of fighting limited wars. As mass public opinion began to play a greater role in determining the legitimacy of the state, governments took actions to minimize the costs to the mass publics. The concept of limited wars seems to make sense when we look at the potential power that the superpowers can bring to bear militarily. Even without accessing their nuclear arsenals, the Soviet Union and the United States (along with the other Warsaw Treaty Organization [WTO] and North Atlantic Treaty Organization [NATO] states) possessed enormous military capabilities. Over the last fifty years, many states have been involved in wars that did not seem to require an all-out military effort. Much like the wars fought before Napoleon, the recent wars have been limited in nature to one degree or another. Rather than seeking the total defeat of the opposing force, states have tried to attain more limited objectives using limited means, that is, minor border adjustments, concessions of islands, and trade or other political concessions. While it makes sense to use limited means to gain limited ends, what happens if the two sides are fighting different sorts of wars?

On one hand, a state that is fighting for its very existence will not be inclined to fight a limited war using limited means (and, by extension, be willing to bear limited costs). On the other hand, a state fighting for issues that do not land on the pole of power, or issues that are not directly threatening to the state's national security, will not fight a total war but rather a limited one. In this case, they will also be unlikely to be willing to accept limitless costs due to the potentially limited benefits of victory. The combination of the war aims of the two sides will play a critical part in the war's outcome if the two sides are fighting over issues that fit into different issue areas and are fighting with different means. We cannot assume, as most have in the past, that the costs and benefits for both sides are symmetrical and zero-sum.

Just as the potential costs and gains of fighting are asymmetrical across the two sides involved, so too are the net costs for the mass publics and the elites within a single state. Mass publics and decision makers gain potentially different things from victory in war. Mass publics may be fighting to keep their way of life or the reputation of their country. State leaders are almost always fighting for their political survival. While this erodes the notion of a unitary actor and an identifiable national interest, there is strong theoretical and anecdotal evidence for the complex balance between domestic and international interests and mass/elite interests. If a state loses a war, it is a rare occurrence for the leaders that led the state into war to keep their hands on the tiller of the ship of state. This argument boils down to the fact that dominant leaders attempt to defend their positions at home. This is also similar to the position Ned Lebow takes in *Psychology and Deterrence*. Lebow argues that the fundamental cause of the Falklands Island War was the externalization of domestic instability in Argentina. This approach is a direct attack on the neorealists' structural approach. Until recently, there has been little support for this argument in the quantitative literature, although Bueno de Mesquita and Lalman (1992) show theoretical support for the argument in very specific sets of circumstances.

The traditional issues or stakes that states fight over include security, material wealth, territory, and reputation. Distinguishing between them will probably prove difficult as a result of the states' constant manipulation of the *apparent* stakes throughout a war. With rare exceptions, states' leaders argue at the outset of the war that, in some way, the state's security is at stake. Time however, as discussed earlier, tends to bring clarity to these ministrations. As states go through the machinations of trying to maintain support, the political characteristics and behavior of the state serve as an intervening variable that can either enhance or reduce the state's credibility. Recall from the previous section that the legitimacy of the state is critical to determining whether or not the state will be able to successfully manipulate its mass publics' beliefs about the expected benefits of war.

$H_{Salience}$:   The less salient the issues at stake for a country, the less likely it will be to win.

Time: Costs Increase Monotonically

Time has both direct and indirect effects on the conduct of war. Rather than trying to capture the role of time by using a proxy variable such as distance, I will initially measure its effects directly. After establishing the empirical effects of time, I will then present a model of war duration. As costs tend to rise for both sides in a war, regardless of the anticipated benefits, the longer a war drags on the greater the chance of a draw occurring. States whose aim is to provoke a long-lasting stalemate with the hope of achieving their policy aims through negotiation will likely choose military strategies such as punishment strategies that are associated with long, drawn-out wars.

How does the passage of time affect the costs associated with fighting for both sides in a war? The effects of time on costs and therefore outcomes is tangled and complex. Time affects the interaction of military strategies, rendering once innovative strategies ineffective (hence one reason for both military and civilian organizations' preferences for quick and hopefully decisive strategies). Maneuver strategies that were once able to efficiently inflict costs upon the opponent may be adapted to, rendering them less effective. Time also affects the ability of states to convey the anticipated net benefit of fighting a war to their mass publics. Time also comes into play in an indirect way as decision makers update their beliefs about their state's mass publics' net assessment of the cost-benefits of the war. The reappraisal of the costs and benefits may alter decision makers' willingness to continue fighting. The longer a war drags on, the more decision makers may update their beliefs about their ability to absorb and inflict punishment.

Given the notion of monotonically rising costs over time, we should then expect to also see the probability of both sides quitting rising over time—in turn leading to a rising probability of draws. As time passes, the opponent will be able to adapt to the type of war, and therefore its ability to absorb and/or inflict punishment should rise over time, thereby further reducing the initiator's expectations of victory over time. The initiator, faced with rising costs, is likely to try to slow the rate of losses, thereby increasing the amount of time it will be involved in the war, which actually plays into the hands of the defender (Maoz 1990, 148). An example of this occurred during World War II. The Germans knew they had to win during the first or second summer. If they did not, the Soviets would then have the time to be able to adapt to the blitzkrieg and develop a defense capable of withstanding the Nazi offensives. Additionally, the Nazis would have to face a state that was able to mobilize greater and greater proportions of its populations, while the Nazis were limited in their ability to bring more and more troops to the front (Maoz 1990, 151). Maoz points out that "wars are duels of wills and wits, and even the most masterful plan might run aground because it forces the opponent to resort to strategies that render the initial plan useless" (Maoz 1990, 165). If enough time elapses for the side on the defense to adapt to the initial offensive thrust of the attacker, we should expect the probability of victory to drop significantly.

H_{Time}:   The longer a war lasts, the greater the chance of a draw occurring.

Up to this point, I have spoken only in broad theoretical terms about the theory of outcomes presented in chapter 2 and the factors that I have identified in this chapter as having an effect on each state's cost-benefit analysis during a war. In chapter 4, I will go into greater detail about the operationalization and measurement of the factors associated with each of the specific hypotheses outlined in this chapter.

CHAPTER 4

Testing the Model

To this point we have accomplished several important tasks. First I reviewed the previous work on war outcomes. Second, I developed a theory of war termination and outcomes that builds upon this theoretical literature. Finally, in the preceding chapter, I explored sets of hypotheses that derive from two of the main approaches to studying international relations: the realpolitik approach and the domestic politics approach. In this chapter, I will explain how each of the specific hypotheses discussed in chapter 3 will be tested. In doing so I will explain how each concept is to be operationalized and measured in the context of the costs and benefits decision makers are likely to associate with waging war. Before doing so, I need to identify what sort of statistical model will be used to test the various hypotheses listed later in this chapter.

Most authors assume that war outcomes are a monotonic function[1] of the two states' or coalitions' military capabilities, usually controlling for distance (Bueno de Mesquita 1981; Organski and Kugler 1980). These measures can correctly predict outcomes with roughly 70 percent success, depending on the data set used and when the outcomes are simply coded win or lose. While this may seem to be an acceptable degree of accuracy, most would, I think, agree that forecasts based on simple measures of capabilities are crude at best. As I will demonstrate in this chapter, these simple models' ability to forecast outcomes accurately declines dramatically when we add the third possible outcome, draw. Believing that simplicity is a good thing in itself, I will show that more complex models dramatically outperform simple models based on capabilities indices.

We can think of several cases in which the side with a preponderance of military and industrial capabilities did not win the conflict. The United States fought to a draw in Korea and in Vietnam. France and Britain were beaten in Suez, as was the Soviet Union in Afghanistan. China's conflicts with Vietnam were hardly resounding victories for Beijing. The point here is not to argue the historical facts of any particular war but rather to show that the assumption that war outcomes are best modeled by military capability ratios is weak and potentially misleading.

Here, I assume that most of the factors will have declining marginal returns to costs and therefore outcomes. As a result, I will fit the econometric models to the logit function (Hanushek and Jackson 1977). A state that is truly preponderant will not be much less likely to win depending on marginal changes in its capabilities. In a conflict between two states that have very similar capabilities, marginal changes in these capabilities may shift the probability of one or the other side winning by a great deal. Because of the curvilinear nature of the logistic function, I am able to capture the notion of declining marginal returns and can also estimate the independent effect of the variables on draws as well as on victory or defeat. More specifically, I will use the multinomial logistic model to estimate the effects of each of the independent variables. The multiequation logistic estimation will allow us to see, for example, if capabilities or some other factor have a different effect on draws versus victory as hypothesized in chapter 2.

In order to construct a reasonable model, we need to lay out the assumptions that form the backbone of the study. The selection of the independent variables and the statistical model tested in this chapter flows from three basic assumptions commonly made in the literature on war and war outcomes:

1. War outcomes are probabilistic and asymptotically certain.
2. A state's probability of winning a war is a function of a finite number of independent variables that affect the costs of fighting and the expected benefits of winning.
3. Holding costs and benefits even, decision makers will make choices that will maximize their net benefits during and after the war. Because losers are typically punished domestically and winners rewarded, these actors prefer to win rather than to draw and to draw rather than to lose ($W > D > L$).

Much of what I believe accounts for the outcomes of wars results from the effects of the structure within which leaders make their decisions. In the following empirical chapters, I will demonstrate that *both* the choices and the structure within which the choices are made determine outcomes. If we ignored one component or the other we would end up reaching flawed or biased conclusions about the processes by which wars are won. Keith Dowding addresses the role of the structure in which decision makers find themselves and how that structure will influence the decisions they make:

However it is the structure of the individual choice situations that does most of the explanatory work. It is the set of incentives facing individuals which structurally suggest behavior to them; by studying those incentives together with assumptions about the way actors make decisions we come to understand why people act as they do. The worth of a model is measured by its structural correspondence to actual conditions, and not by its behavioral assumptions, which can be varied with greater ease. . . . Critics of rational choice theory have been too eager to discard its general assumptions; proponents have perhaps been too reluctant to jettison simplistic models (Dowding 1991, 18)

The model I describe and subsequently test is a good compromise between the need to rigorously apply empirical analysis to a set of exceedingly complex cases and the desire to incorporate some of the richness found in more traditional approaches to the study of the conduct of war.

The Data Set

The cases that I use are interstate wars following the Singer and Small (1982) definition of war. The Singer-Small criteria for a militarized dispute to be coded as a war are that both actors must be recognized as independent nation-states, and the total number of battle deaths must exceed one thousand. The one case where the latter criterion does not hold is the Falkland Islands War, where the casualties are just below the Singer-Small inclusion level (approximately 950). This case meets all other criteria for inclusion and is an important example of a developing nation initiating a war against an established Western power. I believe that the Falklands War also meets an intuitive sense of what an interstate war is compared to militarized intervention of a small nature such as the U.S. incursion into Panama under the Bush administration or the rescue of the medical students in Grenada under the Reagan administration. Some dyads from the Singer-Small data set are also deleted.[2] I am concerned with the effect that the principle actors and their choices have on the outcomes of wars.

Outcome codings are based on secondary historical sources, primarily the Dupuy and Dupuy (1986) military encyclopedia of wars. The general coding rule is such that the state that benefits in the new territorial status quo after the war is the winner while states that seek to change the status quo and prove unable to do so are coded as losers. In a draw, both sides formally agree to cease fighting in an internationally recognized and binding treaty. Cases (the Iran-Iraq War during the 1980s, for example) where fighting ends, usually after a long period of time, without an internationally recognized or enforceable agreement to codify the outcome are coded as draws as well.

Recall that the four quadrants in the outcome diagram presented in chapter 2 model three discrete outcomes and the situation where fighting continues. Obviously, in order for a case to be entered into the data set, the protagonists stopped fighting at some point. Cases where no winner is apparent and the resulting outcome is codified by formal agreement are coded as draws. The cases are coded into three categories; accordingly, I use a multinomial logit distribution with two discrete equations in order to represent the four possible outcome categories (in which three outcomes are observed). I then compare the predicted probabilities with the actual results in the cases. According to convention, I would count the outcome with the highest predicted probability to be the forecast outcome. I then compare this group to the pool of actual outcomes. This simple test captures the nature of the discrete outcomes that the theoretical model developed earlier implies. In order to test the basic notion of three outcomes, I will use a calibration table in addition to the more standard contingency table (Yates, 1990).

Many of the data used to test the hypotheses for the individual factors are drawn from the Correlates of War (COW) interstate war data set developed by Singer and Small, and the Polity II data set developed by Gurr et al. (Singer and Small 1982; Gurr et al. 1989). The temporal domain extends from 1823 until 1985. Some of the outcome codings differ from those found in the COW data set to capture more accurately the status quo at the end of each conflict.[3] The COW data set treats World War II as one multilateral six-year war that included the United States, Germany, France, Poland, and others. Following Dupuy, I break the war down into a series of sequential smaller wars, treating Germany versus Poland in 1939 as one war, Germany versus France in 1940 as a separate war, and so on. In the COW codings, Poland is coded as having won its war against Germany during World War II. This is an attempt on the part of the COW researchers to capture the notion that Poland was on the side that won. It does not capture the plain and simple fact that Germany annihilated the Polish army in a matter of weeks and that the Polish government was driven into exile in England for the duration of the continental war. Accordingly, I coded Poland as the loser.

These dyadic wars within World War II were quite distinct militarily and in time, with each war being violent and brief as far as the military organizations were concerned. In 1940, France formally surrendered to Germany, thereby ending the war between those two countries. To include France as a continuing participant in World War II until 1945 is, from my perspective, a historical misstatement. Similarly, in the other case that differs from COW convention, the Vietnam War, the United States and North Vietnam reached a negotiated settlement in 1973. Following that, the North Vietnamese routed the South in a what I consider to be a separate war two years later.[4] Variables not found in the two data sets, such as strategy, doctrine, surprise, distance, and issue area were coded on the basis of a close reading of both primary and secondary sources, which will be noted in the section of this chapter describing the conceptualization and operationalization of the specific indicators.

One criticism of quantitative work such as this is that the analyst may miss differences in the ways in which wars have been fought over the last two hundred years. If this were true, the logical deduction would be that the inferences we draw from the data set and then apply to all wars might actually only be reasonably applied to a small subset of all the data. It is also possible that if the effect of some variable were negative prior to World War II and positive after World War II then the model might split the difference and estimate the effect at zero, in which case our inference about all the cases would be incorrect. I will test for this by using the parameter estimates generated by the model to make outcome predictions for cases outside the sample. I will return to this point in greater detail in the next chapter.

In another instance, historians might argue that because all wars are unique events, we cannot possibly draw inferences from one time period and apply them to another. Concerns that cases in one time period may differ fundamentally from cases in other eras should be assuaged by Maoz's findings in his work on the paradoxes of war. He finds with few notable exceptions that "there are no significant differences in the associations between the various independent variables and dispute outcomes across centuries, types of initiators, types of targets, and types of disputes" (Maoz 1990, 215). I also find that the model works equally well for all historical periods contained in the data set.

Sampling and Selection Bias

For the quantitative test of this model, I took a stratified random sample of cases from the Singer and Small data set of interstate wars. In order to prevent correlation among errors from case to case, I randomly sampled one case from each war. Each war is an event with multiple cases, with each actor constituting a single case. Thus, in the Franco-Spanish War there are two cases. It is easy to see how there is significant correlation between the outcome of every case in any particular event. The chances of one side winning is dependent to some degree on the chances of the opponent losing. More specifically, in my model, the position of one actor on the cost-benefit quadrant, in figure 6, is partly determined by its opponent's attributes and vice versa. By randomly sampling only one case from each event, we circumvent this problem. I still have 87 cases out of a total of 229 with which I can test the model (Achen 1986).

Another potential source of bias arises from the problem of censured samples (Graves 1989; Heckman 1990). Before most actors decide to initiate a conflict, they weigh their chances of success. In doing so, those actors that judge their chances to be somewhere between slim and none most likely self-select themselves out of the conflict before it begins. Because most conflicts are probably started by actors that judge their chances of success to be high, the estimates of the cost-benefit functions may be biased. For example, we would expect to see fewer cases in the "draw" quadrant if the actors are able to accurately estimate their chances of winning than if they simply started conflicts randomly. If the actors were taken from a random sample of all states and randomly assigned to the two sides in a war, we might reasonably expect to see a more equal distribution of the three outcomes. Some evidence exists for this type of selection bias. For instance, the side that initiated the war won approximately 75 percent of the time. In the fully specified model, however, I will show that initiation drops out as a significant factor influencing the outcomes. The observed difference in outcomes between initiators and noninitiators is an effect of selection bias and not a result of the act of initiation having a significant effect on the process by which the war is fought. There is also some evidence that this is the case with regard to the increased chances of victory we observe being associated with democracies. This will be discussed at length in the following chapters.

This problem of selection bias must be taken into account when we interpret the results of the statistical tests. To better understand the inference problem, a nonwar example may be helpful. Standardized tests such as the scholastic aptitude test (SAT) would be quite accurate predictors of success in selective colleges if the universe of cases includes all students, both those who got into the schools and those who did not. But the tests are less accurate in predicting success if the sample includes only those who attended the school. Among all students, those who score 1200 or higher are more likely to do well than those who score 600 to 1000. But within the selected group, the differences between 1200 and 1600 are not as important as more personal factors such as self-discipline and organizational skills. Depending on one's perspective then, we may either infer that the SAT is either quite useful in predicting academic success or we might infer that the SAT is nearly useless. The correct inference depends upon what population of cases one wants to talk about.

In the same way, between all states, relative military power is probably a very good predictor of potential outcomes. But in the cases where states actually do go to war, other factors may become just as important in determining the outcomes. The role of the military balance may be less useful in forecasting winners and losers, just as the SAT is not so useful in predicting success within the pool of students attending elite colleges. As a result of this selection bias, the inferences I will draw from the empirical results cannot be applied to any pair of states drawn randomly from the pool of all states in the international system but rather only to those where the likelihood of war between them is high, thereby meeting the selection criteria.

In the next section, I lay out the variables, the hypotheses associated with them, and the logic behind the hypotheses. There are two types of variables:

1. Those that affect the costs a state incurs by fighting or the state's ability to raise its opponent's costs.
2. Those that affect the benefits or perceived benefits of fighting for each state participating in the war.

The variables are grouped according to whether the variable is an indicator drawn from the realpolitik literature or from the domestic politics literature. Additionally, within each of these two broad groupings, I distinguish between variables or factors that decision makers have some choice in (such as choosing to repress the mass publics or choosing one strategy versus another) and resource constraints, which are out of the hands of the leaders of the states at war (such as terrain or industrial capabilities).

Measuring the Factors that Determine War Outcomes

As in chapter 3, the theoretical complexity of the various indicators varies tremendously. As a result, the detail of the conceptual explanations will vary also. Population, for instance, is a fairly straightforward concept, both in terms of understanding what it is and how I will measure it. Accordingly, the discussion of variables such as population will be brief. Military strategy and doctrine are far from straightforward, however, both conceptually and in terms of how they can be quantified for the purpose of the statistical test. As a result, I define these terms and variables in detail, both in terms of how to think about them in relation to war and also in terms of how to think of ways to categorize them so they will allow me to make reasonable inferences from the quantitative results.

Choices that Decision Makers Face prior to or during a War

During the period prior to a war breaking out and then later during the war itself, leaders face a constant series of challenging decisions. Some of these I will show have a direct and significant impact on the likely outcome of the war. Factors such as strategy, repression, and whether or not to form alliances are viewed by many scholars as critical components of international relations theory. In this section, I divide the types of choices into two groups. First are those factors that realists or scholars in the realpolitik tradition view as important (strategy, alliances, surprise, mobilization, and technology and training). The second group contains the sole domestic choice that I will model, political repression.

Realpolitik Choices

Doctrine and Strategy: Introduction

$H_{Strategy}$ =   The higher ranked the actor's strategy is, the greater the probability of victory.

$H_{Doctrine}$ =   There is no inherent advantage to either the offense or defense. Under some circumstances the offense will have the advantage, under others the defense will.

Unlike many of the other indicators in this study, strategy and doctrine are very complex factors, both in terms of defining what they are and also in terms of how I will go about measuring them. Military strategy has been studied to a great extent by military historians. For the most part, the work has been confined to specific wars or battles, and relatively little systematic research exists. Outside the "Cult of the Offensive" literature, which discusses the origins of World War I, not much work has been done by political scientists on conventional military strategies. One result of this has been that understandings of strategy and doctrine have developed on an ad hoc basis rather than in a rational and cumulative manner. I consider the various definitions of strategy and doctrine to overlap somewhat but nested in a hierarchical fashion.

Definitions: Doctrine and Strategy

The apparent paradox of a state's need to develop a nonthreatening international foreign policy while retaining retaliatory military capabilities has plagued the security studies field. One reason for this is a frequent misunderstanding about the relationship between grand strategy, doctrine, and strategy. Much of the research in this area has been driven by normative concerns about the possibility of major power confrontation during the cold war. Some who write on the subject tend to tailor their definitions of strategy and doctrine to fit their particular argument.[5] While everyone uses the same terms, they are not all used in the same ways. Barry Posen (1984) talks about three fundamental types of doctrine: disarm, deny, and punish. Van Evera, for example, uses the terms *doctrine* and *strategy* interchangeably.

Here, military strategy refers to the way in which a state uses or plans to use its military forces within a particular theater in a war. Military doctrine refers to the state's military goals (maintaining or altering the status quo) and plans for attaining them. Grand strategy refers to the state's larger plans from theater to theater over time, but will not be tested here. It is important to distinguish strategies (means to an end) from goals (ends for which actors have preferences) even though the two may interact. Within the political science literature, no one has made a real attempt to synthesize the differences and the implications of the failure to differentiate between the different concepts. Unfortunately, the conflation of grand strategy, doctrine, strategy, tactics, operational doctrine, and a whole host of other terms that all refer to both aims and means has muddled the discussion. Next, I carefully define and explain how both doctrine and strategy have been measured in the data set.

Doctrine: Military doctrine refers to the state's military goals (maintaining or altering the status quo between the two sides in the war) and its plans for attaining them. A state's doctrine can be either offensive or defensive. Every state conducts foreign policy of some sort or another. This foreign policy is typically based on the state's outlook on how the world works or how it believes it ought to work. There are states that see the world as a fundamentally conflictual place and wish to ultimately rearrange the system's status quo, whether it be territorial, economic, or political, either in the short or long run. An example of this is the Soviet Union during the postwar period. Its state ideology held that while war was not inevitable, there was conflict between the two sides in the system. If there were a war ultimately, then the Soviets felt that they should be prepared to destroy the capitalist world. Their military plans flowed from their ideology or how they viewed the world.

The ultimate military goals that reflect a state's ideology and worldview are intimately related to its doctrine. Doctrine reflects, in part, how a state believes the world's territorial and economic assets should be distributed. A state that seeks the ultimate alteration of the general system status quo (aside from changes resulting from self-determination and domestic political systems) usually represented through territorial aims, has an offensive doctrine. This offensive doctrine may be pursued using a sequential or reactionary grand strategy, with a variety of military strategies. A state that does not seek to change (at least through war or military means) the system's territorial alignment and instead seeks to maintain the existing territorial distribution has a defensive doctrine.

It is important to note that this discrimination between offensive and defensive doctrines makes no distinction between how these aims will be accomplished. Note also the relation between doctrine and ideology: both involve foreign policy aims. These doctrinal objectives (maintain or disrupt the status quo via cooperation or defection, respectively) are met through the use of either diplomatic or military means, hence military or diplomatic doctrine. How these tools are used refers to a state's military strategy. Within a particular doctrine category, a state has several military strategy options. A state with a defensive doctrine can try to use military or diplomatic means to maintain the system.

Strategy: In using its military to execute a defensive doctrine, the state has essentially three choices of military strategy. The state can defend the status quo by adopting one of the following three strategies:

1. Maneuver: A state may choose to defend itself by attempting to disarm an opponent by focusing on mobility. In a mobile disarming strategy the location of the battle is not important. From the perspective of the defender of the status quo, whether this battle takes place on its soil or on the attacker's is immaterial (except that it is preferable to have a war on someone else's front lawn rather than your own in terms of minimizing the costs that the state must bear). This strategy in many ways can be an apparently offensive one, using more common definitions. In its execution, the defending state will seek out and attempt to destroy the attacker's military forces, either within the attacker's or within the defender's territorial boundaries. The goal of this strategy is to destroy the attacking state's ability to continue its attack militarily. The key here is the counterforce nature of the strategy. Using common parlance, this defensive strategy appears to be an offensive strategy in

that the defending nation will take the initiative in destroying the attacker's military forces rather than wait for these forces to cross the defender's borders. NATO's Follow on Forces Attack (FOFA) strategy is perhaps the best example of this model of a defensive maneuver strategy. NATO may not have had the assets to deny the Soviets the ability to penetrate its borders. Because of this, NATO's strategy depended in great part on locating and destroying the potential attacker's forces before they crossed into NATO territory. While this is certainly an "offensive" strategy in that it depends on local surprise and fighting on the attacker's territory rather than on the defender's, it is part of a defensive doctrine. If NATO forces succeeded in disarming the attacker, there was no provision to fight past that point, nor did NATO possess the military assets necessary to take and hold large areas of territory.

2. Attrition: A state may also choose to defend itself by attempting to deny its opponent the ability to cross its border with a forward defense. This form of denial strategy aims to result in a war of attrition with a recognizable front line or forward edge of the battle area (FEBA). The French Maginot Line in World War II was an attempt at this type of defensive doctrine. The French believed that they could make a defensive line so robust that the Germans would not be able to penetrate the massive and fixed fortifications. The French had no intention of crossing their own border and taking the fight into Germany. They felt that a strong denial capability would lead the Germans to the conclusion that an attack on France would be a futile exercise. Other parts of the security literature refer to this as a prewar strategy of deterrence by denial.

3. Punishment: A state can attempt to defend itself by raising the attacker's costs so high through a strategy of punishment that they will cease the attack. This is the type of threat underlying the concept of mutual assured destruction (MAD). Under MAD, even if a state is attacked with nuclear weapons, it is still able to mount a punishing counterblow against the attacker's home territory. This counterstrike would raise the cost to the attacker far higher than any conceivable gain that might result from defeating the defender. Followed to its logical conclusion, this strategy would not require any forces beyond those needed to punish the aggressor and hence raise its costs. We should note that this type of strategy can be carried out with conventional weapons as well, that is, the conventional bombing of cities as the United States did in World War II in Dresden and Tokyo or in the war in Vietnam with the bombings of Hanoi.

While a state exercising a defensive military doctrine has three choices of military strategy, so does a state with an offensive doctrine. The three strategy choices under an offensive doctrine are roughly analogous to the three defensive strategies:

1. Maneuver: A state may attempt to alter the status quo though the use of force by adopting a maneuver strategy based on speed and mobility. In this strategy, based on a series of sequential actions, the attacking state seeks to occupy as much of the defending state's territory as possible. A subtle point is necessary here. The intention of the occupation is not to hold the land for its own intrinsic value but rather to be able to disrupt the opponent's command, control, and communications links as widely as possible. Physically being on the territory and fragmenting the enemy's unity of command is more important than destroying enemy forces. This is the strategy that the Germans utilized in their defeat of France in World War II. The Germans occupied so much of France so quickly that the French military collapsed into disorganization. This strategy is riskier than the other options, however. Due to its sequential nature, failure to execute the entire plan in order can lead to defeat. Strategies predicated on movement, whether blitzkriegs or encirclement, will degenerate into attrition battles and wars if the initial movements prove unsuccessful. "If a blitzkrieg fails to achieve decisive results, it will evolve into an attrition strategy, as it did on the eastern front in World War II. After 1942 the Germans were clearly no longer capable of effecting a blitzkrieg against the Soviets" (Mearsheimer 1983, 52).

2. Attrition: A state can try to change the status quo by adopting a strategy based on attrition. By destroying the defender's forces and taking its army prisoner, the attacker hopes to render the defender unable to continue the war by raising the opponent's costs above its benefits threshold. This was the German strategy in Russia after 1942. Hitler ordered his forces to take as many prisoners as possible and to destroy as many forces as they could rather than bypass large battles as they had in France. Due to the immense size of the Soviet Union, a territorial strategy based on mobility would probably have been impossible to carry out. The new counterforce strategy based on the rapid envelopment, capture, and destruction of Soviet troops almost proved to be Stalin's undoing. Interestingly, the German generals resisted this strategy change, but to no avail. Unlike the sequential blitzkrieg strategy, a disarming strategy does not depend to such a great extent on the success or failure of any

individual battle. Because of this factor, disarming strategies are less risky than a strategy based on a series of fluid mobile maneuvers. In this strategy, no attempt is made to avoid the opponent's forces because avoiding the forces would decrease the ability of one side to impose cost, via attrition, on the other. Rather, large confrontations are sought out (Mearsheimer 1983, 34).

3. Punishment: A state can try to alter the status quo by adopting a punishment strategy, of which there are two basic forms. In this strategy, the attacker is counting on being able to break the resolve of the defending state. In one form, the attacker tries to do this usually with airborne or missile assets. This strategy was developed in the West from the theoretical work of Duhey and Mitchell prior to World War II. Under Nixon, the United States adopted this type of strategy in Vietnam in the latter part of the war, when the United States brought home most of its ground troops and tried to coerce the Hanoi government into capitulation with a series of punishing bombing raids. The mass bombings of Dresden, Tokyo, and London in World War II were also results of the execution of this strategy.

Another example of the punishment or coercive strategy is the guerrilla strategy advocated by Mao Tse-tung in China during the communist's war against the nationalists after World War II. The punishment strategies that the Western powers pursued required high-technology weapons and massive uses of military force, typically delivered from the air. Mao's punishment strategy relied on the same logic but differed somewhat in its execution. Rather than using high technology such as helicopters and jet aircraft to inflict costs upon the opponent, Mao's punishment strategy was based on soldiers living among the civilian population. The Maoists extracted food and shelter from the civilians as they needed and punished their opponents when opportunities presented themselves. While the means of delivering the punishment may have varied, Mao's guerrilla strategy was similar to the punishment strategy outlined by coercion theorists such as Schelling (1966).

Strategy Index
Each combination of offensive and defensive strategies can either convey a net advantage by imposing costs on the defender or the attacker or can lead to neither side having an advantage. Figure 14 represents graphically (on a quadrant diagram similar to figs. 6 and 7 used in chap. 2), how changes in the costs associated with fighting end up affecting the actual outcome. Figure 14 demonstrates where the various

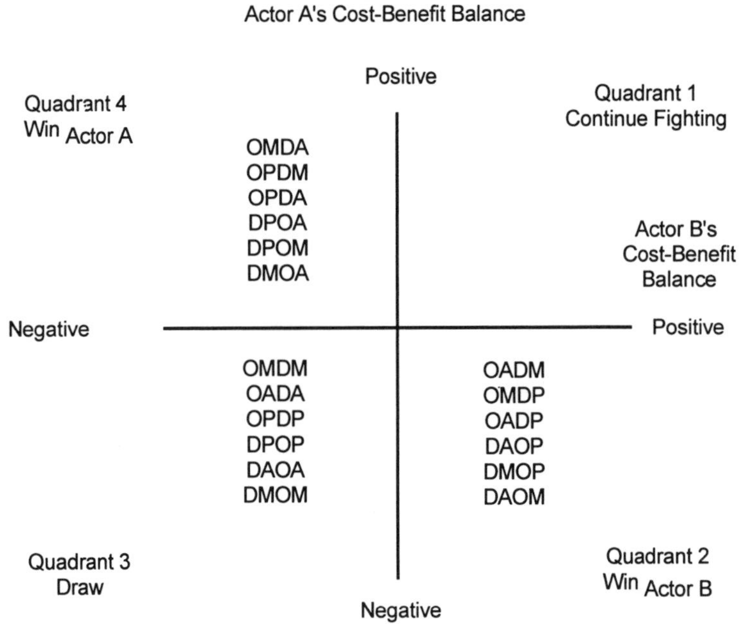

Actor A's Cost-Benefit Balance

Positive

Quadrant 4
Win Actor A

Quadrant 1
Continue Fighting

OMDA
OPDM
OPDA
DPOA
DPOM
DMOA

Actor B's
Cost-Benefit
Balance

Negative ———————————————————————— Positive

OMDM	OADM
OADA	OMDP
OPDP	OADP
DPOP	DAOP
DAOA	DMOP
DMOM	DAOM

Quadrant 3
Draw

Quadrant 2
Win Actor B

Negative

Fig. 14. Expected change in Actor A's cost-benefit balance as a function of Actor A's strategy and doctrine choice and the corresponding change in the expected outcome

strategy combinations should appear on the cost-benefit diagram, with the likely outcomes associated with each. The particular combinations, such as OMDM, correspond to the strategic and doctrinal combinations of the two sides at war. OMDM, for instance, codes a situation in which the side with an offensive doctrine (O) is fighting using a maneuver strategy (OM), as is the side with the defensive doctrine (DM). The remaining codes are explained later in this section. This is an important point: there are best strategies in war just as there are best strategies in chess. Equally important is the fact that by coding the strategies in this way, we will be able to test not just a single strategy per se but the interaction of various strategy types as viewed from the two perspectives of an offensive or defensive doctrine.

Strategy will be operationalized as a scaled variable for each state. The scale is an ordinal one, the rankings deduced from preference rankings of military organizations and partly on assumptions about the advantages of mobile forces over more static ones. In the next chapter, I will show that the rank order of the strategies deduced here matches the relative effectiveness of the strategy combinations observed in the real world. In the statistical model, I test each of the ordinal categories as a dummy variable because the scaling interval is unknown. The relative size of the coefficients should correspond to the ranking in the strategy scale. The hypotheses flow from the ordering in the strategy scale.

Each side in the conflict has three strategic options: a sequential maneuver strategy (M), a disarming attrition strategy (A), or a strictly coercive punishment strategy (P), creating nine possible strategy combinations for both states with offensive doctrines and those with defensive ones. In order to rank the relative effectiveness of the nine combinations of strategies, I must make three basic assumptions based on the notions that states want to minimize costs and maximize the benefits associated with fighting. The assumptions are listed in assumed order of importance:

1. The strategy that leads to the minimum military losses maximizes the opportunity to continue to fight in the future. All other things being equal, the side that can fight more battles wins. Punishment strategies (P) avoid direct exchanges whenever possible, leading to the fewest direct battle losses. Maneuver strategies (M), predicated on disrupting communications and control while avoiding direct confrontations, minimize battle losses compared to attrition strategies (A).

2. Quicker outcomes are better than slower ones for the side trying to alter the status quo (offensive doctrines, the opposite for defensive doctrines). This is due to the difficulty of maintaining domestic political support in the face of mounting casualties. Maneuver strategies (M) lead to the quickest outcomes, followed by attrition (A), then punishment strategies (P). This rule is used to rank strategy combinations within groups of winners, losers, or draws.

3. Each side is able to execute the strategy it chooses at the war's outset. In reality, failed maneuver strategies (M), in cases where the sequential nature breaks down or command and control is lost, evolve into disarming, attrition strategies (A). This results when maneuver strategies fail to achieve quick victory.

Using these assumptions, I deduce a nine-point scale for each side depending on whether it is the side defending the status quo (defensive doctrine) or seeking to alter it (offensive doctrine). Table 2 shows how each actor (Actor A or Actor B) will be assigned a score for its strategy: on an ordinal scale, 9 would be the highest, or most likely to win, and 1

TABLE 2. Ordinal Scale of Strategy Combinations

Side A on Offense-Side B on Defense		
Side A		Side B
Offense-Defense	Rank	Defense-Offense
OM-DA (win)	9	DP-OA (win)
OP-DM (win)	8	DP-OM (win)
OP-DA (win)	7	DM-OA (win)
OM-DM (draw)	6	DP-OP (draw)
OA-DA (draw)	5	DA-OA (draw)
OP-DP (draw)	4	DM-OM (draw)
OA-DM (lose)	3	DA-OP (lose)
OM-DP (lose)	2	DM-OP (lose)
OA-DP (lose)	1	DA-OM (lose)

would be the worst doctrinal and strategy combination, or the one most likely to lose. Each of the observed strategy-doctrine combinations will be tested as a dummy variable. We can also test if there is a fundamental advantage to being on the defense versus the offense. If defensive doctrines are easier to execute well and hence more likely to lead to victory, as is frequently asserted by some scholars, on average they will have larger coefficients than the offensive doctrine combinations. If there is no clear separation in the ordering of defensive and offensive doctrines, then the hypothesis that defense is better cannot be supported. For example, if we see that the coefficients for defenders utilizing mobile strategies are of the same sign and size as states with offensive doctrines using mobile strategies, then we should conclude that there is little net advantage to adopting one doctrine over another.

Maneuver-Attrition-Punishment (M-A-P) Coding
I first recorded each side's doctrine by coding which side sought to alter the status quo or preserve it (determining offensive or defensive doctrine), based on Dupuy and Dupuy (1986) and Holsti (1991). I then coded states' military strategy using Dupuy and Dupuy (1986), Dupuy (1983), and Clodfelter (1993). Instances where the historical consensus was that a state used a blitzkrieg strategy or where the actor encircled and divided the opponent's forces were coded maneuver (M).[6] If there was doubt or lack of consensus among military historians about the strategy choice, I coded the modal strategy of attrition (A). Instances where a state followed a Maoist guerrilla strategy or where civilians were the principal military target were coded punishment (P). In cases where states used multiple strategies, I coded the strategy that absorbed the

majority of the state's military assets. If there was more than one country on one side of a war, I coded the strategy of the largest state (in terms of capabilities). In making my codings I am as broad as possible. For example, a counterforce attrition strategy of searching out enemy submarines and a countervalue attrition strategy of searching out enemy shipping are both coded as attrition strategies.[7] Attrition is the most common strategy, accounting for about two thirds of all cases. Punishment strategy is the least common.

John Arquilla notes that while strategy is important, it is the interaction of the two sides' strategies that is critical to determining the war's outcome. From this assertion, he concludes that there is no "best" strategy, or even an optimal one. Rather, Arquilla simply concludes that because strategic interaction is important and it may have long-term but unintended consequences, we simply cannot tell what will happen (Arquilla 1992, 3). Obviously, I disagree. While I agree that the effect of strategy choice is interactive in that how one side fights will affect the efficacy of how the other side fights, for any given situation I will show that there are, in fact, optimal choices that can be made. In other words, some interactions are better than others. In the next chapter I show the empirical and systematic effects of strategy interactions on war outcomes.

One potential objection to this approach is that it relies on ex-post codings of strategy. While it is true that in the cases used in this analysis the strategies or doctrines of the actors in question were inferred from their actual behavior, Posen asserts that "military doctrines and capabilities are hard to hide, while the political intentions that lie behind the military preparations are obscure" (Posen 1984, 16). A state's doctrine before the outset of a war is far more transparent to the ex ante analyst than the more typical indicators of success in studies of war outcomes such as ratios of battle deaths. Strategy combinations such as when the defender is fighting an attrition strategy and the offense is fighting with a maneuver strategy will spell likely doom for the defender, holding all other factors constant and equal.

Alliance Contributions

$H_{Alliances}$ = Alliance contributions will increase a state's chances of victory. They should have similar, but smaller, effects on the actor's chances of victory than the state's own military industrial capabilities.

Allies allow a state to increase the costs their opponents must bear and reduce the costs that they must bear. Figure 15 shows how

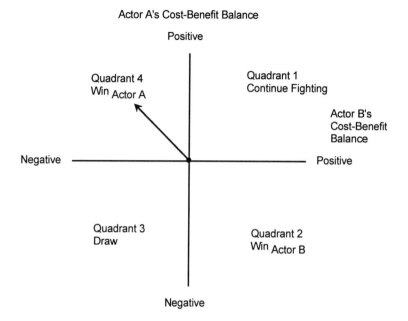

Fig. 15. Expected change in Actor A's cost-benefit balance as a function of the contributions of Actor A's allies and the corresponding change in the expected outcome

this affects an actor's position on the cost-benefit quadrant diagram. Morgenthau, mentioned earlier as the preeminent realist, believed that alliances were one of the central features of international relations. Alliances, Morgenthau argued, allowed states to increase their power quickly simply by aggregating the collective power of the alliance partners. I believe this to be true to a certain extent. Ally contributions help states win but not as much as a state's own capabilities. This ability to increase one's effective power simply by concluding an alliance with another is the central tenet of balance-of-power politics. Morgenthau and others felt that states would try to keep the peace by balancing one's power against another. But because the domestic determinants of power were slow and evolutionary in nature, a state's only recourse was to adjust its relative power through ever-changing alliances. Taking the analogy one step further, we must deduce that realists like Morgenthau feel that alliance contribution to a state's power would be significant and could be measured simply by adding up the resources of the states in question (Morgenthau 1978, 80).

The reason why ally contribution must be discounted compared to a state's own capabilities can be found in the work of collective action scholars. Contrary to the realist assumption about the nature of alliances, Olson and Zeckhauser argue that the relative capabilities and the domestic characteristics of alliance partners will affect the actual contribution of the alliance partner in question. While realists assume that the power of the alliance is an additive function of the capabilities of the alliance partners, Olson, like Maoz, argues that since different countries have different evaluations of the purpose and value of the alliance and bring to the alliance different and frequently noncompatible capabilities, in the final accounting (the war's outcome) the contributions of alliance partners may be significantly less than the sum of their parts (Olson and Zeckhauser 1970, 185). Organski and Kugler (1980) make similar arguments about the relative lack of importance that alliance contributions should make to war outcomes, but their interest is essentially in hegemonic war, where any alliance partner would have relatively little to offer anyway.

At the operational level, it is likely that differences in command structure, differences in technology and training, and differences in things as simple as communications equipment may all hinder allies from working as well with one another as they do with themselves. It is conceivable, but unlikely, that allies might actually hinder a state's ability to utilize its military power during a war. If an ally is unable to meet its commitments in a tightly scheduled operation, the whole battle plan may fail. Due to the highly interdependent and interactive nature of war fighting, units from different countries using different equipment and speaking different languages will likely have a very difficult time working with one another.

Given these hypotheses about the role of domestic politics and other state-level attributes such as technological advantage and strategy, I argue that unless we are able to control for the differences between alliance partners, we will not see the same relationship between alliance contribution and the probability of victory that we do between a state's own capabilities and war outcomes. This is not to say that alliances cannot make a difference; that would be to deny the invaluable contribution of the United States to Britain during World War II. I mean to argue that alliance contributions cannot simply be added together as realists assert without some kind of discounting factor. Rather, alliance performance is a highly complex problem, where relative technological development, doctrine, strategy, training, and political systems will all make some difference. But that is a topic for future research. Alliance contribution is measured here in the same way I measured a state's military-industrial capability, using the COW composite capabilities index, where the alliance partner's contribution is the fraction of the total capabilities of all states involved in the war. The alliance contribution is a separate term in the logistic equation in order that we may be able to measure the independent effect. The ally's technology level is measured in the same way as it is for the state in question, in spending per soldier.

Surprise

$H_{Surprise}$ =   Surprise will have a small positive effect on a side's chances of victory.

It is ironic to note, given the initial devastation of the Soviet armed forces at the outset of World War II, that Stalinist doctrine and attitudes maintained that surprise made at best a marginal difference in the likely outcomes of wars. One of the problems is that the supporters of the surprise doctrine argue that the element of surprise means defenders will be at a disadvantage because their carefully laid defense plans will no longer be appropriate for the new situation. As a result, the action plans of the defenders will constantly be updated to plan for a fluid situation. The problem with this approach is the implicit assumption that the attackers will not be facing a similar situation. The surprise proponents assume that in a surprise attack, all will go as planned and the attacker will not have to adapt to changing conditions. While surprise certainly enables one side to dictate the conditions of battle, at least for a short time, these gains may be offset by other negative aspects associated with strategic surprise. Or, conversely, an initiator who uses surprise to great effect and achieves quick initial victories might upset or change previous plans in an attempt to grab more territory than had been initially planned for. An example of this can be seen in the way the United States became emboldened by the success of the Inchon breakout and hence modified its plans, which ultimately brought the Chinese into the war and led to the final stalemate.

As soon as the initial actions of the surprise attack are over, both the attacker and the defender will find themselves having to adapt to conditions in flux. In many ways, the defender will have the advantage as it fights into its rear, and the attacker fights farther and farther from its logistical trains. In this light, the gains from surprise are likely to be ephemeral. Richard Betts makes the point that surprise may make a difference at the end of a war as well as at the beginning. Betts cites the examples of Dien Bien Phu and the Tet offensive in Vietnam as cases where a surprise attack led to the eventual end of the war in Vietnam for both the French and the United States by changing the attacked side's expectations about the future costs of the war. While authors like Maoz argue that surprise at the outset of war can increase the resolve of the defender, the argument that the defender's resolve or will can be broken by a surprise during the war is novel and interesting (Betts 1982, 10). Strategic surprise, something actually quite rare, is coded as a dummy variable, either present or not, based on a close reading of secondary history sources. The surprise codings try to capture strategic surprise at any time during the war.

Mobilization

$H_{Mobilization}$ = Military mobilization during a war will have a positive impact on war outcomes.

A state's ability to mobilize its resources for war is perceived to be a key factor in the state's ability to prevail in a conflict (Tractenberg 1991). Differences in states' mobilization rates have also been blamed as a cause of war, particularly in World War I (Snyder 1984; Van Evera 1984). The argument that mobilization significantly influences war outcomes or duration has been discussed at length in the historical literature, but to my knowledge it has not been broadly tested using empirical data.

Figure 16 shows how, as the number of the state's troops rises (both in absolute and relative terms), its chances of victory should rise as well. This is because the greater the military capabilities a state possesses, the greater the costs it will be able to inflict upon its opponent and the greater the costs it should be able to absorb before running out of soldiers to fight with. Mobilization is measured in two ways: first, by the number of soldiers under arms, and second, by the ratio of the two sides' number of soldiers. The two terms allow us to measure the absolute and relative effect of mobilization on outcomes.

Military Quality: Technology and Training

$H_{Technology\ and\ Training}$ = Initially, the higher the relative training and technology level, the greater the likelihood of victory. Once the point of diminishing marginal returns is reached, the probability of a draw will increase.

Initially, more spending by a state for technology and training leads to greater costs for the state's opponent. But, like almost all monetary

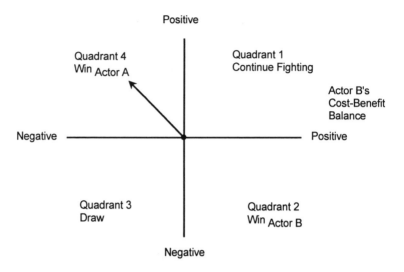

Fig. 16. Expected change in Actor A's cost-benefit balance as a function of the number of troops that Actor A mobilizes and the corresponding change in the expected outcome

investments, these investments are subject to declining marginal returns. At some point, the last dollar spent will no longer result in increased costs for the opponent. At this point, costs will continue to rise for Actor A as it spends more on technology with no return. As a result, the costs relative to the expected benefits will start to rise for Actor A (because the benefits are fixed). Whether the money is spent on training or technology, at some point diminishing returns will result. With respect to training, after soldiers know their jobs and can perform them flawlessly, further intense training offers little return on the investment. Similarly, some technological problems cannot be solved simply by spending more money; the infrastructure and people executing the research will eventually limit the pace of innovation regardless of the money spent.

In this study, I use an indicator for technology and training that can be measured using ex ante information. I estimate the relative level of training and technology with the ratio of the two sides' military spending per soldier. I assume that states with higher spending rates per soldier relative to their opponents will have a correspondingly higher relative degree of technological endowment and higher levels of training. Realistic training is terribly expensive, approaching the cost of actually fighting a war. The state with the higher technology and better training should have a greater probability of victory. One problem with this measure lies in the high degree of error involved in measuring currency rates. The military spending and troop numbers come from the COW data set, and the degree of uncertainty is quite high. If my hypothesis is supported using this crude measure, we can be fairly certain that with more accurate measures the effect of the underlying concept will be at least as great as that found here.

While the logic behind the argument is straightforward, in practice the role of technology is quite complicated. For the most part, it is very difficult to determine the advantage that a particular weapon may or may not have for the offense or the defense in a war. Before World War I, some strategists argued that advances in artillery would reduce mobility to zero, while others such as Foch argued the opposite, that infantrymen walking behind blankets of artillery could advance at will (Maoz 1990, 161). It took the war to sort out who was right or wrong, and even then the results were not clear-cut. What emerges from this is that it is not so much the absolute level of technology present during a war that affects the outcome but rather the relative degree of technical skill and technological investment that the two sides possess. This is why the empirical measure is a ratio of the two sides' resource expenditures.

In *Dubious Battles*, Arquilla recognizes the importance of "skill" in affecting likely outcomes. But, rather than trying to develop an ex ante indicator, he relies on the ratio of battle deaths from previous wars, a decidedly ex post indicator. Instead of using information that can only be learned after the fact, I employ an indicator that is based on information that both sides have available before the war begins. In addition to "skill" or relative degree of technical expertise, technology is a factor implicated in the vast majority of studies on war, whether it be the initiation or outcome, which must be accounted for. Again, Arquilla relies on ex post information culled from the observation of wars. He simply codes the sides with the better observed technology as a 2, equal technology as 1, and 0 when the other side holds a technological edge (Arquilla 1992, 81–85). In this study, the variable is both generated from ex ante information and is continuous, hopefully capturing more subtle differences between the two sides' capabilities.

I estimated the quality of military forces for a country as military expenditures (in constant U.S. dollars) divided by number of military personnel. Following Huth et al. (1992) and Stam (1993), I argue that additional spending per soldier reflects additional troop training, equipment, and relative technology endowment.[8] I then created a ratio of the better side's quality to the worse side's quality.

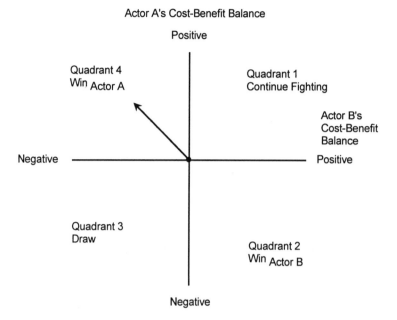

Fig. 17. Expected change in the mass public's perception of Actor A's cost-benefit balance as a function of Actor A's level of political repression and the corresponding change in the expected outcome

Domestic Politics Factors

While the realpolitik factors are those one encounters most frequently when reading military history or the political science literature on war, domestic politics should also play a direct role in the state's ability to successfully wage war. In this, the "choice" section, there is only a single indicator, political repression. Decision makers in time of war must choose whether or not they will repress the dissenting voices among their publics and how severe that repression will be.

Repression

$H_{Repression}$ =   Higher rates of political repression should be correlated with higher probabilities of victory.

In figure 17, Actor A is able to hide the costs of fighting from the mass public (or coerce them into discounting the costs of fighting compared to the costs of *not* fighting). As the apparent costs decline (or the mass public discounts these costs compared to domestic costs of resistance), Actor A's cost-benefit balance shifts toward the Win quadrant. Repression increases the chances of victory because it allows states to hide the costs of war from the mass public and limits discussion among the mass publics about the nature of the benefits of the anticipated victory. I use the Gurr et al. (1989) "competitiveness of participation" variable as the measure of the repressiveness of a state's government. For each state, Gurr's variable ranges from a 1, indicating that no significant opposition activity is permitted in the state, to 5, indicating significant and regular political competition in opposition to the ruling leaders.[9]

Resources

While many of the factors I identify as having direct effects on war outcomes can be directly manipulated by state leaders, some factors are essentially fixed, at least in the short run. For instance, most states do not get to "choose" their industrial capabilities. They are a basic characteristic of that particular country. These types of factors serve as resource bases or constraints on a state's ability to inflict costs on its opponent.

Realpolitik Factors

Military-Industrial Capability

$H_{Capabilities}$ = There should be a positive monotonic relationship between a state's proportion of the military-industrial capabilities available to all the war's participants and the probability of victory.

I model each actor's military and industrial capabilities as a proportion of all the capabilities available to all the war's participants. The indicator of capabilities is measured using the Correlates of War (COW) composite capabilities index. The index is composed of industrial production, military forces, energy consumption, and proportions of urban and rural populations. One characteristic of this measure is that it is almost perfectly collinear with states' gross national products (GNP) for almost all states. This relationship breaks down to a small degree with the very largest states like the United States, the Soviet Union, and China. For most practical purposes though, it is close to interchangeable with most estimates of GNP (Kugler and Domke 1986). This measure, in combination with the mobilization variables, allows us to capture both a purely military component (military personnel and

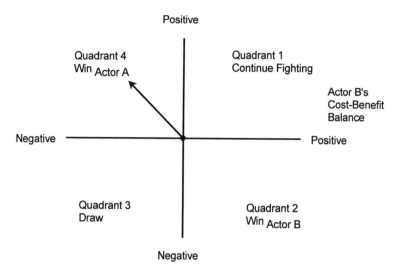

Fig. 18. Expected change in Actor A's cost-benefit balance as a function of Actor A's military-industrial capabilities and the corresponding change in the expected outcome

mobilization) and a civil-military-industrial component (the COW index). I use the COW composite capabilities index (Singer, Bremer, and Stuckey 1972) as an indicator of states' capabilities.[10] I define the balance of capabilities as the ratio of the larger side's total capabilities to the total capabilities of all participants to obtain the balance of forces.

Figure 18 shows how, as the state's proportion of the available capabilities rises, its chances of victory should rise as well. This is because the greater the military-industrial capabilities a state possesses, the greater will be the costs they will be able to inflict upon their opponent. Also, the larger the state's economy is, the smaller will be the proportion of the costs of the fighting to the economy as a whole compared to what they would have been in a state with a smaller economy. The result of these factors will be an increase in the state's cost-benefit balance for fighting.

Population

$H_{Population}$ =   Population levels should correlate with both higher chances of victory and with higher chances of draws.

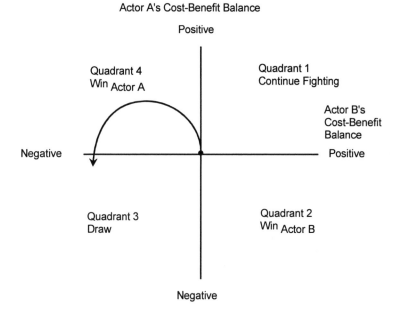

Actor A's Cost-Benefit Balance

Positive

Quadrant 4
Win Actor A

Quadrant 1
Continue Fighting

Actor B's
Cost-Benefit
Balance

Negative   Positive

Quadrant 3
Draw

Quadrant 2
Win Actor B

Negative

Fig. 19. Expected change in Actor A's cost-benefit balance as a function of Actor A's population and the corresponding change in the expected outcome

The arguments behind the role of population and outcomes are relatively straightforward. Within broad limits, measuring population is also fairly simple. The test of the effect of population will be done both indirectly and directly. Population is likely to have an indirect effect through the role of time. Large states should be more likely to fight long protracted wars, being more able to replace losses from fighting without depleting their ability to maintain an adequate employment force at home. Population also should have a direct effect. I could measure population either as a ratio of the two sides' population or by simply controlling for the particular state in question. Here I will not measure population as a ratio (something captured in part by the COW capabilities ratio and as such highly collinear) but rather simply as the number of persons in the state. Using this method, we should see somewhat different results than we might if I used a ratio of the two sides' populations as I did with the two sides' composite capabilities.

Using the single actor's population, we should be able to observe the changes in the sides' cost-benefit balance for fighting in figure 19. As the state's population rises from zero, its ability to inflict costs on the opponent should rise because it has a higher base from which to draw troops, hence the state's chances of victory should rise briefly. But as with most factors, there should be a limit to the number of people that a state can put under arms. Beyond that limit, further increases in a state's population simply dilute the expected benefits that any individual in the society can expect to receive from victory (assuming the gains are divisible in some way throughout the country). At some point, there will be an increase in the likelihood of a draw as the diluted benefits fall below the potential costs of fighting. I measure the total population of the combatants using data from the COW national capabilities data set, coded as billions of people.

Distance

$H_{Distance}$ =   Distance will serve to discount the capabilities of states. There will be a correlation between distance and declining chances of victory that should vary with the size and capabilities of the state in question. Small, weak states should suffer the effects of distance substantially more than states that control a large proportion of the system's capabilities.

Figure 20 demonstrates the direction of the effect that distance will have on Actor A's chances of victory. As I discussed earlier, I argue that distance should have a small independent effect on the probability of victory. Previous findings that contradict this hypothesis, which expects a very strong relationship between distance and outcomes, result from the use of distance as a proxy for a more fully specified model. It is likely that distant disputes and wars were viewed by decision makers and mass publics as inconsequential issues with limited benefits relative to the potential costs involved in prosecuting the war. Distances are measured using map data and distance measurements from the international edition of *Direct Line Distances* (which are measured capital to capital). The routes selected for measurements come from historical accounts of the wars in question and are measured in miles.

Terrain

$H_{Terrain}$ =   Wars fought on difficult terrain will favor the defender and will be of prolonged duration. Where little or no movement is possible, draws will be more likely. In a

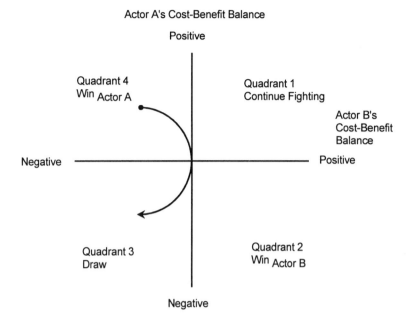

Actor A's Cost-Benefit Balance

Positive

Quadrant 4
Win Actor A

Quadrant 1
Continue Fighting

Actor B's
Cost-Benefit
Balance

Negative

Positive

Quadrant 3
Draw

Quadrant 2
Win Actor B

Negative

Fig. 20. Expected change in Actor A's cost-benefit balance as a function of the distance from Actor A's capital to the forward edge of the battle area (FEBA) and the corresponding change in the expected outcome

situation in which terrain presents few obstacles to movements, victory for one side or the other is more likely.

Figure 21 represents the hypotheses on the cost-benefit diagram. Terrain, as mentioned earlier, affects the war outcome in two ways: first, in the ability to maneuver troops and weapons and, second, in the ability of the attacker to find the defenders. The physical codings rely on map data from *The New York Times Atlas of the World* (1972) and from secondary historical sources such as Dupuy (1983). Terrain that is difficult to travel on and that enables both sides in the war to readily hide will likely correlate with draws. Indirectly, in that it has an impact on time with the interaction of the two sides' military strategies, flat terrain should be associated with shorter, and therefore more decisive, wars, and mountainous terrain or jungles should be correlated with long, drawn-out wars of attrition or punishment. The numerical codings come from the Dupuy (1979) study on battle outcomes.

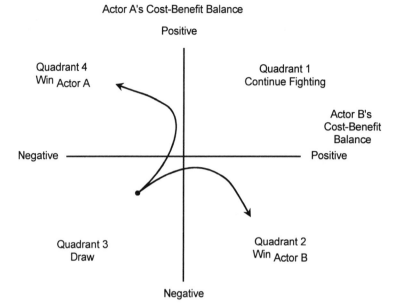

Fig. 21. Expected change in Actor A's cost-benefit as a function of terrain and the corresponding change in the expected outcome. Terrain ranges from impassable to wide open

Terrain codes come from *The New York Times World Atlas*. Terrain codings correspond to the location of the majority of the battles fought during the war. Terrain types were scaled to predicted movement times, using data from Dupuy (1979) who estimated movement speeds on various types of terrain.

Here, the index ranges from 0.7 to 1.2, where 1.0 corresponds to the speed at which vehicles and troops can move on open, rolling terrain, like that found in Eastern Europe. Scores coded 1.0 and above correspond to desert areas with hard-packed surfaces. Codings close to 0.7 match places where movement of vehicles is impossible, such as mountains and jungles. In mountainous or swampy terrain, large numbers of troops can be hidden, slowing the pace of the war and making it difficult for one side to inflict costs upon its opponent.[11] At the high end of the scale are areas where no cover or concealment is available. In these instances, states will be able to quickly inflict costs that lead to quicker, more decisive, outcomes. Dupuy generated the scores by regressing a series of dummy variables for the various types of terrain on codings of vehicle and manpower mobility in several hundred battles.

These data are available in the Historical Evaluation and Research Organization data set (Dupuy 1983).

Interaction of Terrain and Strategy

To measure the interaction of terrain and strategy, I would normally simply multiply the strategy and terrain variables. However, as we have dummy variables marking strategy, the inclusion of each dummy interacted with terrain creates multicollinearity problems. As a result, I multiply a single scaled strategy variable with terrain. This scaled strategy variable is coded 0 through 8, a ranking of the strategies listed earlier. I expect a negative coefficient on the interaction.[12]

Domestic Politics Factors

Here, I will test another direct effect of domestic politics on outcomes. In this instance, however, the factor is not a choice, as repression was, but rather a structural characteristic of the state in question. As I discussed in the previous section, institutional democracy, among other factors, should have a positive effect on a state's chances of victory, whether as a result of changes in the process of fighting or as a result of the war selection process.

Democracy

$H_{Democracy}$ = Higher degrees of democratization should be correlated with higher probabilities of victory.

In a democracy, the mass public is more likely to share in the benefits of victory because the state, in effect, is the people's. Also, in a democracy where the state will be more likely to enjoy greater legitimacy and consent than an autocratic state, the mass public will be more likely to believe the elites about the benefits to be gained. This is shown in figure 22 as a positive shift in the cost-benefit balance for Actor A.

While Spitz argues that democracy is a useful proxy for measuring consent of the governed, he also notes that dissenters will become the targets of political repression, regardless of whether the state is a democratic or authoritarian one.

> On these assumptions . . . consent can be held to be preferable to all other principles of authority. What remains to be considered, therefore, is the relationship between democracy (as the form of state which best institutionalizes the principle of consent) and the

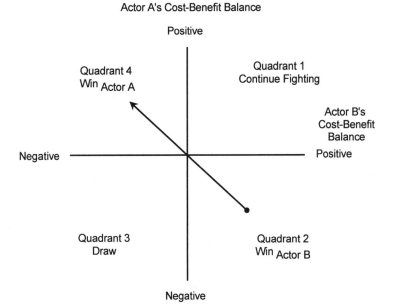

Fig. 22. Expected change in Actor A's cost-benefit balance as a function of Actor A's degree of democratization ranging from Low to High and the corresponding change in the expected outcome

diverse abuses of power. . . . Consent is rarely, perhaps never, unanimous consent. Always there are likely to be some who withhold their approval, not merely to a particular law or a particular government, but to the state itself and the entire system of social order sustained by the state. (Spitz 1958, 11)

Several scholars, Alexis de Tocqueville being the most notable, have wondered about the possible constraining effect of democratic rule on a state's foreign policy. As Spitz points out, good arguments can be made why majority rule will prevail and why the dissent that is supposed to constrain the elite's foreign policy options within democracies will be small. Because the dissent is likely to be limited, political repression will likely be very effective in democratic states for limited periods.

In a democracy, where the notion of political equality is part of the dominant political culture, unanimity in practice is impossible to achieve, but the opinion of the majority must prevail, not so much because the majority is necessarily right or best but because the alternative, rule of the minority, which renders the few superior to the many, is intolerable. If the majority is to inflict its will with a clean conscience, it can do so only if it believes, or convinces itself that it believes that it is right (Spitz 1958, 19–20).

The individual who dissents from the majority and refuses to adhere to the opinions of the ruling power thereby places him- or herself in a precarious intellectual position. As a democrat, he or she argues that all people are equal. As a dissenter, the individual seems to insist that he or she knows better than the majority, thereby affirming the principle of inequality that he or she, along with the majority, had previously repudiated. "His obstinacy no less than his apparent inconsistency serves only to arouse the animosity of the majority" (Spitz 1958, 20).

This explains why, during divisive times, mass publics who are in the majority tolerate and even ask for repressive laws that target the vocal minority of dissenters and also why the number of dissenters is small in number. For evidence of this, we should look to the United States' involvement in the Vietnam War and realize that the public support for the war was overwhelming during the early years. Later, when the efforts became less popular, the number of citizens that actually actively protested against the war was still quite small. Tocqueville presents a similar argument for explaining why mass publics in democracies will go on for so long following a majority-based policy by referring to the disincentives for minorities to speak out against the majority:

> The master no longer says "You shall think as I do or you shall die"; but he says: "You are free to think differently from me and to retain your life, your property, and all that you possess; but you are henceforth a stranger among your people. You may retain your civil rights, but they will be useless to you, for you will never be chosen by your fellow citizens if you solicit their votes; and they will affect to scorn you if you ask for their esteem. You will remain among men, but you will be deprived of the rights of mankind. Your fellow creatures will shun you like an impure being; and even those who believe in your innocence will abandon you, lest they should be shunned in their turn. Go in peace! I have given you your life, but it is an existence worse than death." (Tocqueville 1954, 274–75)

It is interesting to note that Tocqueville then concludes that, in the realm of international politics, democracies will be at a distinct disadvantage relative to authoritarian states or monarchies. Perhaps this might be true in the freedom of decision making, but once war begins Tocqueville's arguments just quoted suggest that, in fact, democracies should be able to absorb greater losses before a significant minority will be willing to speak out against the state's policies. This is of particular interest because it is typically assumed that democracies would be at a disadvantage in conducting foreign policy. In the sense of the mass publics constraining state policy options this may be true. With respect to the outcomes of wars, however, greater degrees of democratization should be an advantage.

Democratization in the Gurr Polity II data set is coded on a ten-point scale, which is an aggregation of the degree of openness of the system, the degree of participation, and the degree of competitiveness of candidate selection. I use the Gurr et al. (1989) "institutionalized democracy" variable as the measure of the degree of democracy of a state government. The variable is a scale ranging from 0 to 10. Zero indicates a state with few constraints on the chief executive, closed executive recruitment procedures, and noncompetitive political participation; 10 indicates the opposite.[13]

Democracy is negatively correlated with repression, but not perfectly. If the correlation were perfect, we would not be able to estimate the effect of either repression or democracy. The reason we need to be aware of this correlation is that there is a chance that the results we observe for democracy, repression, or both may be biased as a result of multicollinearity or correlation of measurement error. I will discuss this potential problem in more detail in the next section.

Issue/Stakes

H_{Issue} = Wars fought over issues removed from the pole of power, where the state will be hard-pressed to demonstrate tangible gains to the mass publics, will be likely to end in defeat or draw.

Figure 23 demonstrates the expected relationship between issue salience and outcomes. Low salience issues will have few benefits associated with them. As a result, both actors will be unwilling to bear high costs, and as a result draws will be more likely. As the salience level rises, the likelihood of the actor being willing to incur more costs rises, as does the chances of victory. Like military strategy and doctrine, the concept of issue area is both complex and has been discussed a great deal, but also, as in the case of strategy, there has been little empirical work.

William Zimmerman suggests the plausibility of coding for cases

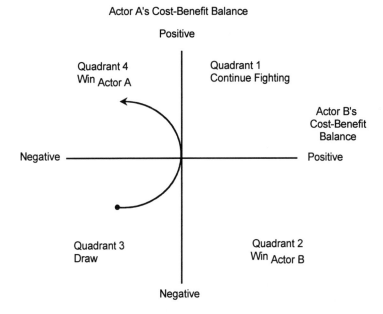

Actor A's Cost-Benefit Balance

Positive

Quadrant 4
Win Actor A

Quadrant 1
Continue Fighting

Actor B's
Cost-Benefit
Balance

Negative

Positive

Quadrant 3
Draw

Quadrant 2
Win Actor B

Negative

Fig. 23. Expected change in Actor A's cost-benefit balance as a function of the issue area that Actor A is fighting over, ranging from low salience to high salience stakes, and the corresponding change in the expected outcome

away from the pole of power versus coding for those in which the issues at stake are close to the pole of power:

> The preservation of the state is a goal highly esteemed by almost all decision makers. Consequently a direct, profound threat to the existence of the state is in most instances to result in power maximizing behavior of the kind anticipated by those in the states-as-sole-actors tradition. What is frequently forgotten is Wolfer's suggestion that it is equally plausible to assume a predictable result in situations where "danger and compulsion are at a minimum." (Zimmerman 1973, 1204)

Because of the likely effects of propaganda, rather than trying to code situations where the survival of the state or regime is at stake (or situations in which the state's structural base of power is at stake such as India for Britain or Middle Eastern oil for the United States), I will code for situations in which the opposite is true. These codings come from

Kalevi Holsti's (1991) *Peace and War: Armed Conflicts and International Order, 1648–1989*. He studies the changes in the issues that wars have been fought over for the last three hundred years. Two particular issues stand out as ones that would be far from the pole of power or instances where the survival of the state would be at stake. One, instances where one side is fighting over the extension or maintenance of empire holdings are likely to be unrelated to the survival of the state, and it is likely that it would be difficult for the state to convince its mass publics otherwise. Two, in wars fought over government policy, for instance, the United States' war in Vietnam, which was fought to maintain the policy of containment, the state in question will be hard-pressed to maintain a positive cost-benefit balance for fighting.

Time

H_{Time} =   The probability of victory is inversely related to the length of the war. The longer the war, the lower the probability of victory, the lower the probability of defeat, and the greater the chance of a draw.

As time passes, holding all else constant, the costs of fighting increase while benefits remain constant. This reduces both actors' willingness to continue fighting, which then increases the chance that an actor that initially thought its chances of victory were high may later believe it may lose, decreasing its willingness to fight. This situation should also lead to more likely draws as well as demonstrated in figure 24. Draws may occur when both sides' costs rise above the expected benefits, which would likely remain fairly constant, while the costs rise monotonically with the passage of time. According to Maoz, "wars are duels of wills and wits, even the most masterful plan might run aground because it forces the opponent to resort to strategies that render the initial plan useless" (Maoz 1990, 165). If enough time elapses for the side on the defense to adapt to the initial offensive thrust of the attacker, we should expect the probability of victory for the initiator to drop significantly.

As I mentioned previously, time is an ex post indicator, meaning that the duration of the war in the data set is what was actually observed at the conclusion of the war rather than an expected duration based on prewar or ex ante beliefs about how long it should have lasted. I will show in the empirical section in chapter 5 that time can be accurately modeled as a function of the military strategies, terrain, population, and industrial capabilities of the two sides.

Several factors affect the duration of wars, one of the prime factors

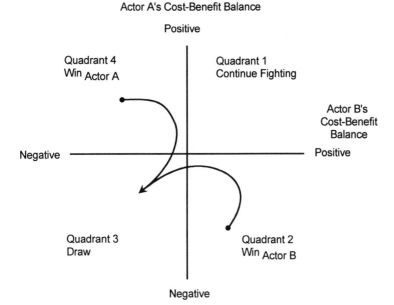

Actor A's Cost-Benefit Balance

Positive

Quadrant 4
Win Actor A

Quadrant 1
Continue Fighting

Actor B's
Cost-Benefit
Balance

Negative

Positive

Quadrant 3
Draw

Quadrant 2
Win Actor B

Negative

Fig. 24. Expected change in Actor A's cost-benefit balance as a function of the war's duration and the corresponding change in the expected outcome. Time ranges from short to long

being the two sides' military strategies. Maneuver strategies offer the potential for quick and decisive victories under several plausible scenarios. An actor may be able to quickly secure victory by concentrating on a narrow point, hoping to penetrate defenses that would prove to be impenetrable with a broad attack. Once a narrow salient has been opened, the maneuver forces will speed as quickly as possible toward the rear areas of the defender. Quick advances do not guarantee quick victory, however. They may also lead to equally quick defeats. Rapidly advancing columns are very vulnerable in that they typically are long single files of men and equipment whose sole flank defense is speed (Luttwak 1985, 100).

Maneuver strategies are likely to lead to quicker outcomes one way or the other. If we focus on a single column, which leaves capable defenders on either side of the salient opening, we can understand the vulnerability and high-risk nature of a mobile attack. In a successful execution, the quickly advancing single columns eventually link up with other attacking columns, and the ability to distinguish the encircling from the encircled becomes difficult. In unsuccessful maneuver-based assaults, the defenders are able to attack toward one another, and are then able to pinch off the advancing columns, which would wither on the vine and die (Luttwak 1985, 100). These high-speed assaults do more than just affect the duration of the assault. If the defenders withdraw from the advancing columns in an attempt to consolidate and defend a new position, they lose all the advantages of an integrated defense network and become simply a series of isolated outposts with no flanking support from formerly neighboring units.

In these ways, we can see that a maneuver strategy will likely end relatively quickly. Either the attacker will completely fragment and disrupt the defender, thereby completely disabling him or the defender will be able to let the initial attack pass and then counterattack the flanks of the attackers' columns, thereby isolating the columns from each other and, more importantly, isolating the columns from their following logistical trains (Luttwak 1985, 100–101).

Terrain both hinders the mobility of the invading and defending forces and potentially gives the defenders the opportunity to hide, allowing the attackers to create ambushes for the retreating forces. Wide-open, flat terrain is likely to lead to short and quick wars. Forces can move quickly and decisively, and no time is lost searching for opponents.

Summary

We are now ready to test the hypotheses and the overall notion of a three-outcome model of war termination. In the next chapter, I will present the results of the logistic regression. Following a discussion of the empirical results, I will investigate the cases where the model fails to predict the correct outcome for the test sample and the cases in which the model makes particularly good forecasts. Then I will use the regression estimates to forecast the cases excluded from the analysis. In chapters 6 and 7, I will present the individual effects of the independent variables.

CHAPTER 5

Empirical Results

Model Specification

This chapter steps away from discussing the substantive issues of winning and losing during wartime and examines the econometric techniques used to test the proposed model. Although a bit technical, this discussion is important because it makes explicit the assumptions and processes used to examine the data; it presents information that is critical to understanding the origins of the empirical results that are presented in chapters 6 and 7. Those willing to take the results on faith may move to the following chapters. For those interested in the statistical procedures used to estimate the various factors' effects on outcomes and the level of confidence that we should have in these estimates, continue on.

In this chapter I address two basic research questions. The first question has to do with the overall fit of the model to the data. In other words, how well we can understand the outcomes we have observed with a given set of independent variables. For this, I will compare the results of several different statistical models and will show that the multinomial logit model, selected on the basis of the discussion in chapter 2 about the nature of draws, allows us to predict, with reasonable confidence, the outcomes of wars. This predictive accuracy is high both within and outside of the sample used to estimate the model. The second research question has to do with understanding the role that the various individual factors identified in the literature play in determining war outcomes. This task also falls into two parts. In the first, I will address the question of whether or not we should accept or reject arguments about the various factors having significant impacts on war outcomes. The second question with regard to the individual factors has to do with their explanatory power, each relative to the others. I begin by examining the various types of underlying statistical models that the data can be fit to. After selecting what I think is the most appropriate model, I show that each of the factors identified in the previous chapter have significant effects on war outcomes. Each of the various explanations will be shown to be statistically significant in the sense that if we exclude them from the analysis, our understanding of outcomes declines in a systematic and measurable way. Chapters 6 and 7 then discuss in detail the individual effects of the various independent variables that I show to be important factors. In those two chapters, I investigate the relative power of each factor rather than investigating the predictive power of the overall model.

In chapter 2, I argued that the relationship between the independent variables and each of the three possible outcomes (win, lose, draw) should not have the same functional form. More specifically, the relationship between the cost/benefit indicators and winning or losing should not be the same as the relationship with draws. Because of this theoretical assertion, I believe that the most appropriate statistical model should be the multinomial logistic. Multinomial logit regression allows us to estimate two separate sets of regression coefficients or estimate measures of the effects that the independent variables will have on the dependent variable. One set of parameters provides estimates of the effects of the variables on winning versus losing. The second set of parameters estimates measure the effects of the same independent variables on the likelihood of observing a draw as opposed to a loss. Using this approach, we might see some independent variables being negatively correlated with winning but positively associated with draws. Some of the hypotheses laid out in chapter 4 are of this nature. For example, the duration of wars should have a positive effect on the likelihood of observing draws but should have a null effect on observing a loss or a win. In short wars, time should not convey a net advantage to either side, but in long wars we should expect to see draws (an outcome identical for both sides) as more likely. Similarly, it may be that surprise conveys little net advantage to either side but may make draws less likely. It is possible that the multinomial model, which makes no assumptions about the order of the outcomes, is not the most appropriate statistical model to use. Recall that in order to deduce the anticipated effects of the independent variables I assumed that leaders prefer winning to draws and draws to losing. Within this additional assumption, another class of estimators may be used and might possibly turn out to be empirically more appropriate than the nonordered multinomial approach. Most political scientists and historians would agree that the assumptions made earlier about preferences for outcomes are reasonable.

If we rank the outcome categories in the order of the preferences that leaders have for them (win, draw, lose), other estimation possibilities arise. Ordinary least squares (OLS) may be used with the ranked outcome variable. However, it is likely that the coefficients for the independent variables will be biased using a least squares estimator because the relationship between the independent variable and the dependent variable is not expected to be linear. Also, using OLS, we may make predictions that are less than zero or greater than 2, that is, outside the actual range of the dependent variable. Two other alternatives, ordered logistic regression and the similar ordered probit regression allow us to fit a set of independent variables to an ordered categorical dependent variable. Using either of these two estimators, we make the assumption that the effect of the various independent variables can be characterized by a continuous function. The categories (win, draw, lose) are then described by cutoff points or levels above which we expect to see first a draw and then a loss occur, and below which we would expect to see victory. From both ordered logit and probit then, we estimate one set of coefficients for the independent variables as we do using OLS. The procedure also estimates the two cutoff points needed to divide the outcomes into three categories. Using OLS with the outcomes coded 0, 1, 2 (win, draw, lose), we assume the values of the cutoff points that would separate the particular outcomes from one another rather than estimating them. Following this, any predicted outcome between 0 and 0.67 would be predicted to be a victory, 0.67 and 1.33 a draw, and between 1.33 and 2.0 a loss.

Why the great emphasis on model selection? If the model fit for any of the alternative models is better than the overall fit of the multinomial logit model, it will cast doubt on the assertion that draws are fundamentally different than wins and losses. Instead, we would then conclude that, in decision makers' minds, draws are simply an in-between point sandwiched between the other two alternative outcomes. Table 3 presents the four possible model specifications.

The first specification, Model 1, the multinomial logit estimation, has two sets of coefficients that can be found in the first two columns of the table. The first column contains the estimated effects of the independent variables on the likelihood of winning versus losing. Generally, positive coefficients in the first column indicate that the variable has a positive effect on the likelihood of victory. The second column presents the estimated effects of the independent variables on the relative likelihood of observing a draw versus a loss. Here, in general, positive coefficients indicate a greater likelihood of observing a draw. A brief caveat is in order here. As with all logit and probit models, because the relationships between the independent variables and the dependent variable are not linear and most of the independent variables are not distributed normally, the relative effect of any independent variable is not constant over its range. For example, the effect of a shift in relative capabilities

TABLE 3. Testing Model Specification

Variable	Mlogit Estimates Win	Mlogit Estimates Draw	Ordered Logistic Regression Order: Win, Draw, Lose	Ordered Probit Regression Order: Win, Draw, Lose	Ordinary Least Squares Order: Win, Draw, Lose
Duration	-0.053	0.14**	0.0200	0.0112	0.00555
	(-0.06)	(0.07)	(0.0165)	(0.00939)	(0.00463)
Capabilities	27.89***	5.28	-7.49***	-4.43***	-1.42***
	(10.31)	(8.02)	(2.14)	(1.22)	(0.393)
Distance	-0.0015*	-0.00032	.000409***	.000245***	.0000657**
	(0.001)	(0.00049)	(.00015)	(.0000893)	(.0000322)
Population	-0.04**	0.013*	0.00995***	0.00593***	0.00158**
	(0.02)	(0.01)	(0.00298)	(0.00180)	(0.000655)
Troops	0.32**	-0.07	-0.0868***	-0.0516***	-0.0126***
	(0.17)	(0.16)	(0.0325)	(0.0193)	(0.00651)
Military Ratio	-0.21	-0.48	0.0764**	0.0458**	0.0125
	(0.14)	(0.66)	(0.0364)	(0.0222)	(0.00934)
Quality Ratio	1.15	0.00092	-0.290**	-0.173**	-0.0187**
	(0.79)	(0.51)	(0.129)	(0.0789)	(0.00910)
Allies' Capabilities	104.0*	115.1*	-8.74***	-5.35***	-1.62***
	(62.7)	(65.6)	(3.51)	(2.01)	(0.555)
Allies' Quality	-11.53	-33.91	0.0586	0.0698	-0.0323
	(9.23)	(23.5)	(0.778)	(0.439)	(0.178)
Democracy	1.42**	1.71**	-0.331*	-0.205*	-0.0794**
	(0.75)	(0.84)	(0.199)	(0.115)	(0.0365)
Repression	-5.07**	-4.76**	0.812*	0.493*	0.137
	(2.38)	(2.24)	(0.460)	(0.268)	(0.0853)
Issue Area	-3.04	6.05*	-0.333	-0.169	-0.0329
	(3.03)	(3.28)	(1.07)	(0.564)	(0.219)
Terrain	-273.0**	-250.3*	17.9**	10.97**	2.76***
	(145.1)	(146.8)	(8.01)	(4.74)	(0.951)
Strategy*Terrain	92.4*	80.4*	-9.57***	-5.78***	-1.47***
	(48.71)	(48.2)	(3.82)	(2.25)	(0.448)

TABLE 3. *Continued*

Variable	Mlogit Estimates Win	Draw	Ordered Logistic Regression Order: Win, Draw, Lose	Ordered Probit Regression Order: Win, Draw, Lose	Ordinary Least Squares Order: Win, Draw, Lose
Surprise	-0.21 (2.58)	-5.11* (3.0)	0.632 (1.02)	0.345 (0.582)	0.345 (0.582)
OMDA	-131.5** (65.08)	-138.97 —	—	—	3.64*** (1.35)
OADM	20.06 (25.07)	-19.40 —	-16.4** (7.97)	-9.94** (4.72)	1.15** (0.504)
OADA	-0.63 (4.9)	9.58 (6.23)	-14.8*** (5.72)	-8.97*** (3.37)	1.15* (0.644)
OPDA	4.06 —	-6.31 (6.54)	-15.3*** (5.21)	-9.11*** (2.93)	0.620 (1.01)
DMOA	-42.84** (23.1)	-75.81 —	-10.6*** (4.25)	-6.34*** (2.47)	1.98** (0.974)
DAOM	91.14* (50.8)	34.51 —	-22.8** (9.62)	-13.7*** (5.66)	—
DAOA	-8.29 (5.43)	6.27 (5.28)	-12.9** (5.61)	-7.87*** (3.31)	1.81*** (0.654)
DPOA	-64.82*** (10.57)	-43.86 —	-6.82*** (2.80)	-4.05*** (1.66)	2.38* (1.26)
Constant					0.0111 (0.715)
Cut 1			-17.07	-10.18	
Cut 2			-15.35	-9.154	

Mlogit Estimates	Ordered Logistic Regression	Ordered Probit Regression	Ordinary Least Squares
Log Likelihood = -18.69	Log Likelihood = -47.16	Log Likelihood = -46.38	Root MSE = 0.65
Pseudo R^2 = 0.81	Pseudo R^2 = 0.48	Pseudo R^2 = 0.49	R^2 = 0.62
Adj Pseudo R^2 = 0.75	Adj Pseudo R^2 = 0.30	Adj Pseudo R^2 = 0.33	Adjusted R^2 = 0.50
n = 88	n = 88	n = 88	$F_{(22, 65)}$ = 4.88
Prob > Chi^2 = 0.0000	Prob > Chi^2 = 0.0000	Prob > Chi^2 = 0.0000	Prob > F = 0.0000

Coefficients (Standard errors in parentheses):
*$p < 0.10$
**$p < 0.05$
***$p < 0.01$

may be pronounced when the two sides are evenly matched. But the same sized shift might have little effect in a war between two sides with disparate capabilities. Because of this, we cannot directly interpret the coefficients in the logit or probit models as we can with the OLS model. Recall that in an OLS model, for each (and every) unit change in the independent variable we expect to see a fixed change in the dependent variable. This is *not* the case with the nonlinear estimations. In the logit model, the probability of case *j* ending in *win*, is calculated as follows:

$$\text{Probability } [Y = j] = P_j = \frac{\exp(\beta'_j x_i)}{\Sigma_j (\beta'_j x_i)} \, , \, j = \text{win,draw,lose}$$

The change in the dependent variable, P_j, that we expect to be associated with a change in an independent variable depends on three things: 1. the coefficients of the other independent variables, 2. the values of the other independent variables, and 3. the value of the independent variable in question (the location in the independent variable's distribution for that particular question—near the minimum, maximum, or mean). Additionally, unlike in OLS, the probabilities here are a function of the exponential function, e^x, where x is the product of both β and x. Because of the complexity of interpreting individual effects, separate sections for that purpose are contained in the chapters that follow. In general, each coefficient represents the effect of that particular independent variable on the likelihood of observing the various outcomes.

In addition to the nonlinear relationship between the independent variables and the dependent variables, an additional complication in the interpretation of the results exists. The other reason that we cannot directly interpret the coefficients is that there are interactive terms in the models that greatly complicate the interpretation of the individual effects. For example, in the multinomial logit model the sign on the OMDA strategy variable is negative in the Win equation, which might lead us to conclude that the effect is the opposite of that hypothesized earlier. The key is that the negative influence of the dummy variable is more than offset by the interactive strategy and terrain term. As a result of these complications, extended discussion of the individual effects will follow in chapters 6 and 7 following a discussion of model specification and variable selection. Before moving to the individual variables though, we should investigate the overall fit of the four models.

The second model in table 3 is the ordered logistic regression. The third model is the ordered probit estimation, and the fourth is the OLS estimation. While the multinomial model is the most appropriate for testing the theory laid out in chapter 2, several models are presented in order to be sure that the results we observe for the individual effects are not the result of an artifact resulting from the statistical model specification. In certain statistical circumstances, econometric models can be estimated that may appear to fit the data quite well, but that fit, in fact, is simply the result of a mathematical quirk. In these situations, the results are not robust at all and may shift wildly simply by using a different statistical model. We can test for this possibility by checking to be sure that the results that we observe are roughly consistent across a variety of underlying model specifications. By presenting a variety of statistical formulations, all of which lead us to the same conclusions, we can be more sure that the results that I present later in this chapter are due to true correlations between the variables and war outcomes and are not simply the result of some statistical artifact. As table 3 shows, while there are small changes from one model to the next, the results are quite consistent, regardless of whether the underlying distribution to which the data are fitted is a linear model, logit, or probit.

In the latter three models in table 3, only one set of coefficients are estimated compared to the two sets in the multinomial model. Because the multinomial logit model estimates two sets of parameters, or a separate equation for winning and draws, the standard errors associated with each independent variable are expected to be larger than in the single equation models. We are simply trying to extract more information from the same number of cases. In doing so, our level of uncertainty associated with each independent variable necessarily rises to a small degree. Because of this, the standard errors for the three single equation models (ordered logit, probit, and OLS) are a bit smaller. For example, in the probit model, twelve of the twenty-three parameter estimates are significant at the $p < .001$ level, sixteen of twenty-three at the $p < .05$ level, and eighteen of the twenty-three at the $p < .10$ level. In the multinomial logit, the fit of the variables to the data might appear to be worse: only two of the variables are significant at the $p < .001$ level. But this is a misleading comparison for the reason mentioned earlier. Because we are extracting so much more information from the data with the multinomial model, we necessarily expect the uncertainty associated with each of the single variable point estimates to be somewhat larger.

We should also note that significance levels for the variables in this study do not have the same meaning that they might if we were trying to infer from a known sample to an unknown population. In this case, the sample is representative of the population of cases to date. The variables' parameters (regression coefficients) are, in effect, descriptive statistics of the population. The standard errors do capture the sense of uncertainty we have about cases that have yet to occur. For instance, in the data set of wars to date, surprise has a small but systematic effect on the probability of winning and draw. Yet there is quite a bit of uncertainty about what this effect would be in cases we have yet to observe.[1] For wars that may occur in the future, surprise may or may not be expected to have some negative effect on the probability of draw. There is a large possibility that in many possible cases, surprise will have no positive effect on the final outcome. The variables with smaller standard errors are those whose effects on the various outcomes we will have greater certainty about in cases we have yet to observe. Variables with large standard errors, surprise and ally quality for example, will have much greater uncertainty associated with them in cases yet to be revealed by the war generation process.

To judge the overall fit of the model to the data we need to use summary statistics. For each of the estimations a set of summary statistics is provided. For each of the maximum likelihood estimations the standard chi-squared statistic is provided. In each case, the probability of a constant-only model performing better can be rejected with tremendous certainty. Unfortunately, the relative fit between the various models cannot be distinguished using this statistic. To further differentiate, a pseudo-R^2 and an adjusted pseudo-R^2 is provided. These statistics provide a rough measure of goodness of fit. While they are not the same either in precise conceptual terms or in mathematical terms to the standard R^2 generated from OLS estimates, they do provide a rough measure of the overall model fit.[2] In addition (as will be seen in table 5), a general reduction of error statistic (ROE) is also provided. The ROE measures the difference between the model's predictions and a set of predictions based on simply guessing the outcomes to be the modal category. Here, Winning is the modal category in the data set with roughly 41 percent of the cases ending that way.

Another typical way of presenting the overall fit of a model is to show a chart of the predicted outcomes versus the actual outcomes. In table 4, the predicted outcome for the in-sample predictions using the multinomial logit model is that with the highest forecast probability.[3]

In this case, table 4 shows an overall success rate of approximately 95 percent (eighty-four out of eighty-eight cases). This is not bad. In fact, it is probably about as good as we could possibly expect. Because the model is based on probabilistic assumptions, perfect prediction would not mean that we had a better understanding of the process that takes place in war but rather that one or more of the independent variables was simply a restatement of the dependent variable (Greene

TABLE 4. Contingency Table of Predicted Results versus Actual Results (Prediction Is the Outcome with the Highest Forecast Probability)

Predicted	Actual		
	Win	Draw	Lose
Win	36	1	0
Draw	2	13	0
Lose	0	1	35
	38	15	35

Correct: 84/88 = 95%.

1993). At first glance, these results might not appear to be that dramatic an improvement over existing models that are simply based on comparing the two sides' military or industrial capabilities. In this case though, the task in front of us is far more difficult.

With binary outcomes (win-lose), by chance alone we could expect to predict 50 percent of the cases correctly, assuming that the outcomes were split roughly evenly between the two possibilities. With a three-outcome model, by chance alone we might expect to be able to predict one-third of the cases correctly simply by predicting the same outcome for all cases. In this data set, if we simply predicted the most common outcome, win, for every case, we would correctly predict 43 percent of the cases. By trying to predict draws as well as winners and losers, I have complicated things immensely. A multinomial model, with three outcome categories using a single capabilities variable as is commonly used with binary outcome models only predicts 47 percent of the cases correctly. By adding draws into the equation, we have made the model reflect reality much more closely than previous scholars' models have done. Also, because the model is probabilistic, we actually should not expect to get all of the cases correct. For instance, if we predicted that the chances of winning was 75 percent for several cases, we should only expect three-fourths of those cases to end in victory for the side in question. Of course, in-sample predictions *should* be quite accurate; they are, after all, based on the outcomes as we already know them. A far more rigorous test is to go back and predict the outcomes of the cases that are not included in the sample used to generate the regression coefficients. If the model performs well for those cases, then we can be sure that we have learned something valuable. For our purposes, we have 156 out-of-sample cases to test the multinomial model results with (244 cases in the total population, minus 88 used to generate the regression coefficients).

In Table 5, each row represents a particular set of cases, each column a particular statistical model. For each combination of a set of cases and a particular model, I report the percentage the model predicts correctly for that particular sample and the ROE statistic that measures, in percentage terms, the reduction in error over a naive prediction based on the modal category. The first row presents the results of the in-sample predictions. Here we can see that the multinomial specification of the model fits the data in the original sample ($n = 88$) exceedingly well, predicting 95 percent of the cases correctly and reducing the expected error by over 90 percent. The ordered logit and probit models perform well, averaging just over 73 percent correct predictions and reducing the expected error by an average of 55 percent. Compared to the multinomial model, however, they run a distant second-place. It is possible, however, that the difference in the models' predictions is a result of overfitting the multinomial model to the data in the sample.[4] More general, or simpler, models sometimes perform better when making out-of-sample predictions than more specific ones. If this were the case, the simpler ordered models (ordered probit, ordered logit) might actually perform better in out-of-sample predictions than the multinomial logit model.

To test for this possibility, we simply need to make a set of out-of-sample predictions for cases not used to generate the regression coefficients.[5] In these we see that the multinomial model still performs significantly better than the alternatives. If we use the parameter estimates to predict the outcomes of the participants outside the sample used to generate the anticipated effects of the independent variables, we see

TABLE 5.   **Prediction Accuracy for Multinomial Logit, Ordered Logit, and Ordered Probit Models for Various Subsets of the Interstate War Data Set**

Sample		Statistical Model		
		mlogit	ologit	oprobit
Stratified Random Sample $n = 88$		84/88 = 95%	64/88 = 73%	65/88 = 74%
	ROE	91%	54%	56%
All cases $n = 244$		184/244 = 75%	146/244 = 60%	151/244 = 62%
	ROE	56%	32%	36%
Minus sample cases $n = 156$		100/156 = 64%	82/156 = 53%	86/156 = 55%
	ROE	39%	20%	24%
All minus 7 Weeks' War and		180/218 = 83%	143/218 = 66%	148/218 = 68%
WWI $n = 218$	ROE	71%	42%	46%
All minus sample, 7 Weeks' War		97/130 = 75%	79/130 = 61%	83/130 = 64%
and WWI $n = 130$	ROE	58%	34%	39%

that the error rate climbs sharply, as expected. What is important to note is not that the error rate goes up but rather that even when predicting cases with novel information, the multinomial estimation fairs far better than the alternative models. In the 156 out-of-sample cases (row 3), the multinomial model still predicts 64 percent of the cases correctly, a 39 percent reduction in the errors we would make guessing the outcomes. The ordered models average only 54 percent correct predictions, an approximately 22 percent reduction in errors over a chance model. The last two rows drop two wars, the Seven Weeks' War and World War I from the out-of-sample set of cases. For all the specifications, the model does very poorly in these two wars, the multinomial model correctly predicting only three of the twenty-six cases.

For a variety of reasons, the Seven Weeks' War and World War I can be considered outliers. They involved large numbers of states, they changed the nature of the international system, and they were very high-stakes wars compared to many of the other wars in the data set. If we drop these wars from the out-of-sample group, the multinomial model correctly predicts 75 percent of the remaining 130 cases. While it is important not to build models that work only for very narrowly defined types of cases, the two wars in question contain far more actors than any of the other wars in the data set. The alliance variables I have are quite broad in what they measure. It turns out that in cases where the alliance patterns are complex and contain many participants, the model simply does not perform very well. For the remaining, simpler wars, the model performs very well.[6] On the basis of these comparisons and tests, it is fair to conclude that the multinomial model is the model of choice for these data. Before moving on to specification tests of the various independent variables, I will use two other means to be sure that the observed results are robust and not artifacts of the estimation technique.

J. Frank Yates (1991) suggests that an additional and effective way of presenting the results of probabilistic models is to show the accuracy of the model with a calibration table like the one in figure 25.

In a calibration table of this type, the data for the graph are generated as follows: for each predicted probability level, for example, the groups of predictions for victory, draw, or loss that fall between 10 and 20 percent, the total number of predictions are counted. In the 10–20 percent forecast category, for example, there are thirteen observations of the model making a forecast of one of the three outcomes having between a 10 and 20 percent chance of occurring. Of these thirteen observations, one actually matched the outcome predicted. In other words, if the model calibrates with the data, when we predict that there

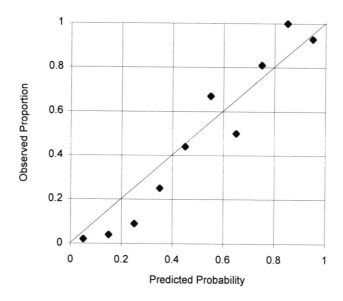

Fig. 25. Calibration table: proportion of cases forecast correctly by forecast probabilities, 45 degree line is perfect calibration. Calibration index = 0.00495.

are a set of cases where we predict the chances of victory to be 10 percent, then we would see 10 percent of those cases end in victory. As you can see, the actual success rate closely matches what we would expect given the probabilistic nature of the predictions. Using the calibration statistic that Yates suggests, the model's fit to the sample data is apparently quite good, with the calibration index being 0.005. If the model fit were perfect, the calibration index would equal zero; if the calibration were completely wrong, meaning that all the cases turned out exactly opposite what was predicted, the calibration index would equal 1.0.[7]

Using a maximum likelihood estimator (MLE) may cause some concern that the results presented in the calibration table are overly optimistic. In effect, the MLE procedures minimize the calibration index. This does not mean that it necessarily perfectly fits the data though; if the wrong likelihood function were being maximized, the calibration index would not tend toward zero. A low calibration index does help assure us that we have selected a suitable likelihood function. One way to check this potential problem is to examine out-of-sample forecasts as we have done. Another way is to visually examine the distributions of outcome forecasts.[8] The next two figures show the distributions of the

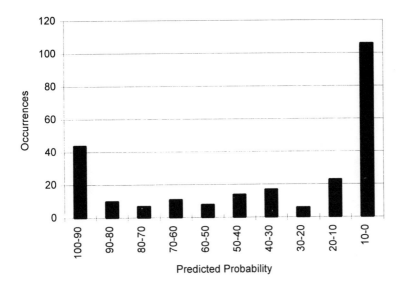

Fig. 26. Distribution of outcome forecasts. Number of forecast occurrences by forecast probability.

three different outcomes compared to the distributions of the aggregate probabilities. If the overall model fit is good, the distributions of the individual win-lose outcomes should be similar, and each outcome should have some proportion of cases forecast that way. For instance, if the model never forecast a draw, but we saw several, then we would have cause for concern. Similarly, if the model made most of the predictions in the 50 percent win, 50 percent lose range, but the observed outcomes were distributed quite differently, 80 percent win and 20 percent lose, for example, we should also be concerned.

Figure 26 shows the distribution of the forecast probabilities across all the outcomes. Each of the 88 cases has three possible outcomes so there are a total of 264 observations for the histogram. From this histogram we can see that the model makes definite predictions, these being indicated by the bars over the 100–90 range and the 0–10 percent range. The model also makes predictions that are less certain, in that it makes predictions across the whole range of probabilities. This reflects the likelihood that many wars are not fought between evenly matched sides (victory almost certain for one side, highly unlikely for the other), but some are. Figure 27 shows the distribution of the predictions for each of the three outcomes separately. An important point should be noted here. If the very low calibration index were simply an artifact of the

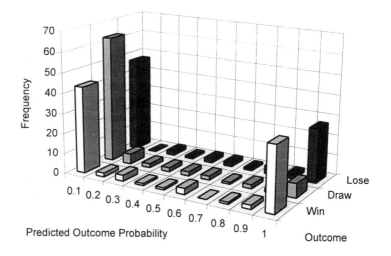

Fig. 27. Distribution of predictions for each of the three observed outcomes

maximum likelihood procedure, we would not expect to see the model make predictions across the entire range of probabilities. For instance, a model that predicts nothing perfectly would have a very good calibration index score. This type of model would be next to useless, however, for the purpose of being able to understand events in which something actually happened. To guard against this concern, the two figures clearly show that for the model in the aggregate (fig. 26) and for each of the three outcomes (fig. 27), definite predictions are made across the whole spectrum of possibilities.

In each of the three outcomes shown in figure 27, we see the same type of distribution as shown for the entire model in figure 26. Although the fit (here Cramer defines the fit as being the similarity of the overall outcome distribution to the distribution of the various actual outcomes) varies between outcome states, the fit is the best for the win and lose categories. Still, the model makes definite predictions for all three outcomes. If it had not, it hardly would have been surprising given the relatively rare occurrence of draws, which make up only 17 percent of all the cases in the sample.

Beyond a discussion of the overall model fit, we can also look at how each of the critical indicators affects the likelihood of the three outcomes. Before we investigate the role that each of the indicators plays in determining outcomes, we need to test whether or not they belong in the model in the first place. The standard way to test whether or not a variable or set of variables is making a significant contribution to the general understanding of the variation in the dependent variable is to use the likelihood ratio test. This test measures the change in the relative likelihood that we observe for the complete model (given the data) versus a restricted model that excludes one or more factors. For each model, we estimate the log of the likelihood function, and this gives us a relative measure of the likelihood that the model fits the data well. The ratio of the logged likelihoods of nested models follows the chi-square distribution. Accordingly, by calculating the ratio of the two models' likelihood, we can calculate the probability that the difference between the two models is the result of random variation, or that the exclusion of the variable(s) in question results in a reduction of likelihood that goes beyond what we might expect from simple random variation.[9]

Table 6 presents a series of multinomial logit models. In these I excluded various sets of independent variables from the full model and examined the effects on the relative likelihood to determine whether the changes we observe in the model fit fall within what we might expect from random variation. Model 1 in table 6 tests the effect of excluding the strategy dummy variables. Several of the strategy variables do not meet the standard levels of statistical significance. In large part this is because, with the exception of the attrition strategy combinations, most of the other strategy combinations are represented in only a few instances in the data set. When we estimate the restricted model without the strategy variables the likelihood statistic drops from -18.7 to -45.6. Using the likelihood ratio statistics we can test how likely we would be to observe a change of this magnitude simply as the result of random variation. The chi-square statistic, with 16 degrees of freedom, is 53.8, which results in a $p < 0.0001$. The p-value represents the likelihood that the differences in the likelihood of the full model versus the restricted model is the result of random variation. In this case, that value is close to zero. Also note that the pseudo-R^2 drops from 0.81, in the full model, to 0.53. As a result, we can be quite sure that the strategy variables make a significant contribution to the overall model's fit. The one change in the effects of the other independent variables that results from the exclusion of strategy is that the sign on the duration variable flips in the absence of strategy controls. With the other independent variables, the magnitudes of the coefficients change somewhat (although the important change would be relative to one another, not changes in the absolute size of the coefficient), but in all other cases the signs remain stable, even though we have excluded a set of variables that account for quite a bit of the variation in war outcomes.

In the second set of coefficients (Model 2), I include the strategy

TABLE 6. Multinomial Logistic Regression Results: Lose Is the Reference State (Testing Variable Specifications)

Variable	Model 1 Minus Military Strategy		Model 2 Minus Surprise	
	Win	Draw	Win	Draw
Duration	0.02	0.045**	−.043	0.07
	(.021)	(0.022)	(.053)	(0.05)
Capabilities	9.46***	5.51*	25.52***	3.40
	(2.8)	(3.11)	(8.43)	(6.73)
Distance	−0.00032	−0.000035	−0.0014*	−0.00022
	(0.00022)	(0.00022)	(0.0008)	(0.00038)
Population	−0.0096**	0.00335	−0.04**	0.0028*
	(0.0048)	(0.0035)	(0.02)	(0.01)
Troops	0.028	−0.0442	0.29**	−0.027
	(0.037)	(0.08)	(0.13)	(0.11)
Military Ratio	−0.10	−0.24	−0.19*	−0.32
	(0.072)	(0.23)	(0.10)	(0.69)
Quality Ratio	0.46*	0.16	1.25**	0.20
	(0.27)	(0.27)	(0.59)	(0.46)
Allies' Capabilities	8.64***	9.23*	98.0*	100.1*
	(3.33)	(5.07)	(54.7)	(57.6)
Allies' Quality	−0.445	−3.91	−11.05	−24.90
	(.714)	(5.56)	(8.1)	(23.5)
Democracy	.401**	0.23	1.32**	1.34**
	(.18)	(.23)	(0.62)	(0.69)
Repression	−0.99**	−0.70	−4.65**	−3.71**
	(.44)	(.55)	(2.03)	(1.76)
Issue Area	−1.48	1.22	−2.73	3.41*
	(1.48)	(1.21)	(2.47)	(2.15)
Terrain	−7.96***	−7.22***	−161.3**	−155.1*
	(2.58)	(2.9)	(81.7)	(83.4)
Strategy*Terrain	2.81***	2.02*	82.5**	74.7*
	(1.02)	(1.14)	(41.2)	(41.5)
Surprise	−0.093	−0.71	—	—
	(1.17)	(1.22)	—	—
OMDA	—	—	−117.7**	−142.20
	—	—	(55.0)	—
OADM	—	—	18.30	−18.28
	—	—	(21.8)	—
OADA	—	—	−0.39	7.82
	—	—	(4.4)	(5.3)
OPDA	—	—	5.67	0.34
	—	—	—	(4.92)
DMOA	—	—	−38.3**	−74.30
	—	—	(19.5)	—
DAOM	—	—	81.5**	31.40
	—	—	(43.2)	—
DAOA	—	—	−7.77*	4.92
	—	—	(4.83)	(4.39)
DPOA	—	—	−56.23***	−42.35
	—	—	(8.86)	—

Coefficients (Standard errors in parentheses):
*$p < 0.10$
**$p < 0.05$
***$p < 0.01$

Log Likelihood = −45.56
Pseudo R^2 = 0.53
Adj R^2 = 0.37
Likelihood Ratio Test:
Chi^2(4) = 31.00
$p = 0.0001$

Log Likelihood = −20.69
Pseudo R^2 = 0.79
Adj R^2 = 0.72
Likelihood Ratio Test:
Chi^2(2) = 4.02
$p = 0.14$

TABLE 6. Multinomial Logistic Regression Results: Lose Is the Reference State (Testing Variable Specifications) (*Continued*)

Variable	Model 3 Minus Terrain and Strategy Interaction		Model 4 Minus Democracy and Repression	
	Win	Draw	Win	Draw
Duration	−.0186	0.0347	−.054	0.07**
	(.028)	(0.0286)	(.045)	(0.035)
Capabilities	12.3***	5.58	19.0***	3.81
	(4.17)	(4.58)	(7.0)	(4.70)
Distance	−0.000342*	−0.0000947	−0.0006	−0.00011
	(0.00021)	(0.000251)	(0.0005)	(0.00029)
Population	−0.0121*	0.00396	−0.024**	0.003
	(0.0066)	(0.00513)	(0.01)	(0.005)
Troops	0.0794*	0.019	0.22**	0.06
	(0.0456)	(0.0739)	(0.11)	(0.08)
Military Ratio	−0.112	−0.459	−0.128	−0.37
	(0.080)	(0.444)	(0.09)	(0.43)
Quality Ratio	0.615	0.130	.67**	−0.076
	(0.459)	(0.445)	(0.34)	(0.34)
Allies' Capabilities	10.8**	16.8	64.90	73.4*
	(5.07)	(10.3)	(44.5)	(44.0)
Allies' Quality	0.434	−13.6	−6.49	−26.98*
	(0.959)	(11.3)	(6.3)	(16.8)
Democracy	0.552*	0.502	—	—
	(0.29)	(.332)		
Repression	−1.01	−1.15	—	—
	(0.687)	(0.849)	—	—
Issue Area	−1.09	3.16*	−2.51	3.18*
	(2.06)	(1.83)	(2.22)	(1.83)
Terrain	—	—	−117.2	−110.0
	—	—	(82.9)	(86.7)
Strategy*Terrain	—	—	61.16	52.20
	—	—	(42.1)	(43.3)
Surprise	−0.689	−2.10	−.34	−2.80
	(1.51)	(1.56)	(1.76)	(1.97)
OMDA	−3.75	−39.8	−92.2*	−109.9
	(3.01)	—	(57.2)	—
OADM	−8.08**	−44.8	7.30	−31.79
	(3.92)	—	(14.4)	—
OADA	−1.82	−0.829	−9.2**	.039
	(1.89)	(2.32)	(4.01)	(2.8)
OPDA	24.8***	18.9	5.11	−.29
	(3.74)	—	—	(2.81)
DMOA	−1.32	−40.0	−32.3	−65.40
	(2.03)	—	(21.9)	—
DAOM	−7.81**	−43.8	54.40	4.19
	(3.37)	—	(42.2)	—
DAOA	−5.24**	−3.27	−13.9***	−1.94
	(2.35)	(2.29)	(5.4)	(2.83)
DPOA	23.27***	22.40	−45.53***	−28.14
	(2.70)	—	(8.76)	—

Log Likelihood = −36.69
Pseudo R^2 = 0.62
Adj R^2 = 0.49
Likelihood Ratio Test:
 $Chi^2(4)$ = 36.02
 p = 0.0001

Log Likelihood = −25.79
Pseudo R^2 = 0.73
Adj R^2 = 0.64
Likelihood Ratio Test:
 $Chi^2(4)$ = 14.2
 p = 0.007

Table 6. Multinomial Logistic Regression Results: Lose Is the Reference State (Testing Variable Specifications) (*Continued*)

Variable	Model 5 Minus Ally Variables		Model 6 Minus Duration	
	Win	Draw	Win	Draw
Duration	−0.027	0.98**	—	—
	(−0.034)	(0.05)	—	—
Capabilities	7.37***	3.66	23.82***	1.07
	(2.94)	(4.09)	(7.33)	(5.10)
Distance	−0.00082**	0.000049	−.0013**	−0.00026
	(0.0004)	(0.00034)	(.00056)	(0.00034)
Population	−0.012*	0.013*	−0.029**	0.00236
	(0.0066)	(0.0079)	(0.02)	(0.0059)
Troops	0.121**	−0.13	0.22**	0.0458
	(0.057)	(0.094)	(0.102)	(0.076)
Military Ratio	−0.26	−0.521	−0.17**	−0.20
	(0.047)	(0.345)	(0.086)	(0.47)
Quality Ratio	0.528	−.0877	1.09**	0.21
	(0.404)	(0.40)	(0.51)	(0.42)
Allies' Capabilities	—	—	89.4**	91.6**
	—	—	(40.3)	(41.1)
Allies' Quality	—	—	−10.25*	−25.50
	—	—	(5.85)	(17.5)
Democracy	0.63**	1.15***	1.30**	0.95*
	(0.33)	(0.48)	(0.55)	(0.52)
Repression	−1.41**	−3.68***	−4.37***	−2.81**
	(0.72)	(1.49)	(1.68)	(1.31)
Issue Area	−1.32	4.17**	−2.30	3.06*
	(1.51)	(2.16)	(2.42)	(1.83)
Terrain	−51.8	−42.7	−141.1**	−137.56**
	(42.1)	(44.4)	(60.1)	(61.0)
Strategy*Terrain	27.03	17.80	70.6**	67.1**
	(21.05)	(22.0)	(29.9)	(30.3)
Surprise	−0.53	−2.60	−1.31	−1.13
	(1.37)	(1.89)	(2.32)	(1.60)
OMDA	−39.98	−50.47	−98.15***	−133.90
	(30.0)	—	(39.4)	—
OADM	8.98	−21.15	15.40	−23.70
	(24.4)	—	(15.9)	—
OADA	−0.072	9.06**	1.11	6.56
	(2.23)	(4.69)	(3.77)	(4.26)
OPDA	16.68***	14.95	5.56	6.19*
	3.90	—	—	(3.71)
DMOA	−14.39	−43.50	−31.3**	−72.30
	(9.94)	—	(13.5)	—
DAOM	25.82	−21.28	70.0**	23.10
	(22.67)	—	(31.9)	—
DAOA	−3.27	5.53	−7.32	3.02
	(2.33)	(4.03)	(4.02)	(3.64)
DPOA	−5.19	16.23	−43.5	−37.5***
	(11.1)	—	—	(7.94)

Log Likelihood = −34.17
Pseudo R^2 = 0.65
Adj R^2 = 0.53
Likelihood Ratio Test:
  Chi^2(4) = 30.98
  p = 0.0001

Log Likelihood = −25.04
Pseudo R^2 = 0.74
Adj R^2 = 0.65
Likelihood Ratio Test:
  Chi^2(2) = 12.71
  p = 0.002

variables and exclude strategic surprise. In the complete model, surprise appears to have little systematic effect on winning versus losing, although it does have a systematic effect on the reduction in the likelihood of observing a draw. Because the standard hypothesis regarding surprise is that it should convey a net advantage that would increase the chances of victory for the state that achieves surprise, and because we do not observe a systematic effect on winning versus losing, it is a possible candidate for exclusion. In the restricted model, the likelihood statistic drops to -20.7. The Chi^2 (2) is 4.02, resulting in a p value of 0.14, above the arbitrary threshold for the rejection of the null hypothesis of 0.05, which is standard in the social sciences. While the standard approach here would be to drop surprise from the equation, there is strong anecdotal evidence and theory for its inclusion. It also appears to have a systematic effect on the likelihood of observing draws, so I keep it in the equation used to estimate the individual effects discussed later in this chapter.

As I discussed in the theoretical and measurement chapters earlier, I hypothesized that terrain and the interaction of strategy and terrain should have important effects on outcomes. When we exclude them (model 3), the likelihood statistic drops by a factor of two. We can reject the null hypothesis that the two variables have negligible impact on war outcomes with almost virtual certainty. These two variables will turn out to be two of the most important variables affecting our ability to forecast and understand outcomes. Interestingly, the effect of excluding terrain and the strategy/terrain interactions on the other variables' coefficients is negligible, the exception being the strategy dummy variables. In their case, two things occur when we exclude the strategy and terrain interaction. The first is that by removing a variable that is somewhat collinear with the dummy variables, the strategy variables' standard errors shrink, in several cases quite dramatically. The second, not unanticipated, effect is that the values and signs of two of the strategy variables change. This is not surprising given that we cannot understand the effect of the strategy variables simply by observing the sign of the coefficient due to the interactive effects of the terrain and strategy variable.

While realists and military historians are almost united in their belief that strategy and military capabilities play significant roles in determining outcomes, no such consensus exists on the role of domestic political factors. Recall that in the complete model (column 1, table 3) there are two variables that get to the role of domestic politics directly. One is the structural variable democracy and the other is a domestic political choice, repression. Some researchers, notably realists and neorealists, argue that we can safely ignore domestic politics from our analysis of war and international politics, while others maintain the opposite.

Comparing the complete model to a restricted model that excludes the two variables, we see that it would be foolish to exclude them from our analysis. Dropping repression and institutional democracy from the analysis (model 4) results in the pseudo-R^2 dropping from 0.81 to 0.73. Using the more reliable likelihood ratio test, we can reject the null (that we should stick with the restricted model) with confidence, the p-value for the chi-square statistic being 0.007. While the signs of the two variables indicate that their effects on outcomes are in the hypothesized direction, the two variables are somewhat collinear with each other. It is possible that the sign on one or both of the variables might flip in the absence of the other variable. To test for this possibility, I ran two other restricted models (not listed in table 4). In each model, democracy and then repression was excluded. For both we can reject the null at $p <$ 0.05. Additionally, even in the absence of the other domestic factor, the sign remains stable on the factor left in the equation. This observation is important because it means that the results for the democracy and repression variables are not simply an artifact of multicollinearity or correlation of errors. The potential problem of multicollinearity will be addressed in some detail later in this chapter.

Unlike the cases of democracy and repression, most international relations scholars would agree that alliances lie at the center of world politics. The statistical results in table 6 supports this view. Recall that two variables measure the contributions of a state's allies. The first is the allies' contribution to the amount of military and industrial capabilities of all the states involved in the war. The second is the allies' relative level of technology and training, measured by the spending per soldier relative to the other participants in the war. If we exclude these two measures (model 5), the pseudo-R^2 drops precipitously to 0.65, an early indicator that they have powerful effects on outcomes. The likelihood ratio test indicates that we can reject the null hypothesis with tremendous confidence (likelihood ratio test Chi^2 [4] = 31.0, p value < 0.0001).

The final restricted model (model 6) eliminates the duration variable. The statistical level of confidence we have in its effect is quite strong (likelihood ratio test Chi^2 [2] = 12.7, $p <$ 0.002). When we exclude the duration from the outcomes equation, we also remove a source of some collinearity. As a result of its removal, our confidence in the point estimates of the other variables increases substantially. Note that in the final model in table 6, all of the nondummy variables (with the exception of surprise) are significant at the 0.10 level or better and all but two at the 0.05 level or better. Why not leave out the variable for time then? The problem in doing so is that our ability to predict draws declines precipitously. It is reassuring to note, however, that whether duration is in the equation or not, the effects of the other variables in the model remain stable. Recall that duration is the one variable that is in no way ex ante or can even be easily accounted for with a contingent forecast as the case would be with the strategy dummy variables. The question then becomes can we successfully model the duration of wars using ex ante factors, at least one of which must be outside of the outcomes model? In the next chapter I show that we can, in fact, model war duration with a solid degree of confidence using variables, some of which are not included in the model of outcomes.

Significance of General Model

Given that the model fits the data reasonably well, what conclusions can we draw before we move on to the more specific findings regarding the individual indicators? Or, to put it more bluntly, of what use is a model such as this? Having confirmed that the basic theoretical model seems to fit a large data set of war outcomes over an extended temporal domain, I could investigate the likely outcomes between two potential adversaries. I could use the model in this light to draw conclusions about the foreign policy choices of various states. Using the model to forecast likely outcomes, I might shed some light on the reluctance of the Americans and the Europeans to become involved in the 1990's Balkan War.

Before using the model to make predictions about contemporary wartime behavior, however, the investigation of the individual effects remains. In this chapter, I have shown that the fit of the multinomial model to the data set is quite good. While the expected error rate increased somewhat, I also showed that the model performs well using out-of-sample cases. Following this, I tested various restricted models to see if there were any independent variables that could be dropped from the model without affecting the overall fit to the data. Using both the changes in the pseudo-R^2 and the likelihood ratio test, I concluded that each of the sets of variables identified in the theoretical section of the book should remain in the model. While each of the independent variables makes a significant contribution to the overall likelihood, I still have not addressed the relative explanatory power of the individual variables, nor have I investigated the expected change in the outcomes that are associated with particular changes in the independent variables. These are the subjects of the next two chapters.

In chapter 6, I will first present summary statistics about the marginal effects of the various independent variables. Following this, each of the structural factors will be discussed, in particular the role of war duration. I will also present an empirical estimation of war duration to demonstrate the feasibility of modeling the duration of interstate war. In chapter 7, the effects of the choices leaders make (strategy, repression, etc.) will be presented. Additionally, a detailed discussion will be presented of the constraining effects and the interaction of the environment that the choices are made in. For example, some states do not have the capabilities to choose particular strategies, and other states may not be able to repress dissent within the mass publics without severely affecting the legitimacy of the state.

CHAPTER 6

The Effects of Decision Makers' Choices

> Nabis, prince of the Spartans, withstood the whole of Greece and a
> triumphant Roman army, and successfully defended his country and
> his own authority against them. All he had to do, when danger threat-
> ened, was to take steps against a few of his subjects.
>
> —Niccolò Machiavelli

In his treatise on statecraft, *The Prince*, Machiavelli argues that the
choice to repress a few subjects in order to maintain the loyalty of the
remaining subjects is a powerful tool during time of war. Interestingly,
Machiavelli argues that repression can be a tool used to demonstrate
compassion:

> So a prince must not worry if he incurs reproach for his cruelty so
> long as he keeps his subjects united and loyal. By making an exam-
> ple or two he will prove more compassionate than those who, being
> too compassionate, allow disorders which lead to murder and rap-
> ine. (Machiavelli 1985, 95)

In addition, Machiavelli in later chapters also discusses the importance
of political organization and military training for both princes and subjects. Machiavelli and many more contemporary analysts tell us that
factors such as strategy, training, and repression are important for waging war, but they do not tell us *how* important. That is the subject of this
chapter. In the previous chapter, I argued that the multinomial logistic
statistical model is the most appropriate method to use to begin to
estimate the relative effect of one variable versus another. In this chapter, I will use the information from the statistical model tested in chapter
5 to show how each of the factors identified here affects the likely
outcomes of interstate wars.

There are two ways to think about the effect that some factor, such
as strategy or time, may have on war outcomes. The first way is to think
about the average impact a factor may have over the course of all wars.

The other way is to think about the possible range of the effect. For example, I will show that historically, on average, time has a small impact on the outcomes of wars. This is not to say that time cannot have a large effect, and I will show that in certain situations it indeed does have a powerful effect, but on average, over all wars, time is usually not the deciding factor. This is because the vast majority of wars are relatively short. Long, drawn-out wars lasting more than two years are quite rare. Because the effect of war-weariness typically does not begin to be a problem for decision makers until the third or fourth year of a war, on average time ends up having little effect. Other factors such as strategy will be shown to have powerful average effects. This is in part due to the fact that leaders or military organizations must choose a strategy for every war, not just some of them.

In this chapter, I first explore the aggregate historical effects of factors critical to determining war outcomes. Next, I examine the independent effects of the two main categories of factors, choices and resources: strategy combinations, alliances, surprise, mobilization, technology and quality, and repression and democracy.

Figure 28 represents the average relative influence on war outcomes of the independent variables that are either choices made by leaders or characteristics of the states they lead. The height of each bar represents the average relative effect. For comparative purposes, the bars are scaled so that the effect of military and industrial capabilities equals one. Remember, the height of the bars does not represent the *possible* effect of a particular variable but rather the historical average effect of the variable in question.[1]

In figure 28, we can see that in terms of historical averages, realpolitik factors such as strategy and alliance contributions have been, on average, by far the most important in determining winners and losers. We see that a state's strategy choice is up to four times as important as the actors' share of military-industrial capabilities. Alliance contributions are also shown to be quite important, as realists anticipate. Strategy and terrain interaction, a factor often ignored by political scientists, has also played a large role historically. A caveat is in order here. We should not place too much stock in the precise ratios between the various variables. The magnitude of the relative effect is somewhat sensitive to the specification of the statistical model. The rank ordering, however, is not at all sensitive to the inclusion or exclusion of one or more independent variables. As Morgenthau and others argue, when we look from a historical perspective, repression and democracy have had far less of a marginal impact on wars than have allies and strategy.

Another interesting point to be made from the information in this

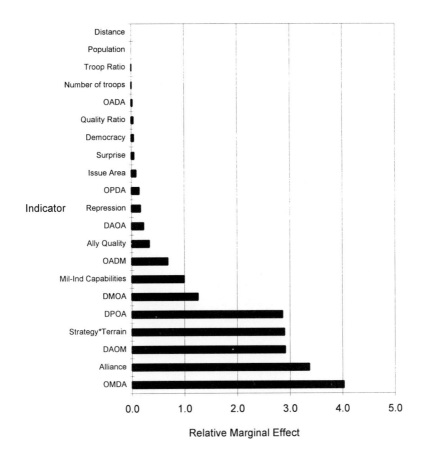

Fig. 28. The historical average marginal effects on the probability of observing a victory

figure is the small aggregate effect of strategic surprise, a fraction of the effect of political repression, which in turn is a fraction of the power we see in the military strategy and capability variables. Figure 29 shows the historical average effects of the variables on the likelihood of observing a draw. Recall that the theory presented in chapter 2 anticipated that draws are fundamentally different than victories and defeats. We see this hypothesis borne out in the data presented here. The factors that lead to victory are not necessarily the same ones that lead to draws.

While we see that strategy and terrain still are the most important factors, their relative effects are not as powerful as their role in determining winners and losers. Alliance contributions have played a far less

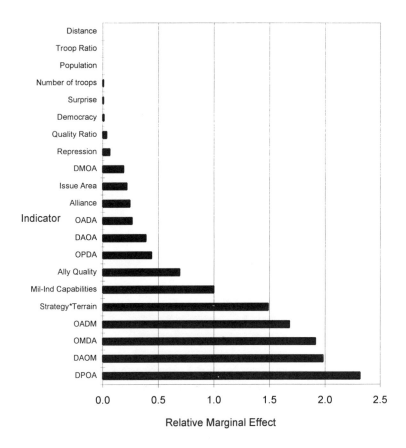

Fig. 29. The historical average marginal effects of the independent variables on the probability of observing a draw

important role historically in determining draws than they have in determining wins and losses. To this point, the empirical evidence supports the realist notion that domestic politics can be safely ignored when we study war. We might reach this conclusion by realizing that repression or democracy have played a comparatively small role, on average, in determining the outcomes of wars. But by stopping here we might fall into the same trap the realists have. We need to go beyond simply describing history as figures 28 and 29 do.

These two figures are useful for thinking about how wars have been fought in the past and what factors have historically been more important than others. We should not conclude from these figures, however, that the factors on the top of the chart *cannot* play important roles in outcomes. In order to see the individual effect that a particular factor *might* have, we need to take a slightly different approach. For example, looking at figures 28 and 29, we might conclude that distance can safely be ignored as an important factor in war. But this may be a hasty and unwise conclusion. Because the vast majority of wars have been fought by states close to or even bordering each other, distance has not played that great a role on average. This is not to say that distance cannot play a critical role when two states are very far apart. In order to estimate the potential effects of the independent variables, we need to set up a system to allow a single independent variable to change from its minimum observed to its maximum and at the same time track the expected change in the outcome probabilities. In the following sections I do just that. Using a series of figures, I graphically show the independent effect of the various choices that confront decision makers prior to and during wars. In chapter 7, I will investigate the effects of the political and resource constraints leaders face during war.

Realpolitik Choices

The Effect of Military Strategy

Historically, military strategy and its interaction with the terrain upon which the battles are fought have been among the most critical factors in determining who wins and who loses wars. We can see this in figures 28 and 29. What those figures do not show is how much the probability of victory or defeat changes as a result of the strategies that civilian decision makers and military leaders make. In figure 30, I demonstrate the specific changes in war outcomes associated with a particular strategy choice. Figures 28 and 29, along with the statistical information in chapter 5, tells us that strategy is one of, if not the most, important factor in determining potential outcomes. But simply knowing that something is important in a historical sense is not the same as knowing what the potential effect may be in any particular case.

In figure 30, and in those that follow, a great deal of information is presented. The height of each bar represents the expected probability of a particular outcome that corresponds to a particular strategy type. Along the bottom axis, running left to right, are the eight observed strategy choices found in the sample used to estimate each factor's effect on outcomes. Reading from left to right, the strategies and doctrine combinations are as follows: OPDA—offensive doctrine with punishment strategy fighting a defender using an attrition strategy; DPOA—the state with the defensive doctrine is fighting with a

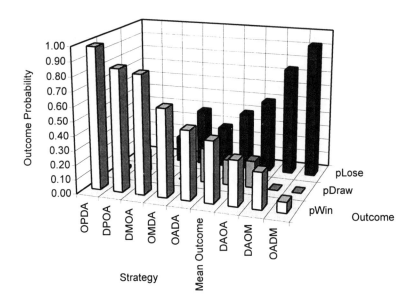

Fig. 30. The effect of military strategy on war outcomes

punishment strategy against an offensive state using an attrition strategy; DMOA, here the defender uses a maneuver strategy, and the state on the offensive uses an attrition strategy; OMDA—cases coded this way are examples of a state seeking to change the status quo (offensive doctrine) with a maneuver strategy fighting a defender using an attrition strategy; and OADA—in these cases the offense is using an attrition strategy against a defender who also uses an attrition strategy.[2] The next category represents the average value of the overall predictions for the data set. This might be best thought of as the average outcome of evenly matched opponents. Following the average outcome values are the three doctrine and strategy combinations that lead to below-average performance: DAOA, cases where a defender fights using an attrition strategy against an offensive state also using an attrition strategy; DAOM, here from the defenders perspective, the defense uses an attrition strategy and the offense a maneuver strategy; and OADM, where the offense uses an attrition strategy in the face of a defender using a maneuver strategy. The final axis represents the three possible outcomes: win, draw, and lose.

For each outcome and strategy combination there is some expected outcome probability. For example, the expected probability of winning for a state coded as fighting with an OPDA doctrine and strategy combination is roughly 95 percent.[3] States that choose a defensive doctrine and attrition strategy combination have a roughly 25 percent chance of winning and a 75 percent chance of losing. Notice that with this doctrine and strategy combination the chance of a draw occurring has dropped to almost zero. In this chart, it is easy to see that maneuver strategies, whether used by states trying to alter or defend the status quo, are among the most effective and are quite a bit more effective than the more common attrition strategies. Punishment strategies, for both offensively minded states and defenders alike have been remarkably successful. Clearly, maneuver and punishment (guerrilla) strategies are more effective than attrition strategies, but what about offensive versus defensive doctrines? While I do not have an explicit variable for whether the system at a particular time is offensive or defensive dominant (this would be a purely speculative ex post coding) we can judge whether historically offensive doctrines have been more effective than defensive ones.

Comparing the OADA combination to the DAOA one (the former are cases where the state in question was attempting to change the status quo against a defending opponent who used an attrition strategy; the latter cases are simply the opposite, with defenders that fight using an attrition strategy against opponents also using attrition strategy), we can see that on average, if both sides fight using an attrition strategy, the offensive side has a 48 percent chance of victory and the defender roughly a 30 percent chance of victory. These results argue quite strongly that when both sides are using an attrition strategy, the offensive side will have the advantage.

Note that military strategies are "strategic" in the game theoretic sense; that is, the effect of military strategy depends on the strategic interaction (in the game theory sense) of the two sides' choices of military strategy. When states begin to use maneuver strategies, however, the advantage swings from the offense to the defense. While both sides of the war gain from using a maneuver strategy against an opponent using an attrition strategy, the defenders gain comparatively more. Fighting against opponents using an attrition strategy, defenders have an 82 percent chance of victory versus a 61 percent chance for states using an offensive doctrine. In both situations, however, the state that chooses a maneuver strategy is at an advantage over an opponent using an attrition strategy.

While the data tell a convincing story, history also provides supporting examples. Conventional wisdom holds that strategy can make an enormous difference in a state's ability to fight wars. In World War II, France used an updated version of its attrition strategy that worked well enough to allow victory in World War I. The French devised a way to exploit their perceived advantages of terrain. By pivoting large numbers of troops to the north, the French hoped to be able to prevent an updated Schlieffen plan of penetration from the north as had occurred in World War I.

The Germans learned different lessons from World War I. The Germans realized that a head-on battle of attrition would spell doom for their grandiose plans. By adopting the blitzkrieg offense in their war against France, the Germans were able to defeat a numerically superior foe in only six weeks. It is important to note that it was not the French strategy in isolation that allowed the stunningly swift German victory to happen. The interaction of a static French defense and a highly mobile German offense doomed the French from the outset. The Germans hoped to be able to catch their opponents off guard. Then, through a series of lightning-quick offensive strikes, they hoped to prevent their opponent from being able to regroup and possibly launch a devastating counterattack against the now spread-out, and hence quite vulnerable, German offensive force.

Given the apparent advantages of the maneuver approach, from the realist perspective it might be surprising that states continue to adopt attrition strategies even after the benefits of maneuver became apparent. But realists fail to take into account the domestic constraints on strategy choice. Maneuver strategies require that tremendous autonomy be granted to lower echelon units, something many military leaders and political leaders are loath to delegate.

Prior to the German attack in 1941 under the name of "Operation Barbarossa," Stalin knew of the enormous potential military advantages of the German blitzkrieg strategy. In fact, the Soviet army in the Far East used the strategy with great success against the Japanese. During the Japanese invasions into Manchuria in 1939, Soviet General Zhukov employed an armored force using a strategy akin to that used by the Germans against the Poles in 1939. The results were similar. Zhukov shattered the Japanese attackers, drove them back across the frontier and inflicted four times as many casualties as the Russians sustained. "This might have been vindication of Tukhachevsky's ideas [use of armor in blitzkrieg-like offenses], but back in Moscow, Stalin did not see it that way. The breaking up of mechanized formations continued" (Messenger 1976, 122). One of the key components of the blitzkrieg strategy is the autonomy of the subordinate units during the attack. This independence of decision making was anathema to the Red Army after Stalin's purges.

The Red Army Air Corps also failed to learn lessons about close-air support for ground troops from the Spanish Civil War and the German defeat of Poland. Stalin's failure to integrate the new strategies his generals developed resulted in the devastating losses the Soviet army suffered during the summer and fall of 1941 at the hands of the Germans. Stalin's refusal to adopt or adapt to the strategies of his opponent or to prepare to defend against the potential German threat left the Soviet army wide open for the massive losses that took place during the initial German invasion. While the Soviets prevailed in the end, their war losses were unprecedented, with over 20 million dying during the war. Without the iron-handed domestic politics of the Stalin regime, replete with its horrific domestic political repression, it is likely that the Russian people would not have been able to continue the fight against the Germans and would have capitulated as they had earlier in March 1918.

Twenty-five years after collapsing in the face of the German army, and after absorbing the crushing blows of the German army, Stalin's Soviet Union was able to eventually repel the German army even without using an optimal strategy. It did this by being able to maintain command and control in the face of the unyielding blitzkrieg onslaught and eventually was able to draw the Germans into a war of attrition. Even though the Soviets lost more men than the Germans did in almost every key battle, the Soviets were able to defeat the Germans through an attrition strategy. It is not clear that the Soviets were responsible for the Germans' change in strategy. The Germans bypassed concentrations of troops in order to increase the amount of territory taken in France but sought out large battles in order to take as many prisoners as possible in the Soviet Union. Given the Soviet Union's significantly larger population and industrial base, it is clear today that the strategy combination of attrition on both sides at the end of the war was to the Soviets' benefit.

More recently, in their war against the mujaheddin in Afghanistan, the Soviet strategy choice of ruthless attrition using an offensive doctrine affected its military's efficiency. The Soviets were able to control far greater areas of terrain and population in Afghanistan than the United States had been able to in its war against North Vietnam, where the United States used a defensive attrition doctrine and strategy (along with a punishing bombing campaign later in the war). Additionally, the Soviets were able to do this while suffering fewer casualties and using fewer troops than the United States did in Vietnam. While the costs for the Soviets' military were lower than for the U.S. military in its comparable war, the costs to the local civilian populations were probably roughly equal. Even though they used far fewer troops in Afghanistan than the United States used in Vietnam, the Soviets were far more brutal in their suppression of local resistance. As a result, they were less vulnerable to attacks in areas that they "controlled" than the United States had been in Vietnam.

From the results above it is easy to understand military organizations' preferences in many circumstances for offensive doctrines and manuever strategies. The rational perspective on strategy choice presented here is not universally accepted though. Using an organizational approach, Posen ties together arms races, war outcomes, war initiation, and strategy by investigating what he believes to be the organizational roots of strategy choice. Posen argues that doctrine (the choice of offense, defense, or deterrent strategies, according to him) is important not just because it affects the likelihood of various outcomes but because it affects the likelihood of arms races and, in turn, the outbreak of war (Posen 1984, 15). Rather than providing empirical evidence to support these claims, Posen believes that it is a foregone conclusion that offensive doctrines lead to arms races and war. His concerns with strategy and doctrine stem from his interests in war initiation. He argues that the links between offensive doctrines, arms races, and war initiation are incontrovertible (Posen 1984, 17). Posen deduces these conclusions from the assumption that the main tenet of offensive doctrines is an irrational belief on the part of military planners that effective first strikes will provide decisive victories for the side that initiates the conflict (Posen 1984, 18).

Rather than investigating the rational links between preferences for a particular doctrine as the doctrines and strategies relate to outcomes, Posen relies on a model of organizational preferences. He maintains that military organizations will prefer offensive doctrine for several loosely supported reasons. Among those reasons are the following:

> Militaries seek advantages over their opponents and offensive doctrines appear to provide an advantage in that the attacker will get to pick the initial battle site.
> Militaries will try to develop active strategies rather than try to estimate the forces needed to overcome the potential resolve of an opponent in a deterrent situation.
> Militaries will prefer offensive doctrines over defensive ones because offensive doctrines will increase the militaries' organizational size and strength.
> Offensive doctrines enhance the military's autonomy from civilian decision makers.
> Offensive doctrines allow the military to develop complex standard operating procedures (SOPs, although it is not clear why defenders will not have SOPs for defense as well). (Posen 1984, 47–49)

Posen ignores explanations for preferences of offensive or mobile strategies and doctrines stemming from civilian leaders' rational preferences for short and decisive wars for domestic political reasons. By possibly limiting the scope and duration of a war, mobile offensive strategies may offer substantial political gains to decision makers at reduced costs when compared to attrition-based strategies. Because of his normative position, Posen ignores most of the factors that lead the military to have rational preferences for decisive, quick strategies.

The empirical findings presented in figure 30 run somewhat counter to the arguments made by supporters of the "Cult of the Offensive" literature. These writers (Mearsheimer 1983; Posen 1984; Van Evera 1984) argue that military organizations' preferences for mobile strategies and offensive doctrine is best predicted by looking at the militaries' organizational interests rather than using a rational choice selection. If these results hold up under further inspection, we should more reasonably conclude that militaries frequently prefer strategies that are based on maneuver because they simply work best. Posen discusses the idea of states choosing the "best" strategy during the European interwar period:

> French statesmen were determined to avoid such costs [as those associated with World War I] in a future war. They intervened in the doctrine of the French army and surrounded it with constraints that would bind the army to defensive warfare. There is more to protecting the security of a state than just "winning." When war costs appear to be terribly high, avoiding them becomes an important national security goal. . . . Moreover, [the French doctrine] was somewhat innovative, certainly a far cry from the army's pre-war offensive preferences. The Maginot fortifications were probably the most remarkable military construction program ever seen on the European continent to that date. (Posen 1984, 235)

The French defenses were remarkable in that they were probably the most extensive and expensive defense network ever defeated in under six weeks in the history of mankind. Posen's assertions are also questionable in that he is willing to brush aside any assumptions about states' preferences for survival because he assumes that forfeiting all national sovereignty could be an "important national security goal" (Posen 1984, 235).

Snyder and other "Cult of the Offensive" proponents argue that militaries prefer offensive strategies for organizational reasons rather than, or as much as, military war-fighting reasons even though they note that civilian leaders are likely to prefer the results of offensive campaigns.

"Offense is difficult and demands large defense budgets. It is also productive in that decisive offensive campaigns produce demonstrable returns on the state's investment in military capability" (Snyder 1984, 24). Snyder also points out that the leaders of the offensively minded German military achieved demigod status in pre-World War I German society (Snyder 1984, 24). This was not because of the organizational preferences of the military but rather because the military had been able to deliver the "goods" that the civilians desired. Military leaders did not need to be constrained by civilians; they selected offensive strategies because offense provided the only means by which they could meet the desires of the civilians for short and decisive wars.

Snyder does note that there may be some rational component of the military's strategy choice, but according to Snyder, it is a small and often inconsequential factor when compared to the myriad other factors influencing the military's policy choices. It is a bit disconcerting to realize that Snyder identifies at least thirteen factors that affect the plans and strategies of militaries and states but falls back to only one case (World War I) in order to sort out and test the various hypotheses related to the many alternative and often competing explanations (Snyder 1984, 33).

We can better understand Snyder's desire to show that preferences for offensive or mobile strategies and doctrines are based on irrational organizational preferences when we realize that his main operating assumption about the role of doctrine is its relationship to the initiation of war. Snyder, along with the other members of the "Cult of the Offensive" group, asserts that "war is more likely, the stronger the offense relative to the defense." Snyder quotes Van Evera, accepting the argument that one of the principal causes of war is the offense/defense balance of the international system. "Defense dominance converts aggressors into status-quo powers by making aggression too expensive, while offense-dominance invites even mildly aggressive states to attack" (Snyder 1984, 214). This argument relies on the assumption that surprise does not matter, which Van Evera, Snyder, and the other "Cultists" maintain is not true, and that there can be no net gains from limited wars. If these two assumptions are false, then Van Evera's and Snyder's assertion about the nature of the offense/defense balance and its role in war initiation may prove false as well.

For example, in the situation where surprise matters and in a defense-dominant world (DMOA) where there are gains to be had from limited grabs of territory, incentives exist for states to aggressively take limited chunks of territory from their neighbors, secure in the knowledge that in a defense-dominant world, with advantages for surprise with vigilant defenders, it will be easier to keep the recently acquired land than it will be for the former defender to take it back. The result of this so-called defense-dominant world with advantages for surprise is a state of heightened vigilance and tense borders. In an offense-dominant world, the opposite could hold true. Empirically, surprise does have a small positive effect on the probability of victory, holding strategy types constant. This effect varies quite a bit throughout the data set though, which is evidenced by the high standard errors associated with the variables' coefficients.

The preceding discussion and the results presented in figure 30 demonstrate that there *are* optimal strategy combinations for states to pursue and they are not always the attrition-based, defensive doctrines advocated by so many political science analysts. To some degree, however, this raises a potential challenge to this study. If there is an optimal strategy or combination of strategies, then why don't states employ the optimal strategy, or at least try to, at all times? The next section in this chapter is devoted to this question. Without a satisfactory answer, the assumption of rationality that serves as the intellectual underpinning of this study and others would come into question.

If There Is an Optimal Strategy, Why Don't All States Use It?

States may pick military strategies that are incapable of winning wars or are nonoptimal due to some sort of value discount that must be applied. While fluid, mobile strategies may be the most efficient strategies if executed correctly, there is frequently a discount factor associated with them as well, due in part to their tremendously complex nature. This discount factor lowers the actual value of the mobile strategies until the utility for them is below a less efficient one, an attrition strategy, for example. Two discount factors come to mind immediately: first, potentially winning wartime strategies (massive offensive ones) may prove so threatening to their neighbors that they may bring a retaliatory response to their deployment. Second, the states in question may not be capable of deploying or executing the potentially winning strategies due to the social and political conditions within their country. Realists might agree with the first, but if the second argument is correct, then we are forced to contemplate an expansion of the realist paradigm. The first possible discount factor has been investigated to some extent; the latter scarcely at all. If states are not capable of executing a high-risk strategy based on mobility and trust due to divisions within the military organization that reflect the social divisions within the society from which the military is drawn, they are forced to choose the next most preferable strategy. We see this phenomenon in countries where class or social divisions within the society are reflected in the military organization, such as Germany in the nineteenth century and Britain and France through World War I. The next two sections briefly discuss these ideas.

Suboptimal Strategy Choices: Class-Based Argument

Most of the European countries prior to the outbreak of World War I had societies with strong class-based divisions (Foot and Western 1973; Bond and Roy 1975). These societal divisions were reflected in the organization of their militaries. In Britain, for instance, the enlisted soldiers and conscripts were drawn entirely from the working class. The officer corps was largely untrained and filled with upper-class citizens who gained their jobs through birthright rather than through demonstrated competence. The general staff was made up of professional soldiers who were among the great military minds of the era. These divisions reflected and exacerbated the distrust between the classes. The general staff felt great contempt for the officers in its charge. The officers could not trust the enlisted soldiers. As a result, strong top-down control was necessary to ensure that orders would be followed. Draconian discipline was necessary to prevent mass desertions. Because of these limitations, fluid, mobile strategies that would require the attacking units to go for days without contact from higher echelons were felt to be impossible.

In the more recent Gulf War in 1991, the Iraqis were unable to use the vast majority of their conscripted troops in anything but the most simple attrition strategies due to an understandable lack of trust between the Baathists who made up the command structure and the rest of the army. Hussein's elite Republican Guard fought using mobile strategies, but they were the only truly politically reliable forces at Hussein's disposal. Fear of mass desertions forced Hussein to leave his other units in static defenses that fell easy prey to the American air and mobile ground attacks after hostilities began. In the United States' segregated army during the Civil War, the world wars, and the Korean War, African-American soldiers fought together under the leadership of whites who had been labeled incompetent. These units were frequently used as cannon fodder. Many high-ranking officers went on record stating their opinion that African-American soldiers could not be trusted and hence could only be utilized to execute the simplest of strategies.

Suboptimal Strategy Choices: Security
Dilemma Argument

Another discounting factor in a state's strategy selection decision-making process is that massive offensive strategies may contribute to inadvertent wars or the vague international sentiment that war is inevitable (Van Evera 1984). This problem has been studied extensively in the security dilemma literature. The general idea behind the concept is that as a state takes steps to ensure that its security will be increased, the act of doing so decreases the security of any neighboring or rival states. Researchers who describe the security dilemma either imply or state that offensive strategies, and the equipment necessary to implement them, exacerbate the tensions that lead to upwardly spiraling arms races. The authors conclude that states can best ensure their safety and maximize their security by developing defensive strategies and equipping themselves accordingly.

If military strategy is not a critical variable in determining war outcomes, then we can recommend the strategy that minimizes the probability of war outbreak without hesitation. But states' strategies have a powerful influence on their ability to prevail in war. The defensive strategies that may help states stay out of wars may preclude them from winning wars that they did not start but became involved in anyway. In this case, we must be concerned with the relationship between peacetime military strategies designed to help prevent war (by minimizing opponents' potential security dilemmas) and war-fighting strategies designed to defeat an opponent.

While many authors feel that military strategies should be chosen with deterrence in mind, unfortunately not all wars are deterred. In this event, the state's military strategy, which had been called upon to help prevent war, must now contribute to defending the state and winning the war or at least preventing the attacking state from achieving its goals.

As Posen states in *The Sources of Military Doctrine*, offensive strategies and doctrines lead to war not on their own per se but because of the way states that share offensive doctrines interact. Posen maintains that offensive doctrines cause states to compete with each other militarily even during peacetime, which raises the probability and stakes associated with war. If only one state had an offensive doctrine and all others had defensive ones, it is unlikely that the effects that Posen and Jervis describe would occur. It is the interactive effects of the strategies during peacetime that may lead to the increased probability of war. Once a war is underway, this interaction between the combatants' strategies is also critical. It was the combination of German blitzkrieg and French forward defense that led to the rapid defeat of France, not either state's particular strategy choice considered in isolation. The findings in figure 30 complicate the debate about the security dilemma. Previously policy recommendations flowed from the assumption that optimal strategies would be defensive. This may not be the case.

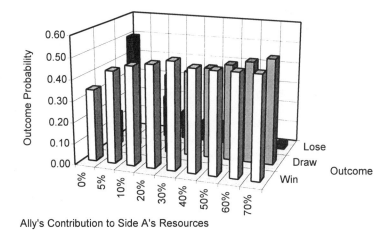

Fig. 31. The effect of ally military-industrial contributions

Military Alliances

While strategy's influence on war and its prosecution may seem logical, realists also urge us to focus on the role that alliances play in determining a state's power. As shown in the aggregate effect (see fig. 28), the realists are correct, from a historical perspective, to emphasize the importance of alliance behavior. Somewhat surprisingly, however, while alliance contributions have been one of the most important factors, on average, when we investigate the independent effect, the relative power of alliance contributions are not as powerful as some of the other factors we have looked at inasmuch as the alliance contribution is subject to apparently dramatic declining marginal returns.

Alliances and alliance behavior are absolutely central to realists and balance-of-power theorists. Because realists ignore domestic politics for the most part, they are forced to some extent to utilize alliance capabilities as the basic currency for the changes in the balance of power that they argue cause changes in the likelihood of war. Accordingly, they believe alliances "provide the primary means of deterring or defeating nations or coalitions of nations that seek to destroy the existing balance" (Holsti et al. 1973, 31). While this does not necessarily imply that we should expect to see a linear relationship between alliance contributions and outcomes, realists clearly assume that more alliance contributions are better. In figure 31 we can see that this is the case to a certain extent.

In this figure, the *x*-axis, running from left to right, is the amount of resources that are being contributed to an actor from its allies. The percentage is the fraction of all the resources available to all the states involved in the war. The higher the percentage, the higher the material contribution of the ally or allies. What we see is that as the amount of ally contributions increases (moving from left to right), the probability of victory for the state in question rises rather quickly from the average outcome. But what realists fail to anticipate is that the allies' ability to influence the war's outcome suffers from dramatic declining marginal returns. From this we can conclude that alliance contribution is important, but having large powerful allies may not be a great improvement on medium-sized allies. There is another possibility as well. Because we do not control for the number of allies in the alliance, it may be that large, complex alliances contribute less on average than a single committed partner. In order to reach the level of ally contribution on the right-hand side of the scale, a state must put together a large coalition of allies, which may not prove to be an improvement over a smaller but more committed group.

Collective action problems may also account for the declining marginal returns as the alliance contribution increases. Olson and Zechauser (1970) address the problem of free-riding in their economic theory of alliances and find that there may be strong incentives for large alliances to be plagued by the free-riding of the smaller partners. So while large alliances may have a large apparent contribution to make, they may be less efficient at delivering the increased chances of victory we might expect. All of this is not to say that allies are a hindrance to fighting the good fight. To the contrary, the data here simply imply that the contribution of allies is subject to diminishing marginal returns, something not anticipated by realists.

Realists implicitly assume that state power, and military power in particular, follows the rules of classical mechanics. Assuming away problems of political vulnerability, they speak in the pseudoscientific terms of physics:

> The format of armored warfare would allow even forces of dubious loyalty to be profitably used; they could be used to hold secondary fronts, add mass and momentum to the vectors of penetration, occupy axes successfully opened, and attract western counterattacks that would otherwise be aimed at the Soviet forces themselves. (Luttwak 1987, 247)

Note that Luttwak assumes that ally contributions will matter, regardless of the quality of the ally, in that they will add mass and momentum to attacks. This hypothesis is not borne out by anecdotal evidence though. During World War II, the German forces stretched themselves to the breaking point in Europe in no small part as a result of the unreliability of their Italian allies.

According to the majority of scholars, alliances exist for the purpose of "aggregating their capabilities for participation in international affairs" (Friedman 1970, 5). Friedman falls in the majority camp when he maintains that alliances contribute to outcomes through the simple aggregation of the two (or more) partners' capabilities. Additionally, he sees instances where the outcome of the alliance might actually be more than the sum of its parts. These might include situations where the allies' capabilities somehow complement each others' or allowed them to pursue strategies that they might not have had the capabilities to execute on their own (Friedman 1970, 11). Friedman and Luttwak are not alone in this view of alliances.

Using a system of power ratios, Rosen deduces a model of war outcomes with four outcome categories similar to the model presented in this book. When Rosen speaks of the effects of alliances on the abilities of states to inflict and absorb punishment, he sounds at first like a realist: "They combine their destructive potential, and share the costs of being harmed (though not necessarily equally). In essence, their strengths and cost-tolerances operate in tandem, though they remain separate parties" (Rosen 1972, 234). Remember, though, that Rosen's model is essentially a theoretical one, with no explicit test of propositions such as this about the relation between alliance contributions and war outcomes. Stephen Walt, making an observation about the role of alliances from the realist perspective, notes that "a state whose security position is threatened will probably attempt to increase its relative power (e.g., by spending more on defense) while simultaneously seeking an alliance with another state" (Walt 1987, 9). The implicit assumption here is that alliances function in an additive manner to increase the power of the participating states.

In addition to controlling for the capability contribution, recall that we also have controlled for the relative quality of the allies' contribution. What we find is that alliances made up of states with gross disparities in their relative levels of technology may not be as successful as alliances where the states are relatively equally endowed in technology and training.

Figure 32 demonstrates this problem. Moving from left to right on the x-axis, first we encounter situations such as the United States faced in the Korean War and the Vietnam War, where we were fighting with

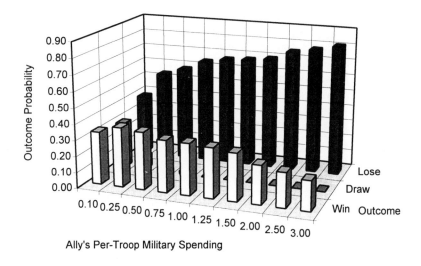

Ally's Per-Troop Military Spending

Fig. 32. The effect of ally quality on war outcomes

allies whose military spending per troop was very low. In these cases, the probability of victory drops off a small amount from the average outcome, but also the probability of observing a draw becomes quite a bit higher than average, roughly 30 percent. As we move to the right, the quality of the ally improves and initially so does the likelihood of victory; this is a result of the probability of draws dropping rapidly. Moving further to the right of the figure, the allies are now spending more per troop and we can see that the probability of winning begins to drop quite quickly. Again, as with previous and later figures, because the models are somewhat sensitive to variable specification, the actual location of the maxima and minima for the respective outcomes cannot be estimated with great consequence, but the general pattern is something we can have strong confidence in. In other words, the specific ratio at which a state's chances of victory begin to decline as a function of its allies' quality is somewhat uncertain. That the likelihood of victory begins to decline eventually is not uncertain. This figure tells us that merging forces of disparate skills and technology will not be an easy task for states to accomplish.

These two presentations of the effects of ally contribution do not directly challenge the realist argument that alliances matter. What they do tell us is that by simply aggregating alliance contributions we may be missing an important part of the picture. The military returns of an alliance are dependent upon a number of factors, some controlled for here (quality), others not (number of partners, political similarity of allies, etc.) More sophisticated empirical models of alliance are clearly called for here. We can be quite sure that although alliances do matter, simple explanations may be ignoring a large part of the story with regard to alliance contribution to war outcomes. We may expect to find similar results when we move on to other factors that realists and military historians regard as critical to outcomes. Compared to alliance politics and effects, the debate about surprise is much less extensive or controversial. Nearly all agree that surprise does and should matter a great deal.

Surprise

Within the political science literature, military surprise appears frequently as a source of great concern. Military writers such as Clausewitz address and openly embrace it; Betts opens *Surprise Attack* with the observation that

> Even very impressive forces may be insufficient for successful defense because surprise can neutralize much of their capability. . . . Pearl Harbor burned this necessity [i.e., be prepared] into the minds of United States military planners. . . . A striking lesson of history, however, is that nations often fall victim to surprise attack despite ample warning. (Betts 1982, ix)

This assumption, that surprise is a critical factor in determining the ability of a state to defend itself and to maintain its security, without much systematic empirical evidence to support it, leads to heightened concerns about the security dilemma, perhaps unnecessarily.

Betts offers the standard argument about surprise, that "military surprise is among the greatest dangers a country can face" (Betts 1982, 3). Betts considers surprise to be a force multiplier by allowing the state taking the initiative to envelope or destroy its opposition's forces at the outset of the conflict. The initial advantages of surprise are assumed to continue on throughout further stages of the war by disrupting the defender's plans for defense. Betts cites studies that argue that the benefits of surprise can have anywhere from a doubling to a quintupling effect for the attacker's forces (Betts 1982, 5).

The historical roots of analysts' beliefs about surprise run deep. Clausewitz, writing in the early nineteenth century, was an ardent believer in the importance of tactical and strategic surprise. He argued that achieving surprise "is more or less basic to all operations, for without it superiority at the decisive point is hardly conceivable. Surprise therefore becomes the means to gain superiority, but because of its psychological effect it should be considered as an independent element" (Clausewitz 1976, 198).

Empirically, however, the data are not as supportive of the surprise hypothesis as many might suspect. As I showed in chapter 5, the statistical effect of surprise is quite uncertain, the p-value being quite a bit larger than that generally accepted in the social sciences. While the effect is in the expected direction, the actually estimated change in outcomes is less than 4 percent, the smallest effect of any of the independent variables in the data set. States that achieve surprise strategies increase their chances of victory only by an average of 4 percent, so small an effect that it is negligible given the level of uncertainty associated with the variable's effect. One definite effect of surprise is that it does decrease the chances of observing a draw by quite a large amount. In the absence of either side achieving strategic surprise, during the course of a war, the likelihood of observing a draw is 20 percent; when either or both sides achieve surprise during the course of a war, the likelihood of a draw being observed drops to less than 7 percent.

Maoz presents one of the many logical reasons why surprise should give the initiator an edge in combat and war: the initiator of a successful surprise attack will catch the defender unaware and unprepared, hopefully unable to mobilize its defenses. By achieving surprise, the initiator is better able to dictate the location, timing, and strategy of the attack. The state that has been surprised typically has its command, control, and communications systems disrupted by the attack. In an attack that has been anticipated, these systems can usually be sheltered (Maoz 1990, 171).

But support for the surprise hypothesis is not universal. Maoz argues that even with the benefits just cited, surprise should not provide much net advantage in affecting the ultimate outcome of the war. He argues that surprise proves as disruptive to the attacker as it does to the defender. The effect of early success leads the attacker to let down its defenses and the surprise bolsters the defender's resolve. The initiator's expectations of the costs and benefits of the war do not include the change in the defender's resolve that results from the surprise attack (Maoz 1990, 176). Examples of this kind of increased resolve might include the Soviet response to the German surprise attack in 1941 and the visceral American response to the Japanese attack on Pearl Harbor. The American response was so strong that, according to Maoz, the U.S. mass public ignored the fact that the Roosevelt administration tied the war in Japan to the war in Europe (Maoz 1990, 186).

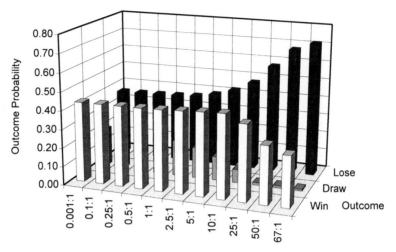

Fig. 33. Military mobilization: How the relative number of troops effects outcomes

Given the logical arguments that can be made both for and against the surprise hypothesis, it should not be too startling to find that surprise has historically increased the chances of observing a definitive outcome (nondraw), but the increase in a state's chances of victory are much less certain.

Mobilization

Military mobilization is an important factor in determining outcomes. It also has the potential to create domestic political conflict or to exacerbate existing domestic political tension. Mobilizing troops for war is expensive both in monetary terms and in domestic political terms. People who are fighting in a war are not available, for the most part, for service to a country in other ways. If a war is unpopular, mobilization of more troops may be unfeasible for political reasons. Recall that we measured mobilization or the effect of the number of troops in two ways: first, in a relative sense and, second, in the absolute sense. The first approach provides some interesting results.

Figure 33 demonstrates the effect of the ratio of the two sides' troop levels. Reading from left to right we move from the situation where an actor is facing an opponent with significantly more troops than its own army to the situation on the right where the opposite holds. The somewhat surprising result is that the ratio of the number of troops appears to have little effect in most cases. From a ratio of 1:10 to a ratio of 10:1, there is little effect. This can be understood because in battle it is typically the local ratio of soldiers rather than the ratio of the total size of the armies that will effect the outcomes of the battles and hence the war. The anticipated effect of the size of a state's army is shown in figure 34. Before examining these results, a puzzling result appears in the extreme values shown in figure 33.

Figure 33 contains what appears to be something of a paradox that may be the result of the troop ratio variables serving as a proxy for another, unmeasured factor. After the 10:1 point we see that the chances of a state winning actually drop off. This observed effect is likely the result of selection bias rather than the soldiers falling all over each other while waging war. Situations in which one side greatly outnumbers the other—gross mismatches—are rare encounters and typically involve issues outside the variables controlled for in the data set, specifically, domestic political variables. An example of this is the 1948 war between Israel and Egypt where England and France tried to intervene but were unsuccessful for political reasons within the European alliance. In another example, Vichy France was unable to fight to victory against Thailand during the World War II. Clearly there were intervening events taking place on the European continent at the time. This is not to say that the number of troops has no effect. If we look at the absolute number of troops that a side has available, we then see the expected results.

Figure 34 demonstrates the strong monotonic relationship between the size of a state's army (while simultaneously controlling for the relative size of the opponent) and war outcomes.

Here we see the anticipated effect of the number of soldiers a state has at its disposal. It is not so much the relative number of troops available but rather the number itself, or the ability to quickly and easily replace losses incurred on the battlefield, that matters. As the number of troops at the disposal of a state's military leaders rises from one thousand to over 6 million, the probability of victory rises from roughly 25 percent to over 80 percent, a powerful effect to be sure. The number of troops that a state chooses to mobilize has a powerful effect on the likely outcomes of any war that state is involved in. Typically, this is also a choice that political leaders must make. There are strong incentives for a state's leaders to deeply mobilize a state's population, as figure 34 demonstrates. At the same time, in the absence of some way to control for the domestic unrest that full-scale mobilization may engender among the

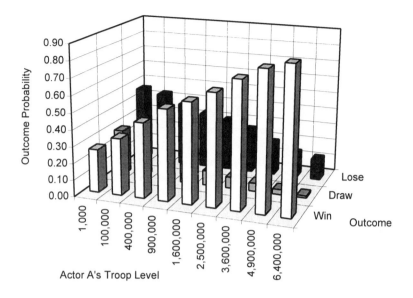

Fig. 34. The effect of the absolute number of troops on war outcomes

state's population, there may be domestic political incentives to mobilize the minimum number of troops that a state's leaders believe will be necessary to successfully prosecute a war. In order to mobilize large parts of a state's population, elaborate plans may be necessary, which in turn may have dramatic effects on both the timing of the war and its outcome.

For example, prior to the outbreak of World War I, Russia developed an aggressive and offensive military strategy that depended a great deal on the quick and complete mobilization of its armed forces (particularly its reserve forces). Its strategy choice and the mobilization plans that went with it had a significant impact on the costs the Russian mass public was forced to bear. "On July 28 1914, Russian leaders announced that partial Russian mobilization against Austria would be ordered on July 29. They took this step to address threats emanating from Austria, acting partly to lend emphasis to their warnings to Austria that Russia would fight if Serbia were invaded" (Miller 1985, 86). Unfortunately for the Russian czar, who had no real desire to take on the Germans as well as the Austrians, he did not realize that he did not have the option of a partial military mobilization. "General Yanushkevich flatly told Sazonov that general mobilization 'could not be put into operation' once partial mobilization began" (Miller 1985, 86). The military commanders based their arguments on the tremendous interdependence of the separate parts of the mobilization plans. Trains taken out of the general mobilization plan to be used for a partial mobilization might not be available in the right place at the right time for the tremendously complex train schedules used in the general mobilization. As a result, the Russian leaders were forced to choose between a full offensively oriented mobilization or a complete retreat in the face of Austrian intransigence. They chose complete mobilization, and World War I was under way.

While Russian involvement in World War I may have been inevitable, because its prewar choice of strategy was predicated on a full-scale mobilization it ultimately became involved in a war far larger and more costly than it could politically afford at home. The domestic political costs of the war, resulting from the enormous burden being borne by the Russian peasantry who made up a large portion of the conscript army, led to the October Revolution and the Russian Red Army's subsequent withdrawal from the war. The Russians' prewar strategy choice of offense based on massive deep and quick mobilization led them into a war in which victory was far from certain and participation not desired. From the perspective of Russian history, this is not an isolated case. While large-scale mobilization provides military benefits, it also may have significant domestic costs associated with it. In part because of this, wars between large armies are relatively rare events.

Along with the decisions of how large an army to mobilize comes the decision of how much to spend on training and equipment for that army. The next indicator, training and quality, also is subject to domestic political constraints. But, first, the empirical results.

Technology and Quality

Technology is a critical component or indicator of a state's ability to overcome wartime friction. For instance, units maneuvering in the desert have a terrible time knowing where they are at any particular moment. Typically, the soldiers responsible for a unit's navigation frequently compare the terrain features they see before them with the ones described by thin, red contour lines on their maps. This is a difficult skill to master even when moving at foot speed in hilly areas with many known terrain features. In locations that are flat, featureless expanses of sand and rock, it occasionally borders on the impossible. Maps of the desert have few if any terrain features or roads with which a small unit leader can orient himself while traveling at potentially high speeds. Knowledge about one's location is critical information because other

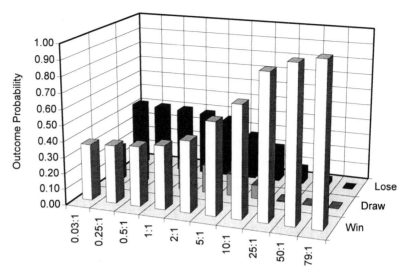

Ratio of Actor A's Spending per Troop to Opponent's

Fig. 35. The effect of relative technology and training levels

units will alter their behavior depending on the location of other friendly units. For instance, artillery units will shift their fire off potentially critical targets if they are told that friendly units have moved into close proximity of the target location. Elaborate fire control plans depend upon all the unit leaders in the area knowing where they are at all times. Small units that have become lost have actually called artillery shells in on their own locations accidentally by giving their own position incorrectly. Both investment in technology and realistic training can help military forces overcome wartime friction. Accordingly, high levels of technology and training provide systematic advantages to a state at war. Figure 35 demonstrates this effect. The relationship between increased relative spending is shown as we move from left to right across the x-axis, the ratio of Side A's spending to Side B's. The effect appears to be quite small for small changes in the spending ratio, and large for large changes.

Be aware that the scale from left to right is not linear in nature. The intervals change as the spending ratio rises, and this is what accounts for the apparent jump in returns on spending near the 5:1 area. If the scale were a linear one, the effect would appear linear as well. The more a state spends on its forces compared to its opponent, the greater that state's chances of victory. The effect is dramatic and quite certain as the tables in chapter 5 demonstrate. Most analysts agree that technology is a critical, and historic factor in determining war outcomes.

The military advantages of the politically constrained choice to invest in technology and training is not just a contemporary phenomenon. The role of technology and wealth emerged early on in the history of organized warfare. William McNeill argues that levels of training and logistical sophistication were important contributors to war outcomes from the beginning of organized warfare. He also maintains that "technology and economics were . . . subordinate to politics, not vice versa" (McNeill 1988, 8). Political decisions tend to drive technological innovation in that they allow for the concentration of economic wealth that facilitates technological advances. McNeill cites the development of the catapult in 399 B.C. in Syracuse. The politicians at the time gathered the cream of the area's crop of skilled workers, paid them high wages and offered large bonuses for practical innovations. As a result, according to contemporary historians, this concentration of wealth and talent was responsible for the development of the most technologically advanced engines of war to date. These siege engines led to the decline of the fortified defense (McNeill 1988, 8–9).

Returning to the example of the troops navigating in the desert, in this instance, high technology can help solve the problem. During the Gulf War against Iraq in 1991, U.S. tankers and special operations units used global positioning system satellites to estimate their position on the ground far more accurately than they could have without the equipment. Beyond land navigation, technology can play a role simply in locating one's opponents. In the same war, U.S. tank gunners were able to locate and engage Iraqi tanks before the Iraqi gunners could even see the U.S. tanks. The Iraqi tank commanders and gunners were forced to rely on outdated passive infrared sighting systems. These sights require secondary illumination of the target for maximum efficiency. The U.S. tanks carried highly advanced active thermal sights that amplify the relative radiant heat of the objects in front of the tank. This tremendous advantage resulted from the relative technological disparities between the United States' thermal-based sighting system and the Iraqi's Soviet-supplied infrared sighting system.

Not all analysts agree on the role technology plays in determining outcomes, however. Mary Kaldor is representative of a small but vocal minority that is highly critical of the argument that increased technology improves military efficiency. Kaldor and others argue that, on the contrary, the increased costs of more sophisticated weapons do not correlate with higher performance, rather, they become a significant handicap on a state's ability to wage war (York 1970). She argues that

. . . cost and complexity become military handicaps: sophisticated weapons are difficult to handle; they go wrong; they need thousands of spare parts; they absorb funds that could otherwise be used for training, pay, ammunition, etc. (Kaldor 1981, 5)

Kaldor is certainly correct in arguing that high-technology (relative to the time period) weapons hold little advantage for soldiers not sufficiently trained in the complexities of operating sophisticated equipment. Realistic training, although shockingly expensive,[4] can make the difference between stochastic failure and controlled success. Practicing combat standard operating procedures (SOPs) over and over during peacetime will reduce the likelihood of random failures under the pressure of combat. A brief example illustrates the potential benefits of rigorous and realistic training. A tank platoon leader must be able to talk over and monitor at the same time at least three separate radio networks (platoon, company, and battalion) through his headset; communicate to the tank's crew on the tank's internal intercom system; maintain visual contact with both the platoon's tanks and the nearest vehicles of the adjacent unit; keep an eye out for possible airplanes overhead; visually identify enemy targets, control the gunner, loader, and driver of his own tank; and aim and fire at least one machine gun—all while keeping track of the unit's position on a map, monitoring the current time, and calling in to higher units on the radio as his vehicle passes over various checkpoints on the ground at speeds up to 40 miles per hour. Add to this mixture the possibility that an opponent might open fire at our overstressed lieutenant and it becomes apparent that events can easily spin out of control. As you can see, there are likely to be many, many things all happening simultaneously; all mutually dependent on the performance of the others moving around him. Only with frequent and realistic training can individuals hope to be able to perform all these tasks and others with a high degree of reliability.

Kaldor extends her theoretical argument regarding the potential combat disadvantages resulting from technological advantage to the comparative case of the United States and the Soviet Union. She feels that the relative backwardness of Soviet weapons would have been an advantage to Soviet soldiers in a confrontation pitting the two forces against each other. The logic behind this assertion rests on the assumption that simplicity, ruggedness, and reliability dictate efficiency (Kaldor 1981, 224). Just the opposite turned out to be the case in the war in Iraq in 1991. Technology and training were critical elements in the American attempt first to achieve air superiority and then to gain dominance on the ground.

Of course, many states do not have the money to acquire the latest technology. Powerful domestic constraints may limit states' ability to maximize their power relative to potential opponents. Military spending comes at the expense of some other part of a state's budget, something that realists tend to ignore. At the same time, there have been instances where technologically backward states have fought more sophisticated opponents to a draw. The confrontation between the United States and China in the Korean War is an example. China was at a technological disadvantage relative to the United States, but many argue that China was powerful, not because of her troops' technological edge, or lack thereof, but because of the enormous population base from which China could draw her troops. It is important not to draw erroneous inferences from searching for monocausal relationships between a particular variable and outcomes. Technology, like the other factors identified and discussed here, is just one of many variables that influence the outcomes of war. Identifying an imbalance in one variable alone cannot account for the outcomes or demonstrations of state power we are trying to understand.

Domestic Political Factors

Repression

To this point, we have essentially investigated strictly military factors—variables that realists would agree are or should be critical to understanding war and international politics. In many of the instances discussed, I have briefly identified ways in which domestic politics have an indirect effect on outcomes by providing a constraint on a state's ability to maximize its wartime performance. Military spending comes to mind as an example. In addition to these indirect effects, however, there is a domestic political choice that I will show next has a powerful effect on outcomes. That choice is whether or not to repress domestic opposition to the war.

Figure 36 shows the effect of a state's choice to repress the opposition during a war. Moving from the left, where states repress the most and the probability of victory is expected to be over 60 percent, to the right where repression is absent, we see the probability of victory drop to just over 20 percent. States that choose to violently repress any opposition to the war effort almost triple their chances of victory compared to states that do not repress. This is a powerful factor in the waging of war, and something that is not anticipated in the realist paradigm. While the average effect of repression is small compared to other factors (as shown

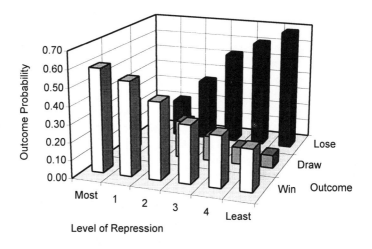

Fig. 36. The effect of political repression on war outcomes

in figure 28), we see in figure 36 that the possible effect is greater than the historically observed average. Leaders face powerful incentives to repress the dissenting segments of their state's mass public during war. Of course, we do not always see this type of behavior. While prolonged fighting leads to costs being incurred by the warring states, over time deaths mount, and opposition may begin to appear even in states fighting what may have been popular wars at the outset. Dissent against a war provides a direct challenge to the legitimacy of the state.

As Machiavelli and others have argued, even what would be coded in the data set as very low levels of repression can be quite effective during periods of conflict. The laws passed in the United States during World War I were particularly harsh in their penalties. While the U.S. involvement in the European war was somewhat limited, there was initially strong domestic opposition to the war effort. Trying to suppress the dissenting voices, "in 1917 Congress passed the Espionage Act which provided imprisonment of up to 20 years for persons who willfully made false reports to aid the enemy or obstructed the operation of the military draft" (Stohl 1976, 92). In a section of the law dealing with the U.S. mail, the postmaster general was empowered by Congress to block groups from using the mail system, which in his opinion advocated treason, insurrection, or forcible resistance to the laws of the United States. Arthur Link asserts that "in effect the Espionage Act became a tool to stamp out dissent and radical, but never conservative criticism" (Link 1967, 210). This act was followed by the

Sedition Act of 1918, which forbade any language intended to obstruct the war effort (Stohl 1976, 92).

The Korean War appears to be an excellent example of consensus through crackdown. Like the War of 1812, the Korean War generated one flash of opposition. This took place in the form of an enormous rally in New York City, which authorities put down viciously, violently, and quickly. Little dissent followed, which was not particularly surprising given that the war started during what some scholars characterize as the period of greatest peacetime repression the United States has ever experienced (under McCarthyism) (Stohl 1976, 94).

One of the problems of the gradual loss of political trust or legitimacy evidenced by popular protest against a war is that the loss tends to feed upon itself. By taking some action that erodes the political trust of the mass public, decision makers incrementally lose the ability to act to regain the trust without the prior consent of the mass public. As the mass public becomes more skeptical of possible state actions directed toward them, seeing the policies simply as vehicles to restore trust in the government, the government becomes further constrained in its ability to act. As a result, there are tremendous incentives to repress any initial vocalizations of loss of legitimacy or lack of trust on the mass public's part. Distrust tends to breed more distrust (Gamson 1968, 45).

While the data appear to be supported by anecdotal historical evidence, for example, that repression tends to help a state's war efforts, there is a powerful alternative explanation to the one just presented. The correlation between repression and outcomes might be the result not of how it affects the process of waging war but rather of the decision-making process that leads to states beginning wars in the first place. Highly repressive regimes may simply choose to fight in wars where the chances for victory are objectively high and where there may be large potential domestic political gains to the repressive elites if the state pulls off a quick victory. Similarly, leaders who cannot suppress opposition over the long haul (democracies) will be acutely aware of the postwar domestic costs of losing (Bueno de Mesquita and Siverson 1995). As a result, they too will be less likely to become involved in highly risky wars. This possibility will be investigated in greater detail in the next chapter when I demonstrate the effect of institutional democracy on outcomes.

The empirical evidence presented in this chapter suggests that states can increase their probability of winning an interstate war by increasing their level of political repression. There is anecdotal evidence that they do so to a limited degree. The Red Army Air Corps failed to learn from the Spanish Civil War and the German defeat of Poland. Stalin's failure to integrate the new strategies his generals developed resulted in the devastating losses the Soviet army suffered during the summer and fall of 1941 at the hands of the Germans. In the absence of domestic political repression to quell any and all anti-war dissent, it is possible that the Soviet mass publics would have revolted in World War II just as they had in World War I. This in turn might have led to equally disastrous results for Stalin as the Russian October Revolution had held for the Romanovs.

Where might these findings about repression fit into the international relations literature? Using the typical realist assumption that states prefer winning over losing, then we would reasonably expect to see states repressing their populations as much as possible in order to maximize their chances of victory. According to the standard assumptions of realists and neorealists, states will take the steps necessary to maximize their power or security. During an interstate war it seems difficult to interpret that assumption in any way other than that states should therefore maximize the factors at their disposal that would increase their chances of victory. If this were true, then we would expect to see states repressing their mass publics as much as possible. Typically, this is not the case. While the degree of political repression in the United States or in Britain during their wars in the twentieth century might surprise some readers, those states and most others did not pursue the most repressive policies possible. The degree of political repression in the United States paled in comparison to that in the Soviet Union or in Nazi Germany. How can we account for this seeming contradiction in the motivations of states and the behavior that we observe? The answer lies in the complex relationship between democracy, repression, and legitimacy.

If a democracy represses dissenting groups, the legitimacy of the liberal state falls into question, almost by definition. "To try to force people to embrace something that is believed to be good and glorious but which they do not actually want, even though they may be expected to like it when they experience its results is the very mark of anti-democratic belief" (Lindsay 1943, 45). Legitimacy is therefore the political system's ability to engender and maintain the belief that the existing political institutions are the most appropriate ones for the society (Lipset 1960, 78). The ability to maintain legitimacy in the face of open dissent frequently results in violent repression of the opposition.

This brings us to the end of the discussion of the factors that political or military leaders have direct control over and the choices that they must face either immediately prior to or during war. We have seen that most of the factors that realists advocate as being important to understanding war and international politics are in fact quite important. In the case of alliances and the number of troops, however, the relationships in question are not as simple and clear-cut as realists typically maintain. The final factor discussed, political repression, lies outside the realist model and may prove to be a controversial finding; I will return to it again in the next chapter. Chapter 7 continues in the same way as chapter 6 began. Rather than looking at the choices leaders must make, chapter 7 investigates the role that resources and political institutions play in outcomes. We will see that these factors are every bit as important as those identified in this chapter.

CHAPTER 7

Resources and Institutional Constraints

Waging war is a fantastically expensive business, both in terms of the actual dollar cost and the lives spent. The Gulf War in 1991 cost the United States and its allies over $40 billion, almost a billion dollars per day. The ability to deliver well-trained and equipped soldiers to distant places is one of the basic components of state power. There are several other factors that also serve as resources which may limit or constrain the choices that leaders must make in one direction or another.

Aside from the choices that leaders must make either in their preparation for war or during the actual fight itself, the resources at the state's disposal play a critical role in determining who will win and who will lose. While states' leaders may be able to choose how to fight or whether or not to repress their domestic opposition, they cannot choose the industrial and human raw materials they will be fighting with. Typically industrial and military resources that leaders have at their disposal were either earned or developed far before a particular war began. Traditionally, the currency of power has been counted in terms of wealth and manpower. In the previous chapter, we investigated the effects of the choices themselves that confront leaders. In this chapter, I will present the results of the analyses of the role that resources and political structure play—the factors that are fixed, at least in the short run, but which can have a powerful effect on who wins and who loses.

National Capabilities

While technology, training, and politics are considered important factors in the analysis of war and security studies, national capability (frequently equated with power) broadly defined, is probably the most discussed factor of all. This is the variable that realists and many others focus on almost entirely. According to realists, "power is a function of military capabilities" (Kegley and Raymond 1990, 187). Figure 37 demonstrates the effect of a state's relative national capability, as measured by the Correlates of War (COW) composite capabilities index, in determining a war's outcome.[1] I generated this figure and those that follow in

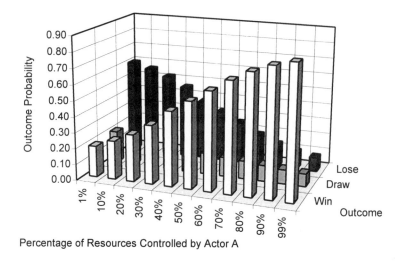

Percentage of Resources Controlled by Actor A

Fig. 37. The effect of relative military-industrial capabilities on war outcomes

the same way as I did the figures in chapter 6. To quickly review, I hold the remaining factors (strategy, troops, population, repression, etc.) constant, and then I allow the factor in question to vary from its observed minimum to its observed maximum, and for each change in the factor in question I calculated the predicted outcome probabilities. These probabilities can be seen in the figures in this chapter.

The most standard indicator of outcomes, national capabilities, has what might be best described as results that match the conventional wisdom regarding power. The relationship between industrial capabilities and the likelihood of winning is monotonic as many have hypothesized. These findings corroborate those in Organski and Kugler's *The War Ledger* and the majority of the standard works on power and military force.

Reading figure 37, as we move from left to right on the *x*-axis, the capabilities of the state in question range from one percent to 99 percent of the combined industrial and military capabilities of the two sides in the war. When a state controls a very small share of the resources available to the two sides in a war, its chance of victory is quite low, as our intuition tells us it should be. As the state's share of the resources rises, so too does its chances of victory. This rise in the likelihood of victory is steady and monotonic, the rate of increase only beginning to decline after a state controls almost 80 percent of the resources available to the two sides. While more is never less, at least with regard to industrial capability, after a certain point more resources provide diminishing returns. This too should not come as a surprise. After some point it becomes increasingly difficult to mobilize and extract the resources of a state for the purpose of waging war.

In some circumstances the ability to produce the tools of war are more important than in others. In a war between industrial powers, slow and steady attrition can be compensated for by increased industrial output. The destruction of war matériel may or may not be a critical component influencing the timing and outcome of the war's end. States that can replace destroyed equipment typically are at an advantage over those that cannot. As H. A. Calahan points out:

> (t)hings wear out with astounding rapidity in a war. The average life of a shovel, for instance is about one day. On a farm in peacetime a shovel lasts three generations. The quantities of war materials left behind in a swift retreat are simply unbelievable. We find that the ability to replace expended materials is always essential to victory. (Calahan 1944, 233)

While most scholars and practitioners would not find anything surprising in the results in figure 37, Maoz, along with a few dissenters from the conventional wisdom, has questioned the validity of the assumption that capabilities and outcomes should be so directly linked. It is interesting to note that Maoz sees that many of the individual factors that have been implicated in war outcomes do not have an intuitive effect and that in many instances the conventional wisdom about factors such as surprise and alliance contributions may be somewhat misguided. Maoz then concludes, erroneously I believe, that the widely anticipated monotonic relationship between "the control of resources and the control of outcomes is either weak or non-existent" (Maoz 1990, 232). I would argue just the opposite, both for theoretical reasons outlined in earlier chapters and because of the strong empirical support demonstrated here.

Population

While industrial capabilities are correctly viewed as an important factor in determining war outcomes, so too has population been considered. You will recall from the hypotheses chapters that there are potential reasons why the same relationship observed between military and industrial capabilities and outcomes may not be seen between population and

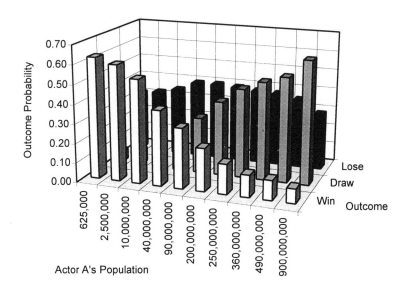

Fig. 38. The effect of actors' population on war outcomes

outcomes. While it is true that people are necessary in order to wage war, never have states mobilized more than 12 percent of their total population for a war. More typically, mobilization rates average in the area of 1 to 2 percent. At this level, the effect of a state's population is largely irrelevant as a constraint on the state's ability to generate soldiers. On the other hand, as hypothesized, it turns out that as a state's population rises, the gains from victory become more and more diffuse at the individual level.

Figure 38 represents the relative effect of population on outcomes. Moving from left to right on the x-axis, the population of the state in question is allowed to rise from 625,000 to 900 million. As the population increases, we observe a decline in the likelihood of victory. What increases monotonically is the likelihood of a draw emerging. Initially (up to a population of 40 million) the probability of loss increases as the probability of victory drops. Eventually though, both victory and loss become more unlikely as the probability of observing a draw increases dramatically.

We should remember that there are many other factors that tend to correlate with population that are being controlled for while we make these changes.[2] The number of soldiers is being held constant as is the industrial capacity of the state in question. If I had operationalized population as a ratio, the more expected pattern would have emerged, when having a larger population than one's opponent is an advantage. This chart shows the way in which the expected benefits of victory decline on a per capita basis as the population increases. As a result, the state's willingness to stay in the war wanes, hence the rise in the probability of a draw. The next indicator to investigate is the distance that separates the two warring sides.

Distance

> It takes twenty pounds of provisions to deliver one pound of provisions to a distant army.
>
> —Sun Tzu

Sun Tzu, in his short pamphlet *The Art of War*, observes a problem that has faced militaries throughout time. Simply moving men and matériel to a distant land requires resources that might otherwise have been used in the fight itself. While Sun Tzu does not argue that fighting distant opponents will lead to failure, he cautions leaders to be aware of the potentially draining effects of traveling to fight in distant battles. Recall from chapter 3 the discussion of Bueno de Mesquita's more recent arguments about the effect of distance. In *The War Trap*, Bueno de Mesquita argues that distance should have a powerful effect on the outcomes of war for a wide variety of reasons, ranging from organizational problems to morale and adaptation. While many of the factors he identifies, such as the issue being fought over and the political system of the warring states, have been controlled for using other variables, the organizational problem is omitted as a separate independent variable and is tested here. Even with controls for most of the factors Bueno de Mesquita highlights there is still an independent effect of distance on the observed outcomes. Figure 39 shows the direct effect of distance on the war's likely outcome.

Moving from left to right, the distance increases from a state fighting a war on its own border (at the far left of the *x*-axis) to a state attempting to project its military power 13,000 miles from its capital. The effects of distance are clear-cut. The farther away from a state that its leaders choose to fight, the greater the chance of incurring a loss. This does not affect the chance of observing a draw. Typically, the farther from home that one side is fighting, the closer to the front the other side is. As a result, we could have reasonably expected that the relationship between victory, loss, and distance would be largely zero-sum, as we observe in figure 39.

Clearly, distance matters a great deal. On average, states have a difficult time projecting their power much farther than approximately

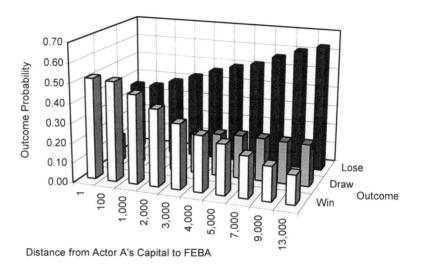

Fig. 39. The average effect of distance on war outcomes

500 miles away from their capital, at which point their chances of victory appear to drop off quite quickly. While anticipating these findings, Bueno de Mesquita also argued that the component that affects outcomes resulting from organization and command and control problems should affect large, powerful states in a different way than smaller, weaker states. According to Bueno de Mesquita, powerful, wealthy states can develop means by which they can more effectively project their power and overcome the effects of distance. During the Gulf War, for instance, the United States made effective use of its Diego Garcia military air bases in the Indian Ocean in its attacks on Iraqi ground positions. Smaller states simply do not have these types of resources.

We can test this argument by changing the capabilities of the states in the data set as well as allowing the distance to vary. If we, in effect, make all the states we use for the predictions powerful states, we can then see the effect of distance on more powerful states. I do this by changing the industrial capabilities variable from the observed values to 90 percent for all cases. I then follow the standard procedure for generating the outcome predictions by allowing the distance to change as before.

In figure 40, the presentation is the same as in figure 39, but the results are quite a bit different because now all states are, for demonstration purposes, powerful in the sense that they control a large proportion of the two sides' capabilities (90 percent). Moving from left to right

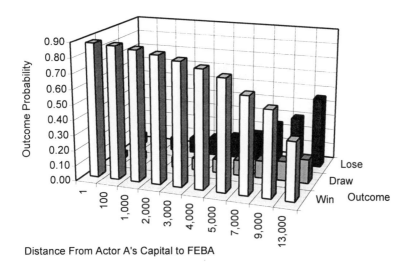

Distance From Actor A's Capital to FEBA

Fig. 40. The effect of distance on war outcomes for powerful states

across the chart (closer to more distant battles), we still see a monotonic decline in the chances of victory as the state is fighting farther and farther from its home borders. But the point at which the decline becomes precipitous comes much later for powerful states (fig. 40) than for weaker states. For typical states (fig. 39), their power or ability to win in war starts to fall off almost immediately (literally any distance beyond their immediate borders) as they attempt to project their forces farther and farther from their borders. In contrast, powerful states do not begin to suffer the effects of distance until the fighting is over 3,000 miles away. After moving past 5,000 miles, the powerful state's chance of victory begins to decline dramatically. Even powerful states succumb to the effects, however, when the distances they are trying to cover exceed 10,000 miles.

Terrain

In a somewhat similar vein to distance, the effects of terrain are something that leaders have little choice over. While it is true that decision makers can choose not to wage wars or perhaps try to choose the location within the borders of the area in which they are fighting, for the most part, terrain, like distance, is something that is set by the geography at hand. Countries do not get to choose where on the globe they are located (otherwise we might all live in northern Maine). Similarly, state

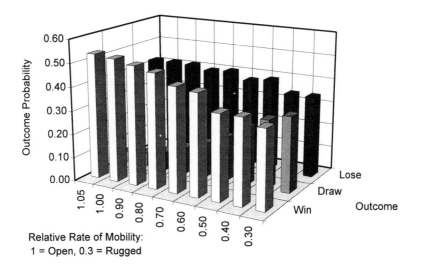

Fig. 41. The effect of terrain on war outcomes

leaders do not get to choose the terrain that is most common in their country. While almost all countries have some open terrain, some are more mountainous or covered by jungles than others. Terrain does differ from distance in an important sense as we shall see in the next section. Unlike distance, terrain tends to affect both sides in a similar way. In other words, both sides must fight on the same ground, for the most part. While distance tends to be a zero-sum variable, increasing for one side as it decreases for the other, terrain acts as a powerful factor on both sides almost simultaneously. As a result the chart will look somewhat different than the previous ones that demonstrated the effects of distance.

In figure 41 we can see the effects of difficult terrain on waging war. In this figure, on the far left (mobility scores around 1.0) are the types of terrain that offer the greatest mobility—deserts and open farmland. Moving to the right, as the mobility index declines toward 0.30 from an observed high of 1.05, the actors' ability to move their men and equipment declines. At the far right, with a low mobility score, are situations such as highly mountainous regions, jungles, and swamps. The results tell us that in situations where the two sides will be able to move their troops easily (the far left side of the chart), the outcome is likely to be decisive. The side in question will probably either win or lose. We will not expect to see draws occurring in locations where the two sides can move their matériel and men quickly and easily. As mobility declines, however, the chances of a decisive outcome (either victory or loss) begin to decline. What is increasing as the terrain underfoot begins to slow progress? The likelihood of draws occurring rises monotonically as the terrain becomes more rugged. When fighting in extreme terrain, holding other factors constant, draws become as likely as any other outcome, an effect many political leaders seem to be willing to ignore or operate in ignorance of.

Terrain affects outcomes both directly and indirectly. In addition to simply slowing the pace of a war, terrain, along with several other factors, may affect a state's ability to execute its preferred choice of military strategy. Strategies predicated on movement are vulnerable to the terrain upon which they are to be executed. For example, open terrain is anathema to the guerrilla warrior. Conversely, Posen (1984) and Mearsheimer (1983) argue that the wide-open terrain in Eastern Europe, in combination with blitzkrieg strategies, is deadly.

A maneuver strategy is predicated on the ability to move quickly and easily. As the data show, one factor that constrains an actor's ability to move its troops and other military resources easily is the terrain upon which a war is fought. While Blainey tried to debunk the notion that terrain determines the outcomes of wars, we see here that this is not necessarily so (Blainey 1973). In fact, in instances where mobility ceases (jungles, steep mountains, and swamps), the likelihood of either side being able to secure a victory declines precipitously. In the extreme, where neither actor would be able to move its troops well, draws become much more likely than they are in wide-open terrain. In areas where mobility ceases, states can fight defensive attrition or punishment strategies without much fear of suffering casualties. In the areas that limit mobility, mountains and jungles, states can hide soldiers and equipment easily. Wars fought in terrain such as this may last for long periods of time, reflecting the difficulty that the two sides will have simply in finding and fixing each other's troops.

This discussion of the interaction of strategy and terrain brings us to the end of the factors that roughly fall into the realpolitik school. The next section begins with institutional democracy, a decidedly domestic political factor. In chapter 6, we investigated the realpolitik and domestic political choices that states had to make during or when preparing to wage war. Just as there are realpolitik factors that serve as resources or constraints on behavior that decision makers do not get to choose, there are also ones that realists would have us ignore or at least treat as clearly less important in the analysis of international conflict. While institutional democracy may appear or disappear over time in a state, in the short run leaders do not get to choose to enjoy the advantages of governing a democratic state. In a similar vein, leaders of democratic states do not typically get to choose or wish away some of the political constraints placed upon them by the checks and balances inherent in democratic systems. In the next section, I will explore the effect of a state's political system on outcomes.

Domestic Political Factors

Democratization

In the last few years, democracy and its relationship to war has been a topic of much interest to both international relations scholars and in comparative politics as the states of Eastern Europe democratize. Rummel (1985), Russett (1990) and others have shown convincingly that there is a strong empirical relationship between the level of democratization and the types of wars and militarized disputes states become involved in. Specifically, Russett and others maintain that democracies simply do not fight democracies. The causal reason for this has been far more difficult to demonstrate to the satisfaction of the security field. Others argue that the finding is simply a spurious one, resulting from the fact that the vast majority of democracies during the postwar period have been allies or have shared many common interests that would buffer any disputes (Farber and Gowa 1995). Maoz and Russett argue that the reason for the lack of wars between democracies has to do with the domestic norms of conflict resolution (Maoz and Russett, 1993).

Another argument can be made to explain the democratic peace as well. If democracies are better able to wage war, both in terms of the wars they select and the ways in which they fight them, then it would be logical to conclude that a war between two committed democracies would be highly costly to both sides, with the likely gains from victory being ephemeral. Limited empirical support for this position can be found in figure 42 This figure supports a rational explanation of the democratic peace, at least in the sense of rational choice approaches to conflict study.

As we can see in figure 42, democratic states stand a better chance of victory than strongly authoritarian states. In terms of the theory, they are more effective at absorbing punishment and inflicting costs. Looking at the graph, as we move from left to right across the x-axis, the level of democracy in the state in question rises from its minimum to its maximum. Typical states that are not considered democracies would be Libya or most countries in the nineteenth century. The most highly ranked democracies include the United States and the Western European states

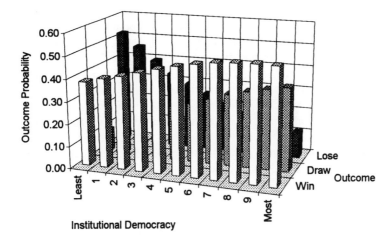

Fig. 42. The effect of institutional democracy on war outcomes

after World War II. What we see is that more democratic states are more likely to win than nondemocratic states; democracies are also more likely to be involved in draws. The decrease in the probability of losing as a state becomes more democratic is greater than the increase in the chances of victory. The difference results from the rise in the chance of a draw occurring as the state in question is more and more democratic. Note also though, that with regard to victory, increases in institutional democracy are subject to declining marginal returns. This is not the case relative to losses though.

There are several possible explanations for this correlation. First, more democratic states may be more likely to win in part as a result of a greater sense of legitimacy surrounding the government's decisions. Second, mass publics may feel that they are more likely to share in the returns from victory. This second explanation may also help account for the increase in the likelihood of draws occurring. If the mass publics (the people that bear the largest burden of fighting) are directly involved in the decision making or can sanction those who make the decisions during a war, then these types of states may be more willing to compromise in wars that appear to be dragging on for an eternity. Finally, as Bueno de Mesquita and Siverson (1995) argue, democratic states may simply choose different types of wars to become involved in than will nondemocracies.

Assuming that the correlation is not just an artifact of the war selection process, this may prove to be an important finding in that it may affect the likelihood of democracies going to war with each other. If the two sides are able to anticipate their opponent being able to absorb almost limitless losses and anticipate the same on their own side, then the leaders may decide that they would be better off negotiating a solution than resorting to the use of force. These findings are also interesting in light of the early thinking about democracy, in which it was generally assumed that democracies would be largely impotent in foreign affairs.

The effects of democracy are particularly interesting given the similar effects of political repression.[3] To begin to test one explanation of the observed effect of democracy (the selection effect) we can look both at the length of wars and also at the likelihood of victory while controlling for initiation (something accomplished in the regression results through the doctrine codings). Both democracy and repression are associated with shorter wars on average. War between highly repressive regimes typically would be fifteen months shorter than a war involving moderately repressive regimes, while we expect a twenty-one month difference between wars involving moderately democratic states and wars between states without democratic institutions.[4]

Some additional evidence that helps to sort out the argument over whether democracies are more likely to win because they fight better or because they simply pick easier wars can be obtained by examining the average duration of the wars that highly democratic or repressive states initiated (selected) versus the wars that they did not initiate. The average length of wars initiated by highly democratic states was 9.2 months, while the average of those that they did not initiate but did participate in was 16.7 months. Wars initiated by highly repressive (risk-acceptant) states lasted 11.8 months on average, while wars that they did not initiate but did participate in lasted eighteen months. Grouping the two extreme types of states together, the average duration of wars started by either highly democratic or highly repressive states was 11.2 months. Wars initiated by states that were neither highly democratic nor repressive lasted an average of 22.4 months, suggesting that the selection argument has strong merit (the difference is significant at the 0.02 level).[5] We can take a cut at the auxiliary question of whether risk aversion and risk acceptance are driving these initiation decisions by looking at the wars' outcomes.

If the risk argument holds, we would expect risk-averse, highly democratic states to pick easy, short wars, which they should win frequently. These expectations are strongly supported by the data. Highly democratic states won ten of the twelve wars they initiated, or 83 percent. While these results are far from conclusive, they point strongly in the direction of the selection bias arguments of Bueno de Mesquita and

Siverson (1995). Looking at the wars which highly democratic states did not initiate, we find they too win more than they lose, although the relationship is not nearly so strong. Of the wars that democracies became involved in but did not initiate, they still won 60 percent of them. This tends to provide support for the legitimacy argument as well. Even in the cases where the selection argument is weakest (wars that democracies do not initiate), democracy appears to provide an advantage. Clearly, the selection argument has strong support, but it does not account for all of the data. In addition to the decisions that lead to war, something takes place in the process of fighting in which democracies fair better than nondemocracies.

A corollary to the legitimacy argument—that democracies fight better and harder because the state enjoys greater legitimacy than nondemocracies—is an extension of the Condorcet jury theorem. Condorcet showed that, on average, decisions made by groups tend to be of higher quality than choices made by individuals. Group decisions are less likely to be high-risk, low-payoff choices. While this argument fits with the selection process position of Bueno de Mesquita, the point may hold during war as well. If democratic states choose better leaders to fight their wars and these better leaders make better decisions during wars, then we can easily understand the finding that democracies do indeed perform better. Unfortunately, this is an area where much further research is required. The somewhat crude measures employed here do not allow for detailed sifting out of the possible explanations for the empirical findings.

Given the interesting results for both the repression and democracy measures, a number of potentially paradoxical deductions follow. For example, democracy may also serve to constrain states' chances of victory as well as increasing them. Recall the findings for political repression. Logically, we might expect the strongest states to be democracies that also powerfully repress their mass publics during wartime. Being able to do so would appear to allow democratic leaders to "have their cake and eat it too," or be able to enjoy the effects of democracy—higher legitimacy and better decision making—and the benefits of repression—reduced dissent. But this is not the case. Democratic leaders are constrained in their domestic options due to the ability of mass publics to sanction their behavior through the ballot box. Bueno de Mesquita and Siverson (1995) have shown that democratic leaders who raise the costs to society by engaging in long duration wars are very likely to be removed from office. Similarly, democratic leaders who strongly repressed citizens would not likely get the chance to do so a second time.

While we never observe high repression scores in democratic states, this is not to say that even without government repression there cannot be strong incentives for dissenters in democracies to remain silent and fearful of the tyranny of the majority thereby confering, indirectly, the benefits of repression to the seemingly open democratic state. For example, in a speech given on July 26, 1918, Woodrow Wilson gave a rationale for antimob violence. Wilson was a harsh critic of those who protested against U.S. involvement in World War I. In his speech, we see the roots of democratic tyranny anticipated by Tocqueville, who argued that even in a democratic state, dissenters would be rare, and those who did dissent from the majority would be actively ostracized:

> We proudly claim to be the champions of democracy. If we really are, in deed and in truth, let us see to it that we do not discredit our own. I say plainly that every American who takes part in the action of a mob or gives support and countenance to them is no true son of this great democracy, but its betrayer. . . . I therefore very earnestly and solemnly beg the governors of all states, the law officers of every community, and, above all, the men and women of every community in the United States, all who revere America and wish to keep her name without stain or reproach, to make an end of this disgraceful evil, (but) not passively, merely, but actively and watchfully. It cannot live here where the community does not countenance to it. (Wilson 1918, 4)

During the months prior to his speech, the U.S. government had been actively prosecuting those who spoke against the war or mass conscription. On April 24, 1918, (four months prior to the Wilson speech), the *N.Y. Evening Post* carried the following in a statement from the Department of Justice:

> On charges of interfering with operation of the draft, 3,465 persons have been convicted or have pleaded guilty, and 181 have been acquitted. Under the Espionage Act, which has been stretched to cover many varying cases of disloyalty, there have been 226 convictions and 17 acquittals. Under the general war statutes, 228 have been convicted and 89 acquitted. (Wilson 1918)

The records of the Department of Justice on June 8, 1918, showed a total of 1,180 persons prosecuted under the Espionage Act. So while democratic states are restrained from using the powerful tool of harsh repression, they still are able to manipulate dissent during wartime, perhaps giving them an advantage over the long haul of a war.

One of the reasons that individuals and groups of individuals choose to dissent from supporting a war effort is that they may feel that the costs of fighting in the war, either for themselves as individuals or for the country as a whole, cannot be compensated for by the potential gains of victory. The notion of gains is something we have not addressed a great deal. For the most part, I have concentrated my analysis on the costs of war and how those costs can be imposed, accounted for, dissipated, or defended against. Reasons for this can be found in the earlier theoretical chapters of this book. This is not to say that the benefits will not have an effect on the outcome. Rather, the issues at stake may be less likely to have observable effects compared to the other more easily measured factors. In the next section, I explore the empirical relationship between the issues at stake and the outcomes of wars.

Issue Area

The notion of issue area is a relational one, much as strategy is. In one war, the two sides may be fighting for two very different things. Both sides may be fighting for different gains and may be facing drastically different downside losses. During the war in Vietnam, the North Vietnamese and the Viet Cong executed a guerrilla strategy for fighting the war. In the war against the United States, the Vietnamese could not have doubted the industrial superiority of the United States. More likely, it was something to be taken for granted. This assumption about the relative physical capabilities forced the Vietnamese to assume a guerrilla posture for the majority of the war. The essential assumption of the guerrilla or punishment strategy is that it is designed for a struggle in which the protagonist is fighting a materially stronger opponent. As described by Rosen,

> [t]he basic idea is that the regime has the guns, but the guerrillas have the hearts of the people. The guerrilla's superiority is not his ability to harm, but in his greater willingness to be harmed. Ho Chi Minh formulated this in a classic way with his familiar prediction that "In the end, the Americans will have killed ten of us for every American soldier who died, but it is they who will tire first." (Rosen 1972, 256)

Rosen evokes a similar example in the case of the French-Algerian struggle in North Africa, where the ratio of deaths was roughly 10:1 against the Algerians, who, according to Rosen's and Ho Chi Minh's logic, nevertheless valued a favorable outcome far more than the French

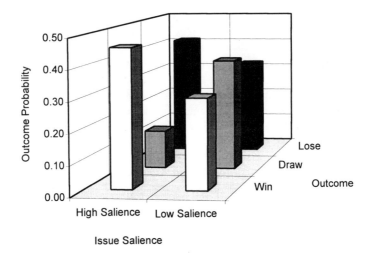

Fig. 43. The effect of issue salience on war outcomes

did and so were willing to suffer far greater casualties. The French suffered a similar defeat against the Vietnamese in their debacle at Dien Bien Phu. Rosen argues that it was not so much the actual casualties suffered at Dien Bien Phu but rather the demonstration of the costs that the French would have to be willing to suffer in order to secure victory (Rosen 1972, 256). Lacking the political will to sustain the high rates of casualties, the French withdrew, to be replaced shortly thereafter by the Americans, who with their faith in their technological superiority felt that a different outcome could be obtained.

The other important factor that contributes to the outcome is the actor's ability to communicate the potential gains or benefits of the war to mass publics. The actor's resolve or willingness to bear the costs associated with fighting depends, to a great extent, on its ability to mobilize the population in support of the war for the duration of the conflict. As mentioned before, issue area, democratization, the ability to suppress dissent, and time all should figure into a mass population's willingness to support losses in pursuit of wartime victory.

Figure 43 shows similar effects when states are fighting over issues that do not directly affect the state's survival. We read the chart by again moving from left to right—from high-salience wars to low-salience wars—and observing the expected probability for each of the three outcomes. High-salience wars tend to be decisive wars. In these cases, note that the chance of a draw is very small. In the low-salience wars, the likelihood of both victory and loss drops substantially, but now the likelihood of loss is marginally higher than the chance of victory. What has changed dramatically is the likelihood of a draw occurring. In low-stakes wars, draws are very likely to be observed; decisive victories become quite rare.

In figure 43, the issue at stake in the low-salience wars for the state in question is related to empire-building or maintenance, or situations involving a particular government policy. All other issues are coded as high salience. For example, the issue at stake for the United States during the Vietnam War was a policy issue, the containment of Communism, which though important was of low salience compared to wars fought for territorial integrity or for the survival of a state's system of government (the stakes that the North Vietnamese were fighting for). The effect on a war's outcome of the two issues contained in the low-salience category is quite clear-cut. Other issues are likely to be more muddled in their effect. In wars fought over territory, for instance, whether or not the underlying stakes are tied to the survival of the regime or the state, the government's leaders will likely be able to convince some of the population that the issue is one of survival. In the case of wars fought over policy (to include reputation stakes) or empire assets, it may be almost impossible for even the most efficient governmental propaganda organs to convince the mass publics that their collective survival is at stake.

Where do these findings fit into the political science literature on issue area? William Potter conducted a review of the issue area literature and found little empirical work of merit that supports the issue area contentions made by either Zimmerman or Rosenau. "The few attempts at actual data analysis using substance-based issue area categories, moreover, have yielded very ambiguous results" (Potter 1980, 427). Potter reaches the conclusion that the solution lies in the data analysis technique and calls for focused comparison case studies. While I agree with Potter that the bulk of the issue area work has yielded few firm findings, I do not agree that the solution is to fall back to case studies. Rather, we simply need to hone our quantitative knives all the more sharply and collect more data so that we may see the distinctions between domestic structure and the issue at stake in conflict, areas that have been conflated to a large extent in other attempts to sort out these topics.

These empirical results, taken in combination with the findings on repression and democratic political institutions, help us sort out a basic question in the field of comparative foreign policy where there are two basic intellectual approaches. On one side of the coin are the scholars who envision that it is the differences in the domestic political structures that account for differences in foreign policy outcomes, war being just one possible type of foreign policy behavior. On the other side of the coin are those authors such as Zimmerman (1973) and Lowi (1964) who argue that domestic structure is not the key but rather it is the issue area at stake which will determine foreign policy outcomes. Rosenau, in his pretheory of international relations, incorporated both domestic politics (democratization, political repression) and issue area into a complex matrix (Evangelista 1989, 147). By controlling for both domestic structure and issue area in so far as they affect war outcomes, we can see that Rosenau was probably correct in maintaining that we need a sophisticated and detailed way to account for both issue area *and* political structure. I am not saying that for other realms of foreign policy the empirical results apply universally but rather that, within this limited area, I think I show that Rosenau's assertions were correct. This shows that both Katzenstein (in the domestic structure camp) and Zimmerman (issue area) may have focused their analytic lenses a bit too narrowly.

Zimmerman recognized the possible shortcomings of his approach in predictive or ex ante situations. As he pointed out, in many instances, states will attempt to escalate a conflict or convince their mass publics that the issue at stake is one close to the pole of power, where the survival of the state is in question. By doing so, the state would be able to raise the level of costs that would appear to be worth sustaining, while raising the apparent benefits of victory (Zimmerman 1973, 1209). This complicates the analysis a bit. Remember that rather than coding for instances where the survival of the state is at stake, I coded for the instances in which it would border on the impossible to make that argument. Cases in which the issue was a government policy, reputation, or empire expansions in which the benefits and therefore the means to achieve them were likely to be limited were controlled for. I could have tried to code instances where the state's survival was at stake, but making that judgment ex ante would be exceedingly difficult, and in most instances governments make that argument to their publics whether it is true or not, thereby depriving it of some of its substantive impact on the outcomes. By making the cut in the way I have here, Zimmerman's "Note in Search of a General Theory" has found some empirical support.

While the issue being fought over is of great importance in affecting the ability to mobilize popular support for the war, we must be aware that states will use propaganda to manipulate the perceived issue versus the actual one. Thinking back to figure 4, states manipulate mass public preceptions of the benefits bar's height. For example, during the latter parts of World War II, Germany and Japan had not won a single major engagement for over two years. But this had little effect on the resolve of the two states because of their careful use of propaganda. "As long as the Germans believe that New York has been heavily bombed, as long as the Japanese believe that their forces are holding Los Angeles, our minor but continued successes will be effective only against the higher command which, supposedly, is correctly informed" (Calahan 1944, 241).

Advances in communications technology has made it more difficult to hide information from a state's mass public, limiting the effectiveness of domestic propaganda such as that used to great effect by Japan and Germany. One result of this has been that the costs of limited war have become apparent in several cases. For example, while the Americans and the Soviets fought limited, low-salience wars in Vietnam and Afghanistan, respectively, their opponents were fighting total wars, as the Soviets did in World War II. The North Vietnamese population was completely mobilized as was the Mujahideen in Afghanistan. In fighting their total wars, the Vietnamese and the Afghans were prepared to bear far higher costs than were the superpowers they took on. By mobilizing their populations to such a great extent, the smaller countries were able to raise the costs of the wars for their opponents to levels that far outstripped any potential gains that the superpowers may have sought or could convince their respective mass publics to bear. In both cases, the smaller side fighting a total war had war aims beyond the limited objectives of their larger opponents. Because the smaller states fought a total war, with the gains or benefits from victory being enormous, rather than a limited one with concurrently smaller payoffs, the costs that could be sustained by the smaller states (relative to the potential gains) outstripped the costs that their opponents could bear.

President Kennedy endorsed the concept of the limited war when he authorized sending U.S. advisors to Vietnam. President Johnson continued the policy by refusing to raise the taxes of the citizens at home to pay for a war on the other side of the planet. At no time in the war with North Vietnam did the United States use all of its military capability. In contrast to World War II when the United States was on a wartime footing, complete with domestic food and fuel rationing and blackout curtains, during the Vietnam War, citizens at home never had to bear the burdens of the war taking place in Asia (aside from the loss of a small portion of the country's young men and women). The Soviets used a similar approach in Afghanistan, ironically with similar results. In both instances, the United States and the Soviet Union fought limited wars with limited objectives with limited means against opponents fighting general or total wars with all the capabilities and resources they could muster. Neither state ever brought its complete power to bear in the wars and neither side had the unconditional surrender of its opponent as an ultimate goal. The Soviet war aims in the Great Patriotic War stand in sharp contrast to their aims in Afghanistan. In World War II, the Soviets fought a total war with devastating costs for all involved. Soviet losses exceeded 20 million lives. In addition to fighting with a completely mobilized population, the Soviets' goal was complete and unconditional surrender by the Germans.

This discussion of issue salience raises the following puzzle: while states may be uncertain about their opponent's costs and potential gains before the war occurs, once fighting begins these will become more readily apparent. Why then are states willing to stay involved in wars for long periods when quick and decisive victory becomes an elusive goal?

One way in which wars are able to drag on over long periods of time, when the accumulated costs would appear to have far outstripped the anticipated gains at the outset of the war, is that states will change their aims during the war to reflect larger expected benefits from success. This may also account for the previous ambiguous findings regarding the role of issue area. By changing the expected payoffs via changing war aims, states are always able to keep the anticipated payoffs from success in the war greater than the anticipated costs. In this way, states will stay in the war as long as they have the ability to make their mass publics believe that the aims of the war will provide payoffs greater than the costs incurred. However, as the legitimacy of the state declines, the mass publics' perceptions of the net costs of fighting will become harder and harder to manipulate, and the state's ability to manipulate expected benefits from the war will decline. At the same time, costs will be rising steadily, increasing the likelihood that the state will eventually either succeed in winning the war or be forced to seek a settlement (Luttwak 1985, 58). But what accounts for the duration of a war? In the next section I discuss both the effect that time has on the outcomes of wars and also what accounts for some wars lasting longer than others.

Time

> When you do battle, even if you are winning, if you continue for a long time it will dull your forces and blunt your edge; if you besiege a citadel, your strength will be exhausted. If you keep your armies out in the field for a long time your supplies will be insufficient.
>
> —Sun Tzu

The passage of time necessarily results in increased costs for both sides in a war. This in turn leads to an increase in the likelihood of a draw

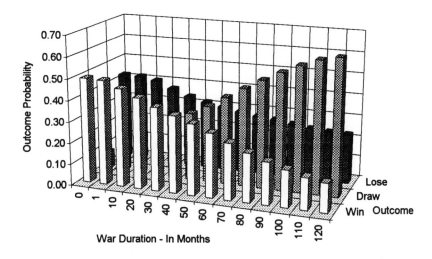

Fig. 44. The effect of war duration on war outcomes

occurring. In figure 44, the effect is demonstrated graphically. As in the previous charts, moving from left to right the observed duration of the war increases from less than a week (0 months) to 120 months. An interesting empirical finding emerges: the passage of time confers no large advantage to one side or the other. Short wars are decisive, one way or the other. The longer a war lasts, the more likely it is to end in a draw. The longer a war lasts, controlling for the other factors, the higher the costs associated with fighting for both sides.

The constraint of time, or the inability of leaders to maintain popular support for any war indefinitely, creates tremendous incentives for civilian leaders to find ways to limit the amount of time that their states will be involved in a war. Posen (1984) argues that the preference for quick wars is a bias inherent in all or most military organizations that leads them to prefer massive, complex offensive strategies that will lead to quicker outcomes. I argue the opposite and demonstrate empirically that these preferences on the part of military organizations and many of their civilian counterparts in the various policy-implementing bureaucracies are not irrational. Rather, they are simply a rational response to the preferences of political leaders to minimize the costs associated with fighting given that it is these people who will make the decisions that lead a nation to war. It is the civilians, not the militaries as the "Cult of the Offensive" practitioners would have us believe, who have the entrenched preference for wars to be as short as possible, and it is not an irrational or organizationally driven preference. Maoz also, like others, notes that it is not necessarily the military planners who advocate swift, short-lasting wars. Rather, it is the civilian decision makers themselves who want the war to be short and decisive (Maoz 1990, 137).

The preference for wars to be as short as possible (with the exception of states using punishment strategies) is simply a rational response to the fact that in any political regime, popular support for death and vast expense wanes over time. The easiest way to ensure that political support will stay above some critical threshold is to limit the amount of time that a war will last or to take all steps possible to that effect. This means that states have powerful incentives to choose the military strategies or mobilization levels that lead to the quickest outcomes. Although the strategies that produce these outcomes are risky, in that the objective probability of the strategy failing is somewhat higher than a more simple, longer duration strategy of attrition or punishment, it is a certainty that political support will fade in a long war. In addition to potential loss of mass public support for the war effort, the passage of time produces essentially two types of problems for military planners, which in the long run may lead to a decline in the likelihood of decisive outcomes. The first is technical adaptation by one's opponent to the strategy or weapons that one is using. The second is political adaptation or the problem of rising dissent as a result of rising costs associated with fighting.

Technical Adaptation over Time

The first way in which time directly affects a state's ability to reduce its marginal costs of fighting, which in turn reduces the likelihood of the state quitting and increases the likelihood of a draw, is by giving the state's opponent time to adapt to its strategy or technology. Given enough time, most adversaries can adapt to the strategy of their opponent. Adaptation can take the form of technological adaptation such as the tank, which emerged in an attempt to adapt to the barriers posed by barbed wire and machine gun-filled defenses. Some adaptations are tactical like the ones developed by the Israelis during the war in 1973. "The same Israeli tank battalions that the antitank missile had seemingly made obsolete by October 9, 1973, or at least made incapable of offensive action, were penetrating the Egyptian front one week later, and advancing uncontested to encircle entire divisions just one week after that" (Luttwak 1987, 38). During World War II, American bombers in the Eighth Air Force tried to bring the German war machine to a halt by interdicting its supplies of ball bearings through destruction of the Schweinfurt industrial works, which was assumed to be a supply bottleneck for the German war matériel industry.

After the loss of 137 out of 367 planes in two days, the American pilots succeeded not in driving the Germans out of the war but rather in forcing the Germans to adapt. Because the Americans had insufficient firepower to destroy the German industrial system overnight (as they later developed the capacity to do with the atomic bomb), the Germans had enough time to adapt to the decreased availability of domestically produced ball bearings. The Germans simply adapted to the loss of their ball bearing factories by buying more ball bearings from the Swiss and by developing a new type of slide bearing, making ball bearings obsolete in many applications (Luttwak 1987, 56). Allied bombing of civilian targets actually forced the more complete mobilization of German society. Massive bombing raids forced the closing of restaurants and small shops that, among other factors, led to the evacuation of urban residents to the country. This freed large numbers of domestic servants for factory work. Luttwak argues that this explains, in part, the paradoxical increase in German industrial output after the initiation of Allied bombing of civilian and industrial targets, an unanticipated result of forced adaptation. The initial advantage of introducing a new technology or tactic is fleeting, with diminishing returns over time as the enemy is able to adapt to the changing wartime conditions (Luttwak 1987, 57). Axelrod directly addresses the importance of the fleeting nature of military advantage resulting from strategic and tactical surprise in his article "The Rational Timing of Surprise" (Axelrod 1979).

Political Adaptation over Time

While time can be the best friend of a state desperately trying to adapt to its opponent's war-fighting apparatus, time can also be a politician's worst nightmare. Bruce Russett addresses the role of time in war, particularly in reference to the popular support for the war effort. He finds that after a brief spurt of increased popular support, the "Rally 'Round the Flag Effect," wars produce increased levels of social dislocation, dispute, and violent political protest. "Governments lose popularity in proportion to the war's costs in blood and money. Of the two, blood seems more important" (Russett 1990, 46). This is likely because governments can manipulate the economy in the short run and defer economic costs to later periods, thereby mitigating the otherwise apparent economic costs to civilians of fighting a war. This is exactly what the Johnson administration did during the Vietnam War. Of course, as a war drags on, the ability to defer payment diminishes. As the economic bill comes due, the costs of war become more apparent back home as once delayed economic distortions become impossible to hide.

As far as political support goes, "in every case candidates of the party initiating a war did less well both during and immediately after the war than would have been predicted by the models that predict election results from the state of the economy" (Russett 1990, 47). It is important to note that this effect is not limited to either unsuccessful wars or to the United States. During World War II, Roosevelt, directing arguably the most popular and successful war effort the United States has ever been involved in, saw his popularity decline in linear fashion during the years after the war began. In England, where elections had been suspended during the war, Churchill's party was voted out of power as soon as the restrictions were lifted, even while he was in Potsdam negotiating the settlement of one of Britain's greatest military victories.

In an example of the effects of time in the United States, Kriesberg and Klein (1980) find that support for spending on national defense declined monotonically during the Vietnam War, beginning in 1964. At this point, U.S. involvement in the war was minimal and the costs to society low, but from the moment the war began support started to decline over time. Support bottomed out from 1969 to 1974.

In May 1964, only 4 percent of the U.S. public favored withdrawal from Vietnam. By June 1965 this proportion rose to a still small 13 percent. This percentage dipped during 1966 to a low of 6 percent in the fall of 1966. In July 1966, 85 percent surveyed in a Harris poll favored the bombing of Hanoi and Haiphong, while only 15 percent were opposed to the effort. Repression of this small minority must have been tempting. Later, the minority grew quickly into an eventually overwhelming majority as the Johnson and Nixon administrations struggled to maintain control of public opinion. By October 1967, the number opposed to the war grew to 35 percent. The Tet offensive reduced those opposed to the war to a small but significant minority. In June 1969, only 29 percent favored immediate withdrawal, 62 percent being opposed. Finally, in January 1971, the tide had turned against the war after years of U.S. involvement. Seventy-two percent in an Opinion Research Corporation survey supported withdrawal by the end of the year. Even when the efforts became less popular, however, the number of citizens who actually actively protested against the war was still quite small (Mueller 1973). In 1975, as soon as the United States ended its involvement in Vietnam, support for a stronger defense and greater defensive spending began to grow again (Kriesberg and Klein 1980, 81).

Another reason why time is a problem is not related to technological adaptation but rather to domestic mass publics' adaptation to political repression. Authoritarian regimes must repress more and more in order to maintain authority and the appearance of legitimacy during an unpopular war. Leaders in democracies may also be tempted to harshly suppress dissent against the war. Of course, in democracies this type of behavior would almost immediately show that the legitimacy of the state's action is declining. The state's legitimacy and its decline in the face of potentially rising domestic political antipathy is critical for the state's ability to convince the mass publics (who bear much of the costs of war both collectively and as individuals) that the net benefits of continuing to fight are still positive. Russett uses the example of the Israeli mass publics' support for the war in Lebanon during the 1980s:

> Israeli backing for the war in Lebanon shows how drastically and rapidly popular support can be withdrawn from an unsuccessful war. Initially in the summer of 1982, two-thirds of the population supported it. Three years later that support was down to 15 percent, and the greatest drop-off had occurred in the first ten months—by May 1983. (Russett 1990, 46–47)

Declining support for a war leads to increased incentives for elite repression of mass dissent. Max Weber pointed out that mass compliance is not entirely predicated on the fear of coercion, and indeed there are likely diminishing returns to increased political repression. (Page, 1992) As Leslie Green notes, a state administration that had to perpetually rely on force to maintain order would not survive long:

> In normal circumstances many people accept the state as legitimate, others are attracted by the facilities it provides, and still others obey habitually. In none of these cases do coercion and fear of sanctions figure prominently among their motivations. At most coercion has an indirect and secondary effect: it offers assurance to those who are law-abiding that they will not be taken for suckers and thus reinforces their primary motives for obedience. (Green 1988, 71)

As a result, the coercive effects of repression become more and more apparent as time moves on during a war. In turn we can then also expect to see highly repressive states select wars they believe to be of short duration.

Modeling War Duration

Being able to accurately model the expected duration of wars is a terribly important task. War duration is the only factor in the model of outcomes developed and tested here that cannot be observed directly before the war begins. It is also an endogenous factor, meaning that many of the factors that affect outcome also have an effect on the duration of war, which in turn has a critical effect on the likelihood of observing draws versus decisive outcomes. Empirical analysis provides evidence that we can model the war's duration using a combination of indicators, all of which can be observed before the war begins.

When planning a war, decision makers must make assumptions about the expected duration of the war and the potential costs associated with fighting for the assumed period of time. In wars that last longer than expected, the costs that the actor must absorb will have to exceed those that it expected to sustain. As such, the actor's willingness to continue fighting will then fall as the expected benefits of the war do not change, while the costs continue to mount. Some military strategies reflect this notion of costs versus time. For instance, the blitzkrieg aims for quick, sudden victory. This is a risky strategy choice though, for if the blitz fails, the costs will rise above those expected, and the army may be poorly adapted or trained to fight a sustained war because many large organizations can typically only prepare and train for one complex task at a time (Maoz 1990, 143).

One problem when trying to account for the effects of time is deciding when decision makers update their subjective beliefs of their ability to absorb and inflict costs. Research in this area points to cataclysmic events, or sudden deviations away from existing trends. For instance, a sudden change in the number of ships lost at sea might be the type of event that would trigger an admiralty to update its convoy strategies (Gartner 1992). A sudden shift in the number of soldiers killed in action could also lead to an updating process. Scott Gartner maintains that as a result of information costs, states attend to just a small number of critical indicators such as the number of soldiers killed in action or the number of ships sunk in a year. Perhaps even more important, he also finds that states are not terribly sensitive to small changes in the indicators, only updating their beliefs when some truly devastating event occurs.

It might be plausible to argue that states update their military strategies and their subjective beliefs on a somewhat regular basis, during the winter perhaps, when fighting typically slows. But the empirical research in this area and in the formal learning literature points to a more stochastic triggering process, something that would be exceedingly difficult to forecast (Reiter 1996). At this point we could estimate the likely effects of the updating process but not when we should expect the updating to occur. As a result, in the outcome model presented earlier, I use a far simpler and admittedly cruder approach by simply controlling for the duration of the war itself and ignoring the specific tactical adaptations that take place over time during the war. This point is somewhat troublesome nonetheless and is an area where further research must be done.

The duration of a conflict is the one endogenous or ex post indicator used in the model. As I argued in chapters 3 and 4, the duration of a conflict is likely affected by the population, military capabilities, terrain, and the military strategies of the two sides. Note that there are several excluded variables in the duration model. If the duration model simply contained variables that were also in the outcomes model, in effect we would be generating a system of perfectly correlated equations. The perspective for duration is somewhat different, so rather than focusing on one side's population or capabilities, in the duration model total capabilities, population, and military forces are included. Also included is a variable for the number of states involved in the war, absent in the outcomes model. The results of a Weibull model hazard analysis are presented in table 7, with the log of duration being the dependent variable. The appropriate way to analyze the duration of events (such as wars) is to use a hazard model (Bennett and Stam 1996).[6]

The use of OLS regression on data that take the form of some finite length of time is inappropriate. Because duration data is strictly positive, the assumption of normally distributed errors made by OLS regression is violated. Applying a linear model to duration data would introduce specification error, likely lead to biased coefficients, and the potential prediction of negative values for expected war duration (Hanushek and Jackson 1977; King 1989). Several different parametric functional forms can be specified as the basis for a hazard model, with the exponential, Weibull, normal, log-normal, and gamma distributions representing only a few of the possibilities. There are few firm guidelines for selection of model form. Here I use a Weibull specification in the hazard analysis. As with the multinomial logit results presented in chapter 5, direct interpretation of the final estimated b coefficients is difficult due to the presence of e and nonlinear interactions.[7] At the simplest level, positive coefficients in b predict longer duration and negative coefficients predict shorter durations.

As shown in table 7, the fit of the duration model to the data is quite good, as it was for the outcome model as well. As is the case with outcomes, strategy plays a critical role in determining the length of wars. Punishment strategies lead to longer wars, and maneuver strategies lead to shorter wars. Recall that I mentioned two types of punishment strategies earlier, a guerrilla strategy and a coercion strategy based on airpower or other means of delivering constant punishment. Both means of delivering punishment result in long, drawn-out wars. Punishment

TABLE 7.   Hazard Model Coefficient Estimates: Effects on War Duration

Variable	Coefficient	Standard Error
Realpolitik		
Strategy: OADM	2.87	(0.947)***
Strategy: OADA	3.33	(0.801)***
Strategy: OADP	6.28	(2.05)***
Strategy: OPDA	7.99	(1706.)
Terrain	2.99	(3.65)
Terrain × Strategy	−1.24	(0.995)*
Balance of Forces	−3.98	(1.28)***
Total Military Personnel	0.273	(0.0884)***
Total Population	0.162	(0.716)
Population Ratio	0.00671	(0.022)
Quality Ratio	0.00081	(0.012)
Surprise	−0.219	(0.636)
Salience	0.427	(0.399)
Domestic Political		
Repression	−0.246	(0.168)*
Democracy	−0.118	(0.0661)**
Other Approaches		
Previous Disputes	0.0161	(0.0686)
Number of States	−0.135	(0.0977)*
p (duration parameter)	0.942	(0.122)
Constant	1.26	(1.50)
Log-Likelihood	−126.1	
Mean Error (months)	12.2	
SD of Mean Error	16.2	
Median Error	5.0	
Mean Error (as % of War Length)	4.4%	
Number of Wars	77	

*$p < 0.1$.
**$p < 0.05$.
***$p < 0.01$.

Note: Standard errors in parentheses. Significance tests are one-tailed. A constant-only model estimates $p = 0.618$, log-likelihood −176.7, mean error 18.3 months (27.7%), and median error 15.1 months.

strategies predicated on air power prove difficult to execute due to the difficulty of identifying and striking targets from the air. Ground-based guerrilla strategies are slow because the soldiers must spend a great deal of their energy simply surviving away from a large military supply organization and hiding from those who would eliminate them. Because the guerrilla forces are dependent on the good will of the local populace to support them, two hypotheses have evolved over the best way to counter the guerrilla strategy. Because the guerrilla army has no centralized logistic organization, they are vulnerable to loss of general support from mass publics.

Contrary to the attrition strategy, where the central point is to find and destroy the enemy in a direct manner, the guerrilla-punishment strategy aims for a different sort of vital point. Rear areas, flanks, and vulnerable points (as opposed to masses of troops and equipment) are the primary targets of the guerrilla. The most common techniques are harassment, dispersion, and exhaustion (Mao 1961, 46). Additionally, where conventional strategies depend on movement and positions of troops requiring complex logistical networks to support the large and complex military machine, the guerrilla network depends on the people themselves to organize rather than fitting into a military organization provided by the state. In the guerrilla strategy there is no decisive battle to be sought out, nor are defenses ever established and fixed (Mao 1961, 51).

Mao cited the Russo-French war in 1812 as one of the first examples of a successful guerrilla strategy in action. While Mao acknowledged the importance of the conventional military in the Russian victory, he saw the harassing actions of the Russian partisans as the critical factor in securing victory over the French, perhaps the greatest European army assembled to that point (Mao 1961, 59). Mao anticipated the role that time would play in the defeat of a conventional force. "Historical experience shows us that regular army units are not able to undergo the hardships of campaigning over long periods. The success of guerrilla strategy depends on interdiction of conventional forces supply lines, then letting time weaken the resolve of the conventional forces, the entire time maintaining a harassing pressure" (Mao 1961, 60).

In the hazard analysis results in table 7, the interaction of strategy and terrain helps determine the baseline length of the war, with the number of troops available, their technology and skill, and the strategy they employ affecting the actual duration. Also included in the model are the domestic political variables, democracy and repression. As noted earlier, both highly repressive and highly democratic states tend to select wars that will be shorter in duration. Balance of forces also appears to be a key variable in determining the duration of wars. The more out of balance the opponents' capabilities, the faster the war progresses. The most dramatic changes in war duration occur when force ratios move just away from parity. This finding gives support to those, such as Organski and Kugler (1980), who argue that small shifts in the balance of power when the states in question are closely matched can have a major impact on international politics. Once capabilities have moved from parity, additional increments bring declining marginal returns in terms of speeding up a war's duration.

Finally, as the number of participants in a war increases and the benefits of potential victory become distributed among more actors, the potential gains from victory for any individual state shrink. When many states are involved in fighting, some of them may receive no tangible benefits from victory at all. Because of smaller and possibly more abstract benefits, the leader of an individual state in a coalition will thus be less able to convince domestic audiences to continue fighting than when the state is fighting alone. The more states there are fighting in a war, the more quickly a coalition will fall apart, leading to a shorter war.

Conclusion

The figures presented previously are a useful way of investigating or inferring the effect of each of the indicators used to estimate the outcome model. They allow us to look at the effect of each factor as it varied throughout its range. Remember that these represent the total possible change that could likely be associated with each of the independent variables. It is not the historical average effect as discussed at the beginning of chapter 6. Rather, the charts presented here and earlier represent the possible effect that each of the variables could have. Earlier I presented a summary table of the average effects over the time period the data are drawn from. In those two figures I demonstrated the historical average effect as a means of getting a handle on the average impact each variable has had over time. In this chapter, and in the section on choices, we have seen that some variables that historically, on average, have had a small effect, can, under the proper conditions, nonetheless have powerful effects on outcomes. Figures 45 and 46, while similar to those given at the outset of chapter 6, demonstrate the comparative power of each of the independent variables. Unlike the previous examples, however, these charts represent the relative *possible* or potential effects rather than the relative historical effects.

In figure 45 we see which variables have potentially the most powerful effects (versus those that have been powerful to this point) on winning versus losing.[8] Again, as is the case with the figures presenting the historical averages (figs. 28 and 29), strategy also has the largest potential effect in determining outcomes. One dramatic difference between these figures and those in chapter 6 is the potential role versus the historical role of the domestic political variables. Repression has the potential to be more important a factor than alliance contributions, something that realists would not suspect. Realist factors such as strat-

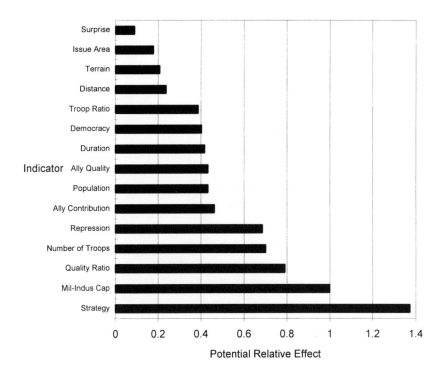

Fig. 45. The potential influence of various factors on winning versus losing interstate wars

egy, the number of troops, and technology are still the most important. But whereas in the historical average figures factors such as duration, democracy, and population had little apparent effect on outcomes, we clearly see here that they can play a dramatic role, even though on average they have not done so historically. It is difficult to understate the importance of this point. Using duration as an example, because the vast majority of wars are quite short (the median duration is under six months) on average, the duration of wars plays little role in their ultimate outcome. But, as shown both in figure 44 (duration effects) and in figure 45 (comparative effects) we can see that states would make a terrible error if they chose to ignore the potential effects of duration and chose simply to focus on the average historical impact. It is interesting to note that surprise plays little role from either perspective. Compared to other factors, surprise has little historical or potential effect on outcomes.

Now we can see, in direct terms, that domestic political factors such

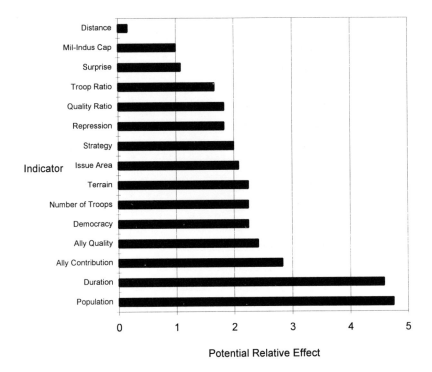

Fig. 46. The potential influence of various factors on draws occurring during interstate wars

as repression and democracy play important roles in war. In addition, the choices that states must make with regard to strategy, military mobilization, and spending on defense are clearly subject to domestic constraint, a clear but indirect role that domestic politics plays in outcomes.

In figure 46 the factors that affect the likelihood of draws occurring can be seen. Compared to the factors that affect the likelihood of decisive outcomes (win or lose), domestic factors play an even more important role in determining draws. Institutional democracy is potentially over twice as important a factor as military-industrial capabilities. The realpolitik factors, alliance contributions and quality, are the third and fourth most powerful factors, respectively. Both democracy and issue area are more important from this perspective than military strategy, something realists do not typically anticipate. Duration and population are key potential factors in determining draws. States that choose strategies that lead to long drawn-out wars (punishment strategies) can be assured that the risk of suffering a decisive defeat is likely to be small.

By furthering our understanding of how wars are fought and what the factors are that contribute to their outcomes, we will hopefully increase our understanding of the conditions under which states may believe they can expect to gain from initiating a war. Simplistic outcome models may be far more parsimonious, but in their simplicity they may lead us to make erroneous conclusions about the conditions that lead to the success or failure of policies. Focusing myopically on historical relationships also may lead us to misunderstand the potential effect of factors that lie within the control of state decision makers. In the final chapter I address some of the larger implications of the empirical findings presented in this and previous chapters.

CHAPTER 8

Expectations about the Outcomes of Wars

Having reached this point in the discussion of the many factors that affect states' ability to wage war, many readers might still be willing to argue that a study of this kind has little use in today's complex world. For all the factors included in the model, it is still only that—a simplification of the actual process at work in the complex reality of war fighting. While the statistical model developed and tested in the earlier chapters represents a step forward in estimating the likely outcomes of interstate wars, it still relies on an enormous simplification of reality in order to permit the kind of empirical analysis presented in chapter 5. Even though the world may have become a more complex place over time, the model developed here works equally well for the period before World War II as it does afterward. Scholars and pundits alike tend to think that the presence of nuclear weapons has somehow magically transformed the field of battle. While nuclear weapons may have altered the strategic planning of the nations that possess them and may have led to a forty-year period of protracted tension between the two most powerful nations on the earth, they did not fundamentally change the forces at work during conventional wars. Of the twenty-five cases of war after the invention of the atomic bomb, the model correctly predicts twenty-three of them. This success rate of 92 percent matches the model's pre-World War II success rate of fifty-seven out of sixty-two cases. The world today may be more complex, but our ability to understand one of the most basic state behaviors does not vary significantly over the history of the nineteenth and twentieth centuries.

Policy and Theory Implications

In another light, by confirming that the basic theoretical model may have merit, we should pause to reconsider the notion of arms races, and more broadly, the security dilemma. One of the more puzzling empirical findings from the last twenty years has been that not all arms races lead to wars. This model may help us to understand this phenomenon. Recall from chapter 2 that I demonstrated that the model predicted that there would be situations in which both sides of a potential conflict could see their chances for victory either increasing or decreasing simultaneously and the likelihood of draws correspondingly increasing or decreasing.

Some arms races may end peacefully because the two actors see their relative chances for victory declining even while they race away. Figure 11 anticipates this type of arms race as the actors might move around the cost-benefit diagram as theta varies from 2.0 pi radians to 4.0 pi radians. Samuel Huntington (1958) anticipated these findings when he found, using case studies, that the beginning of arms races are more dangerous than their ends. He also found that quantitative arms races differed from qualitative ones, something that would be difficult to confirm here given the crude nature of the measures used. This model provides us with a new way to think about arms races and discover the circumstances under which some end in war while others end peacefully.

We have also learned that many factors that have been largely ignored in the past by international relations scholars should command equal respect by researchers developing and using models of war and interstate conflict. Political repression is important for the normative theorist, the comparative specialist, and for the practitioners of security studies. A state's ability to repress dissent within its borders during war is as potentially important as its ability to recruit and maintain allies for the fight. We in the business of studying war have much to learn from our colleagues who study the intricacies of domestic politics.

While the list of variables considered in the previous chapters is quite long, it is far from exhaustive. Some might question how I could have ignored factors within a state as they affect a state's ability to project its power abroad or against its neighbors. For example, I have not addressed the role that ethnic bias or racial bias plays in states' ability to make the choices that would optimize their chances of victory during war. That is material for another book. But why have so few systematically and empirically investigated the indirect role that culture and other domestic characteristics play in the process of waging war? Perhaps the answer lies in a desire to believe that wars are caused and do not result from the conscious decisions by the leaders of the states in question. If wars are caused by factors beyond the control of states' decision makers, then we might be able to understand why scholars have disconnected the study of various sociological factors and the state's ability to project its power. The search for the cure for the disease of war, in this view, could be easily kept separate from the domestic politics of social class, military manpower, and institutional racism.

If, however, we accept that wars are the result of the deliberate choices of rational decision makers who balance the costs and expected benefits of their choices made within the resource and political constraints of the states they lead, then we should be able to more easily see how these decision makers would face pressures both from within the state as well as from outside its borders. If the choice to go to war is simply one of the many various decisions that state leaders must make, and we can understand the domestic pressure for other decisions, then the willingness to include the effects of domestic influence groups (many of which have agendas based on some form of ethnic or racial bias) on the decision to go to war becomes startlingly apparent. Only after balancing these oft conflicting pressures do choices result. In making these choices, in order to be able to generate support for the leaders' preferences, other domestic battles may come to the fore.

For example, during the period immediately prior to the U.S. entrance into World War I, many African-American leaders viewed the war as an opportunity, not so much a chance to make the world a safer place but to display their abilities and valor. Southerners wary of this possibility lobbied successfully for several months for the exclusion of African-Americans from the war effort. Woodrow Wilson, whose desire to enter the war was intense, was willing to make tradeoffs in the realm of power by excluding African-Americans in order to serve his broader interests in maintaining political support for a U.S. presence in Europe.

In addition to understanding the pressures of domestic interest groups, by demonstrating the declining marginal returns for particular factors such as military troop levels and relative defense-spending levels, we can also better understand or anticipate the times during which state leaders will be more likely to exclude various groups from the armed forces. In chapter 7, I showed how sensitive the outcome expectations can be when the two sides in a potential war are closely matched. In these instances, small variations in either sides' troop levels or spending on weapons and training may have a significant effect. When the balance is more skewed, few of the indicators are sensitive to even large changes in their respective values. While the French were literally dying for the want of more troops in World War I, the U.S. military, for a time, could afford to exclude certain groups without unduly affecting its potential wartime capabilities.

By studying the effects of distance, we may also have learned information that can be of tremendous use in studying the likelihood of regional conflicts spilling into larger, more difficult to control situations. While large, powerful states like Russia and China can project their forces great distances without suffering the debilitating effects of distance, smaller, weaker states' power drops off quickly. As a result, it is unlikely that regional wars between weak states could evolve into larger far-flung contests of wills, assuming powerful patron states remain neutral observers. Perhaps the fear in the United States of Iraqi regional domination prior to the war in 1991 against Saddam Hussein resulted from unwarranted fears of Hussein eventually projecting his power far beyond his borders. Even with the large military machine he had assembled, given the weak state of his economy and lack of industrial infrastructure, Hussein would have been hard-pressed to fight much beyond his immediate borders. In this sense there was and is little danger of regional powers like Iraq becoming military juggernauts like those witnessed during World War II. The oft heard journalistic comment that some aggressive nation or another is "another Hitler's Germany" should, in all likelihood, be taken with a large grain of salt. What made Hitler's Germany so dangerous was not its aggressive nature or imperialistic aims (there have been plenty of nondescript states that fit those characterizations), but rather the Germans' ability to project power beyond their immediate borders. There are precious few states in the international system at any time with that capability.

One area where this study may have raised as many questions as it answers lies in the realm of military strategy. By showing that under many observable conditions there are optimal strategies, many of which are offensive in nature if not in goals, people who study the theoretical nature of the security dilemma may need to introduce a new level of complexity into their models. Clearly, both the highly mobile strategies best characterized by the blitzkrieg raids of the Germans in World War II and the slow-working guerrilla or punishment strategies advocated by Mao and Ho Chi Minh are devastatingly effective when the state pursuing them has the means and the will to invest the necessary lives and time in them. Standard attrition strategies, whether offensive or defensive in nature, are tremendously vulnerable to attacks from more persistent or mobile opponents.

Forecasting Outcomes

A final way in which models such as this help us better understand the world lies in an improved ability to forecast or anticipate the possible or likely outcomes of potential wars. During the 1990s, many in the United States have been puzzled by the military's seeming willingness to commit to the war in Iraq but its hesitancy to become involved more broadly in the Balkan War. Using this model, we can forecast the outcomes in the two situations and perhaps better understand the motivations of the U.S. Defense Department.

In order to gain a rough understanding, it is not necessary to resort to a complex data search. For both cases I assume the following:

The United States controls 95 percent of the industrial capabilities available to the two sides (an optimistic estimate).

The United States enjoys a 3:1 spending ratio versus both the Iraqis and the Serbs.

The United States receives an ally capability contribution of 10 percent.

The allies' spending ratio is 0.5:1.

The United States has roughly 1 million soldiers from which it can draw.

In the case of the Balkan War, the United States would pursue a strategy of attrition due to the terrain there (highly mountainous and rugged).

In Iraq, the United States would use a mobile strategy because of the more open terrain.

A U.S. population of 250 million.

A terrain score of 0.3 in the Balkans.

A terrain score of 1.0 in Iraq.

A maximum score on the democracy scale and a minimum on the repression scale for the United States.

In the Serb case the issue is over a government policy.

No assumption about the issue in Iraq, where we could have been fighting for a more tangible stake such as control of critical oil fields or control of critical shipping lanes through the Persian Gulf.[1]

Using these data, the forecast for the Gulf War anticipates an outcome in which the United States has a 98 percent chance of victory, a 1 percent chance of a draw, and 1 percent chance of losing. In the Balkan War, fighting with a different strategy, on treacherous terrain, and over a less tangible issue, the anticipated outcome is far different: 0 percent chance of victory, a 76 percent chance of a draw, and a 24 percent chance of losing. In this light, the U.S. military's hesitation to become more deeply involved in a potential war against the Serbs is much more understandable.[2]

Competing Explanations in World Politics

Lest we think that realism or other nonrational choice approaches are part of a dying fad, writers in the early 1990s continued to carry the torch. While Morgenthau wrote the core of his *Politics among Nations* during the immediate postwar years, and Waltz's *Theory of International Politics* emerged in 1979, writers today still rhapsodize about the virtues of realism. Robert Lieber, for example, offers a somewhat tempered call for the continuation of the realist approach:

> As a means of making sense of the external world and the require-ments of foreign policy, realism provides no iron laws of human behavior, but it does offer an approach to reality in which both theory and policy can be grounded. (Lieber 1993, 166)

Lieber goes on to argue that because the basic nature of the interna-tional system remains unchanged—an underlying condition of anarchy—there will always be situations in which the incentives that states confront may prod them toward war and violence. Lieber concludes from this observation that war is unlikely to become obsolete and that "recogni-tion of these realities is a precondition both for understanding the dy-namics of international affairs and for developing policies that are to have any hope for achieving peace and protecting the national interest" (Lieber 1993, 166). I find it striking that realists simply assume that because we cannot rule out the likelihood of violent interstate behavior in the future, the only way we can understand when these conflicts will occur and develop policies to manage the conflicts is through the applica-tion of realist theory.

"Few, it seems, can consistently escape from the belief that inter-national-political outcomes are determined, rather than merely affected, by what states are like" (Waltz 1979, 61). Perhaps Waltz tries with such diligence to pursue his blind alley because of the logical policy prescrip-tions that would flow from both theoretical and empirical findings that the nature of states would affect international political outcomes. "If the international-political outcomes are determined by what states are like, then we must be concerned with, and if necessary do something to change, the internal dispositions of the internationally important ones" (Waltz 1979, 63). Ironically, the U.S. post–cold war international strat-egy of fomenting institutional democracy is an attempt to accomplish exactly what Waltz apparently feared so much.

Realism fairs poorly as positivist theory. States simply do not be-have all that often the way realists assert that they do. On the other hand, many realists answer this critique of the paradigm by arguing that realism is a normative theory. But if states always behaved in the manner that realists say they should, the states would frequently find themselves in compromising situations. By ignoring the very factors realists press us to ignore (domestic political structure and domestic mass public constraints on elite decisions) and concentrating on those they would have us focus on (alliances and surprise), we might make grave errors both in our predictions of wars that are likely to occur and in our policy prescriptions and recommendations.

Bueno de Mesquita and Lalman close their seminal work, *War and Reason*, with a note about the admitted shortcomings of their theory and its empirical tests. Rather than dwelling on the faults in their work, they leave the reader with the hope that the "volume will encourage the development of more refined tools of measurement. . . . In the absence of data with which to approximate continuous outcomes, we felt it made more sense to build a theory of discrete outcomes" (Bueno de Mesquita and Lalman 1992, 276–77). This book has been an attempt to more fully specify a model of outcomes than both the model used in their work and the most commonly used models in the vast literature on war initiation. While I have not specified a continuous outcome model as Bueno de Mesquita and Lalman hoped for, the three anticipated outcomes I do forecast roughly capture the general types of outcomes decision makers base choices on prior to the initiation of conflict, and they represent a significant step forward from simpler binary outcome models.

How States Behave: Making Judgments about Domestic Costs and Benefits

While most of the discussion in the literature and in this study focuses on the potential tradeoffs between domestic politics and security concerns of powerful, developed nations, there are also interesting and related findings in the field of political development. Saadet Deger and Ron Smith (1983, 335) find that states' military expenditures are strongly and negatively correlated with economic growth. These admittedly controversial findings reinforce the notion that states face tremendous tradeoffs between military power and domestic economic well-being. The results in chapter 6 demonstrate that the declining marginal return for defense spending per soldier further complicates the normative discussion of the relationship between defense and domestic tradeoffs. While many developing states face serious security threats, the internal political threats are frequently even more serious. The result is that these states are not in a position to maximize their power relative to the interstate system in which they find themselves; rather they must take the steps necessary domestically in order to survive internal political battles. In many cases, this will lead to policies that favor domestic economic growth over maximizing military security.

According to Arnold Wolfers, realists have tried to explain nation-states' compulsion to behave as they do in the following way:

> They have offered two different explanations. According to the first, human nature is such that men, as individuals and as nations, act like beasts of prey, driven by an insatiable lust for power or animus dominandi. The will to power, moreover, when transferred from small and frustrated individuals to the collectivity of the state, takes on greater dimensions and generates an all-round struggle for survival. (Wolfers 1962, 83–84)

The second argument simply transfers the goals of the first argument from power to security. Perhaps the flaw in the model can be seen through Wolfer's analogy. While wild beasts of prey do, indeed, feast upon one another, they rarely, if ever, kill for pleasure and rarely kill more than they need to eat as they would pursuing relative gains. The result is that carnivorous animals become domesticated, for the most part, when their dietary needs are sated. In a similar way, when states are feeling secure enough, having satisficed, they will then pursue other policy choices, typically involving domestic politics. But these choices, while placating domestic groups in peacetime, carry through into war-time behavior. As analysts, we cannot ignore the effects of domestic politics when we try to investigate the causes and nature of war. The rational choice paradigm, rather than the realist paradigm, offers an intellectual approach to reality that is far more realistic than the "realist" model.

Implications for Future Research

Having spent the better part of the last seven chapters developing and explaining a set of methodological tools so that we can better understand the past, in what directions does this work point for the future? There are primarily two research agendas within the security studies field that might benefit from an application of this model's results: (1) the rational choice literature on war initiation and state behavior during wartime; and (2) the arms race literature.

The rational choice literature, whether the models represent the choices to go to war or not or the effects that wars have on states' internal politics, are all critically dependent on estimates of the various actors' probability of victory in the war or potential war in question. The model of outcomes developed here represents an enormous leap forward in both complexity and accuracy compared to more standard models of outcomes. It would be quite informative to find out if the accuracy of the current state-of-the-art rational choice models improves or declines with better outcome data.

The literature on the effects of arms races has led to the somewhat dissatisfying conclusion that some arms races lead to wars and others do not. While many authors have speculated about this finding, no one has focused on the likely outcomes of the potential war that might result from the escalation of the arms race in question. To this point, no one has focused on the probability of victory in war as the variable that changes over time during the arms race. Rather than focusing on the increase, whether relative or absolute, of the numbers of weapons available or the technology of the weapons, we might better focus on the changing probability of the outcomes associated with a potential war between the two or more states engaged in the arms race. This approach might prove more fruitful in understanding one of the more important phenomenon in international relations.

Notes

Chapter 1

1. When I refer to resources here, I am referring to them in the broadest sense. Kalevi Holsti addresses the entire range of issues that states have gone to war over in *Peace and War: Armed Conflicts and International Order, 1648–1989.*

2. For an extensive discussion of this issue see Dan Reiter (1995), "Exploding the Powder Keg Myth."

Chapter 2

1. For most advanced players, it is this intractability that makes the game so interesting. If the solution were known, then playing the game would be far less interesting. While tic-tac-toe proves interesting to small children, most adults find it to be a trivial game, and as such, dull.

2. Von Neumann and Morgenstern "pointed out, there is a numerical limit on the number of moves in a game of chess under a given tie rule. (The limiting number is probably around 5,000 moves with typical rules—far more than any game of chess ever played!)" (Poundstone 1992, 47). The number of possible permutations, or strategies, then reaches a scale typically used only by physicists and cosmologists.

3. While conflicts may certainly have more than two sides or participants, for the sake of clarity I will refer to all conflicts as having only two sides.

4. The Nash equilibrium is a position in which neither player can improve his or her outcome through a unilateral move or change in strategy.

5. We also would expect to see very few wars. If the outcomes were certain, and not probabilistic, there would be no need for states to ever go to war. States would be certain that they would either win or lose and would negotiate from that position. It is the probabilistic nature of outcomes that makes the occurrence of war possible in a world where we assume the leaders to be rational.

6. This theoretical approach draws heavily from Bueno de Mesquita and Lalman, 1986.

7. See Doran and Parson (1980) and Goldstein (1988) for extensive treatment of power and economic long cycles.

Chapter 4

1. By *monotonic* I mean that the change associated with capabilities (or other factor) is either always increasing or always decreasing. The increase in the chance of victory, for example, might slowly drop off, but the probability of victory would never begin to decline in absolute terms.

2. For the Korean and Vietnam wars, minor participants were dropped.

3. The listing of cases, actual outcomes, and predicted outcomes can be found in the data set that is archived with the ICPSR and the low data repository that is available via anonymous ftp.

4. While I believe that this coding change is theoretically appropriate, I did check the sensitivity of my results to this change. The results were quite similar even if we dropped the changed wars (dropping them because we believe they are currently miscoded). Two differences emerged. First, because the Vietnam War is the only war in which we observe an offensive punishment strategy (OPDA), we are forced to drop that variable. Second, because this procedure involves dropping fourteen cases (twelve in World War II), all of the standard errors increase slightly. The coefficient estimates were stable, however.

5. See Hart 1967; Clausewitz 1976; Luttwak 1980; Dupuy 1983; Mearsheimer 1983; Posen 1984; Van Evera 1984; Snyder 1985; Sun Tzu 1991.

6. Note that the coding of strategy as described in the historical record leads to a possible problem for my ex ante argument in that the coding is based on an ex post evaluation of the strategies used. There are a few cases in which states initially tried to execute maneuver strategies but were forced to switch to attrition strategies. An example is Germany's World War II strategy on the Eastern front, where it initially used a maneuver strategy but switched to an attrition strategy as the blitzkrieg ran out of steam in the Soviet Union. Unfortunately, purely ex ante coding of strategy is impossible without access to military strategic plans. However, in the empirical record there are relatively few instances where strategy changed between categories, and so the problem affects only a few cases. When states did change strategy, they tended to do so soon after the beginning of a war, and so the magnitude of this problem does not appear to be severe. This does mean that our future predictions will have to be contingent on revealed strategy, however.

7. Gartner's *Strategic Assessment in War* (1992) contains an extended discussion of tactical and strategic change during wartime. The types of strategy change he addresses do not affect the broad strategy codings I employ here. One other factor relevant to coding strategy that I ignore is the offense-defense balance in terms of which strategy enjoys a particular advantage at some point in time. I leave this out of the analysis because it is typically a factor that is revealed during the course of the war and is not usually known ex ante. If it were, the horrific trench warfare of World War I might not have occurred. Ignoring this factor may have the effect of increasing the uncertainty associated with any estimates based on the empirical model.

8. Data on military expenditures and personnel were obtained from the

Correlates of War (COW) national capabilities data set. Exchange rates and an inflation deflator were obtained from Gurr et al. (1989). When there were multiple countries on a side, I created a weighted average of quality on each side where states' contributions to their side's overall quality was proportional to their capabilities.

9. There was significant missing data on the variable; when data was missing, I substituted the mean of the variable across the rest of the data set, or 2.36.

10. This index ranges potentially from 0 to 1 and indicates a country's share of total international military personnel, military expenditures, energy consumption, iron and steel production, total population, and urban population.

11. In cases where there were more than two actors on one side, and so the terrain on which different states fought might have been quite different, the coded value was an average of terrain scores weighted by the size of the forces fighting in particular terrain.

12. Including the scale or individually multiplied dummy variables makes little difference in the overall results of the model, as the model fit remains nearly identical.

13. There was significant missing data on the variable; to allow estimation, when data was missing I substituted the mean of the variable across the rest of the data set, or 2.61.

Chapter 5

1. This high level of uncertainty is not the result of multicollinearity. Dropping independent variables that are correlated with surprise (OMDA for example) has little effect on the standard error associated with surprise.

2. For an extended discussion of the various pseudo-R^2s, see Hagle and Mitchell's article "Goodness-of-Fit Measures for Probit and Logit." There, they compare the results of four pseudo-R^2 measures to the R^2 values one would obtain using OLS. They find that the various measures, with the exception of the Achen statistic, are reasonably close to the estimates one would obtain using OLS. Because the data for the dependent variables is somewhat skewed, the R^2 measure used here is the Dhrymes measure, defined as $R^2 = 1 - \ln L_1/\ln L_0$, or 1 minus the ratio of the log-likelihood of the full model divided by the log-likelihood of the null (constant-only) model. Hagle and Mitchell also suggest using a Reduction of Error (ROE) statistic defined by Brenner, Hagle, and Spaeth (1990) as:

$$ROE = 100 \times \frac{\text{\% correctly classified} - \text{\% modal category}}{100\% - \text{\% modal category}}$$

One problem of the pseudo-R^2 for the nonlinear models is that it does not take into account the number of independent variables or the number of cases. Because of this, following Pindyck and Rubinfeld (1981, 80) I also calculate a corrected R^2 computed as follows:

Corrected $R^2 = 1 - [1 - R^2 \times (N - 1)/(N - k)]$, where N is the number of observations and k is the number of independent variables. Another problem with using the pseudo-R^2 as a single measure of fit is that for each value of the pseudo-R^2, there are several possible "true" R^2 values that would map to it. Because of this, I employ several different goodness-of-fit measures, each of which points in the same direction.

3. By "in-sample" I am referring to the eighty-eight cases that make up the stratified random sample. This sample is drawn from the larger data set of all participants in all wars. The entire data set consists of 244 cases, each of which is a country fighting in a war. There are eighty-eight wars in the data set, so with one participant in each war in the sample used to test the multinomial statistical model, the result is a sample of eighty-eight cases.

4. Because the sample is drawn randomly from the underlying population of cases, we do not expect it to look exactly like the population. We expect there to be some difference between our sample and the remaining population of cases due to random variation. For example, the sample might contain a smaller or greater proportion of one type of strategy choice than in the population. As a result of this expected difference the regression coefficients estimated using the sample are expected to be somewhat different than the "true" or underlying population parameters. If we slavishly fit the statistical model to our sample data, we run the risk of sacrificing the ability to generalize to the population. As a result, we are forced to make a trade-off. If we fit the model to the sample perfectly, it will necessarily not fit the population (out-of-sample predictions) because of the known and expected random variation. As a result, we should always check to be sure that the statistical results also allow us to make accurate prediction (results better than random choice) for out-of-sample cases as well as investigating in-sample model performance.

5. One possible confounding problem is that the out-of-sample cases contribute some information to the in-sample cases. It might be the case, for example, that the model simply predicts the opposite outcome for the two sides of a particular war. Or, if a draw is forecast, each case in such a war is coded as draw. In examining the out-of-sample forecasts we can see that this is not the case. Many of the forecast errors occur not by mispredicting both sides, as would be the case necessarily in the situation described above but by correctly predicting one case in a war and making the same prediction for the opposing side, that is, both sides being forecast as winners or losers. All forecasts, both in-sample and out, are contained in the data set available from the ICPSR.

6. This type of problem is not unique to this study. Various other authors have grappled with this type of problem and have handled it in different ways. For example, in his seminal study *The War Trap*, Bueno de Mesquita treated the Seven Weeks' War as eight different small wars. Similarly, he treated World War I as a single case, with Austria-Hungary fighting Yugoslavia and Yugoslavia winning. He reduces World War II to Germany versus Poland and the Soviet Union versus Finland, with Poland and the Soviet Union being the victors, respectively.

7. For a complete discussion of the calibration table and index, see Yates (1991, 46–58).

8. J. S. Cramer (1991) discusses at length numerical and graphical evaluation techniques for logistic regression models. Because there are no good single measures of fit, Cramer advocates the use of multiple indicators of model fit, both statistical and graphical.

9. The log-likelihood ratio is determined by the following formula: Log Likelihood Ratio $= -2LLR = -2 \ln (L_0/L_1)$, where L_0 and L_1 represent the likelihood value (the relative likelihood that the model fits the data) of the null hypothesis and the likelihood value of the full model, respectively.

Chapter 6

1. Estimating the marginal effects of independent variables is a subject that is often ignored in the quantitative literature. Christopher Achen (1982) argues that in the case of the linear model, if we want to compare the relative power of one independent variable to another, one should use a statistic that captures both the regression coefficients' absolute value and the mean value of the variables in question rather than relying on the regression coefficients alone. Unfortunately, with the logistic model, Achen's simple power statistic leads to a biased result. The problem is that the relative impact of an independent variable changes as we move across the variable's distribution. In the linear model, we assume that an independent variable's effect remains constant throughout its distribution, while in the nonlinear case, the effect may be quite small at one point in the distribution and quite large at another. Following Green (1993), the marginal effects in the multinomial case above are calculated as follows:

The notation P_j is used for Probability $[Y = j]$, which is calculated as

$$P_j = \frac{\exp (\beta_j' x_i)}{\Sigma_j(\beta_j' x_i)} \ , \quad j = \text{win,draw,lose}$$

and δ is used for the marginal effect on outcome j of the vector of independent variables where, $\delta_j = \partial P_j/\partial x$, $J = $ win,draw,lose. In terms of the vector of coefficients,

$$\delta_j = P_j(\beta_j - \bar{\beta})$$

where

$$\bar{\beta} = \sum_{j=0}^{j=J} P_j\beta_j.$$

This measures the average change in the probability of a particular outcome (win, draw, lose) as each of the independent variables is allowed to vary throughout its distribution.

2. The mean value in figure 30 is calculated by averaging the predictions for each of the outcomes over the entire data set. For example, in the first case, the actor (France) is predicted to have had a 99 percent chance of winning, a 0 percent chance of a draw, and a 1 percent chance of losing. Similarly, there is a prediction for each of the three outcomes for all the cases. The average prediction is then calculated taking the average of all the predictions for all the cases in the sample. So, on average, any state has a 42 percent chance of winning, an 18 percent chance of a draw, and a 40 percent chance of losing (for practical purposes, the 42 percent and the 40 percent figures are statistically identical).

3. In this chart and those that follow, the predicted changes in the outcome probabilities are calculated using the formula in note 1 of this chapter. Each of the variables other than the one in question are set to the values actually observed in the data set. The independent variable in question is allowed to vary from its observed minimum to its observed maximum. In the case of the strategy choices, they are listed in rank order based on the hypotheses in chapter 4.

4. Training costs in technologically advanced militaries approach the cost of actual use during wartime. The significant difference being the lower replacement costs during peacetime when casualties and damage to equipment are considerable lower. Estimates of the costs for the United States in the Gulf War in 1991 ranged from $45 to $100 billion. This is certainly a great deal of money but was between one-third and 1/2 of the annual cost of peacetime training and technological development at the time.

Chapter 7

1. The COW composite capabilities index is almost perfectly collinear with states' gross national products (GNP). The difference between the two becomes most apparent for the few very large states within the system. This is interesting to know in that many authors maintain that GNP should be the best overall measure of state power (Kugler and Domke, 1986).

2. It might be the case that the results observed for population are the result of collinearity with the number of soldiers or the capabilities index. To check for this possibility, the regression analyses were performed both with the confounding factors in the model and without the factors. The point estimate for the population variable remains quite stable, although the standard errors vary somewhat as could be expected.

3. As with several of the other indicators, the democracy index and the repression index are quite collinear. To check if the results (the direction of the effect) are a spurious artifact of the multicollinearity problem, the results were verified by estimating the regression models with each of the two political indicators in the model for separate runs. In both cases, the results are essen-

tially the same as those when both repression and democracy are in the equation at the same time. As a result, we can be quite confident that the findings are genuine and not simply the result of correlated measurement error or extreme multicollinearity.

4. I did additional analysis regarding democracy and repression in part to ensure that collinearity was not leading to these results, which some might find paradoxical. While the democracy and repression variable are strongly correlated (Pearson's $r = 0.62$), other tests indicate that the results presented here are *not* the result of multicollinearity.

5. I define states that Gurr codes as scoring 8 or more on the democracy scale as "highly" democratic." I define states scoring 1 on Gurr's PARCOMP index of repression as "highly repressive."

6. Hazard models are also referred to as survival models, duration models, or event history models. Comprehensive sources for duration analysis include Greene (1993), Kiefer (1988), and Lancaster (1990). Recent applications of hazard analysis to political science include Warwick (1992), Bueno de Mesquita and Siverson (1995), and Vuchinich and Teachman (1993).

7. However, as William Green (1993, 722) notes, the expected survival time for any given case (set of values x_i) given a Weibull distribution is $E[t|x_i] = \exp(\beta'x_i)*\Gamma(1/p + 1)$. The best way to interpret the magnitude of the coefficients is to use this formula to calculate and compute the values of hypothetical cases. For example, if we calculated the expected duration of a war to be sixteen months given an attrition strategy, but only twelve months given a maneuver strategy while holding other variables constant at their means, we would estimate the effect of the strategy change on duration as negative four months, holding the other variables at their mean values.

8. The height of the bar represents the relative power of a particular independent variable. They are scaled so that the effect of military-industrial capabilities = 1.0. The values are calculated by measuring the possible change in winning and losing as each of the independent variables is allowed to move from its minimum to its maximum. For example, when democracy is at its minimum, we expect the probability of winning to be roughly 20 percent. When democracy is at its maximum, the probability of winning is roughly 40 percent. Therefore, democracy can be said to have a possible change of 20 percent on the chance of winning. Each bar represent the relative power in this sense as compared to the other independent variables.

Chapter 8

1. See chapter 4 for a discussion of variable operationalization and chapter 5 for a discussion of the expected empirical effects of each of the factors on the expected outcomes. For the Gulf War, I generated a forecast of a U.S.-Iraqi war. For the Balkan War, I forecast a U.S.-Greater Serb war.

2. See table 3 for the regression equations used to generate the forecast probabilities.

Bibliography

Achen, Christopher H. 1982. *Interpreting and Using Regression.* Beverly Hills: Sage Publications.

———. 1986. *The Statistical Analysis of Quasi-Experiments.* Berkeley: University of California Press.

Arquilla, John. 1992. *Dubious Battles: Aggression, Defeat, and the International System.* Washington, D.C.: Crane Russak.

Art, Robert, and Kenneth N. Waltz. 1983. *The Use of Force: International Politics and Foreign Policy.* Lanham, MD: University Press of America.

Axelrod, Robert. 1979. "The Rational Timing of Surprise." *World Politics* 31: 228–46.

———. 1984. *The Evolution of Cooperation.* New York: Basic Books.

Bennett, D. Scott, and Allan C. Stam III. 1996. "The Duration of Interstate War: 1812–1985." *American Political Science Review* 90, no. 2 (June): 239–57.

Betts, Richard K. 1982. *Surprise Attack.* Washington, D.C.: Brookings Institute.

Blainey, Geoffrey. 1973. *The Causes of War.* New York: Free Press.

Bond, Brian, and Ian Roy. 1975. *War and Society: A Yearbook of Military History.* New York: Holmes and Meier.

Bueno de Mesquita, Bruce. 1981. *The War Trap.* New Haven: Yale University Press.

Bueno de Mesquita, Bruce, and David Lalman. 1986. "Reason and War." *American Political Science Review* 80: 1113–29.

———. 1992. *War and Reason: Domestic and International Imperatives.* New Haven: Yale University Press.

Bueno de Mesquita, Bruce, Randolph M. Siverson, and Gary Woller. 1992. "War and the Fate of Regimes: A Comparative Analysis." *American Political Science Review* 86: 638–47.

Bueno de Mesquita, Bruce, and Randolph M. Siverson. 1995. "War and the Survival of Political Leaders: A Comparative Analysis of Regime Types and Accountability." *American Political Science Review* 89, no. 4 (December): 841–55.

Calahan, H. A. 1944. *What Makes a War End?* New York: Vanguard Press.

Carr, Edward Hallett. 1939. *The Twenty Years' Crisis, 1919-1939.* New York: Harper & Row.

Clausewitz, Carl von. 1976. *On War.* Princeton: Princeton University Press.

Clodfelter, Michael. 1993. *Warfare and Armed Conflicts.* 2 vols. Jefferson, NC: McFarland.

Cramer, J. S. 1991. *The LOGIT Model: An Introduction for Economists.* London: Edward Arnold.

Dahl, Robert Alan. 1956. *A Preface to Democratic Theory*. Chicago: University of Chicago Press.

Deger, Saadet, and Ron Smith. 1983. "Military Expenditure and Growth in Less Developed Countries." *Journal of Conflict Resolution* 27: 335–53.

Doran, Charles F., and Wes Parsons. 1980. "War and the Cycle of Relative Power." *American Political Science Review* 74: 947–65.

Dowding, Keith M. 1991. *Rational Choice and Political Power*. London: Edward Elgar Publishing.

Dupuy, R. Ernest, and Trevor N. Dupuy. 1986. *The Encyclopedia of Military History from 3500 B.C. to the Present*. 2d rev. ed. New York: Harper & Row.

Dupuy, Trevor N. 1979. *Numbers, Predictions, and War: Using History to Evaluate Combat Factors and Predict the Outcome of Battles*. Indianapolis: Bobbs-Merrill.

———. 1983. *Analysis of Factors that Have Influenced Outcomes of Battles and Wars: A Database of Battles and Engagements: Final Report*. Dunn Loring, VA: Historical Evaluation and Research Organization, Division of T. N. Dupuy Associates.

Epstein, Joshua M. 1987. *Strategy and Force Planning: The Case of the Persian Gulf*. Washington, D.C.: Brookings Institute.

Evangelista, Matthew. 1989. "Issue-Area and Foreign Policy Revisited." *International Organization* 43: 147–71.

Farber, Henry S., and Joanne Gowa. 1995. "Common Interests or Common Polities? Reinterpreting the Democratic Peace." Working Paper No. 5005, National Bureau of Economic Research. Cambridge, MA.

Fitzpatrick, Gary L., and Marilyn J. Modlin. 1986. *Direct-Line Distances: International Edition*. Metuchen, NJ: Scarecrow Press.

Friedman, Julian R. 1970. "Alliance in International Politics." In *Alliance in International Politics*, 3–33. Edited by Julian R. Friedman, Christopher Bladen, and Steven Rosen. Boston: Allyn and Bacon, Inc.

Friedrich, Carl J. 1972. *Tradition and Authority*. New York: Frederick A. Praeger.

Foot, M. R. D., and J. R. Western, eds. 1973. *War and Society: Historical Essays in Honour and Memory of J. R. Western, 1928–1971*. New York: Barnes & Noble Books.

Gamson, William A. 1968. *Power and Discontent*. Homewood, IL: Dorsey Press.

Gartner, Scott Sigmund. 1992. *Strategic Assessment in War: A Bounded Rationality Model of How Organizations Evaluate Policy Effectiveness*. Ph.D. dissertation. University of Michigan.

Gaubatz, Kurt Taylor. 1991. "Election Cycles and War." *Journal of Conflict Resolution* 35: 212–44.

Gibbs, Brian H., and J. David Singer. 1993. *Empirical Knowledge on World Politics*. Westport, CT: Greenwood Press.

Gilpin, Robert. 1981. *War and Change in World Politics*. New York: Cambridge University Press.

Goldstein, Joshua S. 1988. *Long Cycles: Prosperity and War in the Modern Age*. New Haven: Yale University Press.

Graves, Laura M. 1989. "College Recruitment: Removing Personal Bias from Selection Decisions." *Personnel* 66: 48–52.

Green, Donald P., and Ian Shapiro. 1994. *Pathologies of Rational Choice: A Critique of Applications in Political Science*. New Haven: Yale University Press.

Green, Leslie. 1988. *The Authority of the State*. New York: Oxford University Press.

Greene, William H. 1993. *Econometric Analysis*. 2d ed. New York: MacMillan.

Gurr, Ted Robert, Keith Jaggers, and Will H. Moore. 1989. *Polity II Codebook*. Boulder: University of Colorado.

Hagle, Timothy M., and Glen E. Mitchell. 1992. "Goodness-of-Fit Measures for Probit and Logit." *American Journal of Political Science* 36: 762–84.

Hanushek, Eric Alan, and John E. Jackson. 1977. *Statistical Methods for Social Scientists*. New York: Academic Pres.

Hart, Sir Basil Henry Liddell. 1967. *Strategy: The Indirect Approach*. London: Bader.

Heckman, James J. 1990. "Varieties of Selection Bias." *American Economic Review* 80: 313–18.

Holden, Barry. 1988. *Understanding Liberal Democracy*. Oxford: P. Allan.

Holloway, David. 1985. *The Soviet Union and the Arms Race*. New Haven: Yale University Press.

Holsti, Kalevi J. 1991. *Peace and War: Armed Conflicts and International Order, 1648–1989*. Cambridge: Cambridge University Press.

Holsti, Ole R., P. Terrance Hopmann, and John D. Sullivan. 1973. *Unity and Disintegration in International Alliances: Comparative Studies*. New York: Wiley.

Huntington, Samuel P. 1958. "Arms Races: Prerequisites and Results" *Public Policy* 8: 41–86.

Huth, Paul K. 1988. *Extended Deterrence and the Prevention of War*. New Haven: Yale University Press.

Huth, Paul, D. Scott Bennett, and Christopher Gelpi. 1992. "System Uncertainty, Risk Propensity, and International Conflict among the Great Powers" *Journal of Conflict Resolution* 36: 478–517.

Hybel, Alex Roberto. 1986. *The Logic of Surprise in International Conflict*. Lexington, MA: D. C. Heath and Company.

Jackman, Robert W. 1993. *Power without Force: The Political Capacity of Nation-States*. Ann Arbor: University of Michigan Press.

Jervis, Robert. 1985. "Introduction: Approach and Assumptions." In *Psychology and Deterrence*, 1–12. Edited by Robert Jervis, Richard Ned Lebow, and Janice Gross Stein. Baltimore: Johns Hopkins University Press.

Kaldor, Mary. 1981. *The Baroque Arsenal*. New York: Hill and Wang.

Karnow, Stanley. 1983. *Vietnam: A History*. New York: Penguin.

Kaplan, Morton A. 1962. *System and Process in International Politics*. New York: John Wiley.

Katzenstein, Peter J. 1978. *Between Power and Plenty: Foreign Economic Policies of Advanced Industrial States*. Madison: University of Wisconsin Press.

Kegley, Charles W., and Gregory Raymond. 1990. *When Trust Breaks Down: Alliance Norms and World Politics*. Columbia: University of South Carolina Press.

Kiefer, Nicholas M. 1988. "Economic Duration Data and Hazard Functions." *Journal of Economic Literature* 26: 646–79.

Kilgour, D. Marc. 1991. "Domestic Political Structure and War Behavior : A Game-Theoretic Approach." *Journal of Conflict Resolution* 35: 266–84.

King, Gary. 1989. *Unifying Political Methodology*. Cambridge: Cambridge University Press.

Knorr, Klaus Eugen. [1911] 1962. *Limited Strategic War*. New York: Frederick A. Praeger.

Krasner, Stephen D. 1983. *International Regimes*. Ithaca: Cornell University Press.

———. 1985. *Structural Conflict: The Third World against Global Liberalism*. Berkeley: University of California Press.

Kriesberg, Louis, and Ross Klein. 1980. "Changes in Public Support for U.S. Military Spending" *Journal of Conflict Resolution* 24: 79–112.

Kugler, Jacek, and William Domke. 1986. "Comparing the Strength of Nations" *Comparative Political Studies* 19: 39–69.

Lancaster, Tony. 1990. *The Econometric Analysis of Transition Data*. Cambridge: Cambridge University Press.

Lebow, Richard Ned. 1985. "Miscalculation in the South Atlantic: The Origins of the Falklands War." In *Psychology and Deterrence*, 89–124. Edited by Robert Jervis, Richard Ned Lebow, and Janice Gross Stein. Baltimore: Johns Hopkins University Press.

Levy, Jack. 1982. "Historical Trends in Great Power War, 1495-1975." *International Studies Quarterly* 26: 278–300.

Lieber, Robert J. 1993. "Existential Realism after the Cold War." *Washington Quarterly* 16: 155–68.

Lindsay, A. D. 1943. *The Modern Democratic State*. Oxford: Oxford University Press.

Link, Arthur Stanley. 1967. *American Epoch: A History of the United States since the 1890s*. New York: Alfred A. Knopf.

Lipset, Seymour. 1960. *Political Man*. New York: Doubleday.

Lowi, Theodore J. 1964. "American Business, Public Policy, Case Studies, and Political Theory." *World Politics* 16: 677–715.

Luttwak, Edward N. 1980. *Strategy and Politics*. New Brunswick, NJ: Transaction Books.

Luttwak, Edward N. 1985. *Strategy and History*. New Brunswick, NJ: Transaction Books.

———. 1987. *Strategy: The Logic of War and Peace*. Cambridge: Harvard University Press, Belknap Press.

Machiavelli, Niccolò. 1985. *The Prince*. Chicago: University of Chicago Press.

Mao, Tse-tung. 1961. *On Guerrilla Warfare*. New York: Frederick A. Praeger.

Maoz, Zeev. 1983. "Resolve, Capabilities, and the Outcomes of Interstate Disputes, 1816–1976." *Journal of Conflict Resolution* 27, no. 2 (June): 195–230.

———. 1990. *Paradoxes of War: On the Art of Self-Entrapment*. Boston: Unwin Hyman.

Maoz, Zeev, and Bruce Russett. 1993. "Normative and Structural Cases of Democratic Peace, 1946–1986." *American Political Science Review* 87, no. 3 (September): 624–38.

Mayo, H. B. 1960. *An Introduction to Democratic Theory*. New York: Oxford University Press.

Mearsheimer, John J. 1983. *Conventional Deterrence*. Ithaca, NY: Cornell University Press.

———. 1990. "Why We Will Soon Miss the Cold War." *Atlantic* 266: 35–60.

Messenger, Charles. 1976. *The Art of Blitzkrieg*. London: I. Allan.

McKeown, Timothy J. 1983. "Hegemonic Stability Theory and Nineteenth-Century Tariff Levels in Europe." *International Organization* 37: 73–91.

McNeill, William H. 1988. "Men, Machines, and War." In *Men, Machines, and War*, 1–21. Edited by Ronald Graham Haycock and Keith Erik Neilson. Waterloo, Ontario: Wilfred Laurier University Press.

Miles, Robert. 1984. *White Man's Country: Racism in British Politics*. London: Pluto Press.

Miller, Steven. 1985. *Military Strategy and the Origins of the First World War: An International Security Reader*. Princeton: Princeton University Press.

Milner, Helen V. 1988. *Global Industries and the Politics of International Trade*. Princeton: Princeton University Press.

Mitchell, Christopher R. 1991. "Ending Conflicts and Wars: Judgment, Rationality, and Entrapment." *International Social Science Journal* 43: 35–55.

Mitchell, William. 1921. *Our Air Force, the Keystone of National Defense*. New York: E. P. Dutton.

Morrow, James D. 1987. "On the Theoretical Basis of a Measure of National Risk Attitudes." *International Studies Quarterly* 31: 423–38.

———. 1991. "Conceptual Problems in Theorizing about International Conflict." *American Political Science Review* 85: 923–29.

Morgenthau, Hans Joachim. 1978. *Politics among Nations*. New York: Alfred A. Knopf.

Mueller, John E. 1973. *War, Presidents, and Public Opinion*. New York: John Wiley.

Olson, Mancur, and Richard Zeckhauser. 1970. "An Economic Theory of Alliances." In *Alliance in International Politics*, 175–99. Edited by Julian R. Friedman, Christopher Bladen, and Steven Rosen. Boston: Allyn and Bacon.

Organski, A. F. K., and Jacek Kugler. 1980. *The War Ledger*. Chicago: University of Chicago Press.

Organski, Katherine, and A. F. K. Organski. 1961. *Population and World Power*. New York: Alfred A. Knopf.

Page, Edward. 1992. *Political Authority and Bureaucratic Power: A Comparative Analysis*. New York: Harvester Wheatsheaf.

Pape Jr., Robert A. 1990. "Coercive Air Power in the Vietnam War." *International Security* 15: 103–46.

Pindyck, Robert S., and Daniel Rubinfeld. 1981. *Econometric Models and Economic Forecasts*. 2d ed. New York: McGraw-Hill.

Posen, Barry R. 1984. *The Sources of Military Doctrine*. Ithaca, NY: Cornell University Press.

Potter, William. 1980. "Issue Area and Foreign Policy Analysis." *International Organization* 34: 405–27.

Poundstone, William. 1992. *Prisoner's Dilemma*. New York: Doubleday.

Puchala, Donald James. 1984. *Fiscal Harmonization in the European Communities: National Politics and International Cooperation*. London: Pinter.

Reiter, Dan. 1995. "Exploding the Powder Keg Myth: Preemptive Wars almost Never Happen." *International Security* 20, no. 2: 5–34.

Reiter, Dan. 1996. *Crucible of Beliefs: Learning, World Wars, and Alliances*. Ithaca: Cornell University Press.

Rothgeb Jr., John M. 1993. *Defining Power: Influence and Force in the Contemporary International System*. New York: St. Martin's Press.

Rosen, Steven. 1972. "War Power and the Willingness to Suffer." Reprinted in *The Scientific Study of Peace and War*, 255–73. Edited by John A. Vasquez and Marie T. Henehan. New York: Lexington Books.

Rosenau, James N. 1966. "Pre-Theories and Theories of Foreign Policy." In *Approaches to Comparative and International Politics*, 27–92. Edited by R. Barry Farrell. Evanston: Northwestern University Press.

Ruggie, John G. 1984. *Power, Passions, and Purpose*. Cambridge: M.I.T. Press.

Rummel, R. J. 1985. "Libertarian Propositions on Violence within and between Nations: A Test against Published Research Results." *Journal of Conflict Resolution* 29: 419–55.

Russett, Bruce M. 1990. *Controlling the Sword: the Democratic Governance of National Security*. Cambridge: Harvard University Press.

Schelling, Thomas C. 1966. *Arms and Influence*. New Haven: Yale University Press.

Singer, J. David, Stuart Bremer, and John Stuckey. 1972. "Capability Distribution, Uncertainty, and Major Power War, 1820-1965." In *Peace War and Numbers*. Edited by Bruce Russett. Beverly Hills: Sage Publications.

Singer, J. David, and Melvin Small. 1982. *Resort to Arms: International and Civil Wars, 1816–1980*. Beverly Hills: Sage Publications.

Singer, J. David, and Paul F. Diehl, eds. 1990. *Measuring the Correlates of War*. Ann Arbor: University of Michigan Press.

Siverson, Randolph M., and Juliann Emmons. 1991. "Birds of a Feather : Democratic Political Systems and Alliance Choices in the Twentieth Century." *Journal of Conflict Resolution* 35: 285–306.

Snyder, Glenn H. 1968. "Deterrence and Defense: A Theoretical Introduction." In *American Defence Policy*, 30–58. Edited by Mark E. Smith III and Claude J. Jones Jr. Baltimore: Johns Hopkins University Press.

Snyder, Glenn H., and Paul Diesing. 1977. *Conflict among Nations*. Princeton: Princeton University Press.

Snyder, Jack L. 1984. *The Ideology of the Offensive: Military Decision Making and the Disasters of 1914*. Ithaca, NY: Cornell University Press.

———. 1985. "Perceptions of the Security Dilemma in 1914." In *Psychology and Deterrence*, 153–79. Edited by Robert Jervis, Richard Ned Lebow, and Janice Gross Stein. Baltimore: Johns Hopkins University Press.

Snyder, Jack L., and Robert Jervis. 1991. *Dominoes and Bandwagons: Strategic Beliefs and Great Power Competition in the Eurasian Rimland*. New York: Oxford University Press.

Spitz, David. 1958. *Democracy and the Challenge of Power*. New York: Columbia University Press.

Stam III, Allan C. 1993. *Win, Lose, or Draw*. Ph.D. dissertation, University of Michigan.

Stanton, Shelby L. 1985. *The Rise and Fall of an American Army*. New York: Dell Publishing.

Strange, Susan. 1985. "Protectionism and World Politics." *International Organization* 39: 233–59.

Stohl, Michael. 1976. *War and Domestic Political Violence*. Beverly Hills: Sage Publications.

Sun Tzu. 1991. *The Art of War*. London: Shambhala.

Tocqueville, Alexis de. 1954. *Democracy in America*. New York: Vintage Books.

Tractenburg, Marc. 1991. *History and Strategy*. Princeton: Princeton University Press.

Trotter, William R. 1991. *A Frozen Hell*. Chapel Hill, NC: Algonquin Books.

Van Evera, Stephen W. 1984. *Causes of War*. Ph.D. dissertation. University of California, Berkeley.

Von Neumann, John, and Oscar Morgenstern. 1947. *Theory of Games and Economic Behavior*. Princeton: Princeton University Press.

Vuchinich, Samuel, and Jay Teachman. 1993. "The Duration of Wars, Strikes, Riots, and Family Arguments." *Journal of Conflict Resolution* 37: 544–68.

Walt, Stephen M. 1987. *The Origins of Alliances*. Ithaca: Cornell University Press.

Waltz, Kenneth N. 1979. *Theory of International Politics*. Reading, MA: Addison-Wesley.

Warwick, Paul V. 1992. "Rising Hazards: An Underlying Dynamic of Parliamentary Government." *American Journal of Political Science* 36: 857–76.

Wayman, Frank W., and Paul F. Diehl. 1994. *Reconstructing Realpolitik*. Ann Arbor: University of Michigan Press.

Wilson, Woodrow. 1918. "The President on Mob Violence." American Civil Liberties Union, *War Time Prosecutions and Mob Violence Involving the Rights of Free Speech, Free Press, and Peaceful Assemblage.* New York: National Civil Liberties Bureau.

Wittman, Donald. 1979. "How a War Ends." *Journal of Conflict Resolution* 23: 743–66.

Wolfers, Arnold. 1962. *Discord and Collaboration.* Baltimore: Johns Hopkins University Press.

Yates, J. Frank. 1991. *Judgment and Decision Making.* Englewood Cliffs, NJ: Prentice-Hall.

Young, Oran R. 1980. "International Regimes: Problems of Concept Formation." *World Politics* 32: 331–56.

York, Herbert. 1970. *Race to Oblivion.* New York: Simon and Schuster.

Zimmerman, William. 1973. "Issue Area and Foreign-Policy Process: A Research Note in Search of a General Theory." *American Political Science Review* 67: 1204–12.

Index